AF655342

Monetary and Payments Cooperation in South Asia

ABOUT THE AUTHOR

Rahul Tripathi is a senior faculty in political sceince at Goa University. He holds a doctorate in South Asian Studies from the School of International Studies, Jawaharlal Nehru University, New Delhi. He has been a visiting faculty at College of International Relations, Nihon University, Mishima, Japan and the Project Director, South Asia Together at the International Centre, Goa. He has credited a book entitled *Freedom in South Asia: Democratisation, Peace and Regional Cooperation* (Konark Publishers, 2008.)

Monetary and Payments Cooperation in South Asia

RAHUL TRIPATHI

CONCEPT PUBLISHING COMPANY PVT. LTD.
NEW DELHI-110059

© Rahul Tripathi (b 1971)

All rights reserved. No part of this work may be reproduced, stored, adapted, or transmitted in any form or by any means, electronic, mechanical, photocopying, micro-filming recording or otherwise, or translated in any language, without the prior written permission of the copyright owner and the publisher. The book is sold subject to the condition that it shall not, by way of trade or otherwise, be lent, resold, hired out, or otherwise circulated without the prior publisher written consent in any form of binding or cover other than that in which it is published.

The views and opinions expressed in this book are author(s) own and the facts reported by him/her have been verified to the expert possible, and the publishers are not in any way liable for the same.

ISBN-13: 978-81-8069-650-3 **ISBN-10: 81-8069-650-2**

First Published 2010

Published and Printed by

Concept Since 1974

Concept Publishing Company Pvt. Ltd.
Regd. Office:
A/15-16, Commercial Block, Mohan Garden
New Delhi-110059 (India)
Phones : 25351460, 25351794, *Fax* : 091-11-25357109
Email : publishing@conceptpub.com,
Website: www.conceptpub.com

Editorial Office:
H-13, Bali Nagar, New Delhi-110 015, India.

Cataloging in Publication Data-- *Courtesy:* D.K. Agencies (P) Ltd. <docinfo@dkagencies.com>

Tripathi, Rahul.
Monetary and payments cooperation in South Asia / Rahul Tripathi.
p. cm.
Revision of the author's thesis (Ph. D.)--Jawaharlal Nehru University.
Includes bibliographical references (p.).
Includes index.
ISBN 13: 9788180696503 ISBN 10: 8180696502

1. Monetary policy--South Asia. 2. South Asia--Commerce. 3. South Asia--Foreign economic relations. 4. South Asian cooperation. I. Title.

DDC 332.4954 22

Preface

Any study on regional cooperation in general and monetary and financial cooperation in particular in the context of the on-going global financial crisis, would be faced with a two fold dilemma. First, the crisis comes at a time when perhaps the national, regional and the global consensus on globalization and regional integration has been all pervasive. Last three decades have been a witness to how nations have had a strong desire to join the globalization bandwagon and very often treated regionalism as a stepping stone if they were not ready to face the global impulses as yet. So how come they have been affected by the crisis in an equal measure despite the varying degrees to which they had been integrated?

Secondly, if there were regional instruments in place, then how is it that they have proved to be drastically inadequate not only in comprehending the nature of the crisis, but also figuring out ways and means to tackle it. Regionalism in its true essence is an instrument of maximizing collective gains and therefore naturally should provide mechanisms for minimizing collective loss. Why is it therefore that policy makers and planners were left with no other option but to start thinking of ways and means to deal with the crisis afresh, without taking into cognizance the mechanisms that were put in place decades ago.

The present study, with no pretensions of trying to find answers to these questions, tries to revisit an idea that had been operationalised more than three decades ago with a fair degree of success, till the waves of globalization and liberalization took over and the mechanism was left looking for a new rationale for itself. Located in the larger context of monetary and payments cooperation in South Asia, this book is an attempt to understand and analyze the Asian Clearing Union, an organization created way back in the 1970s, during the heydays of South-South cooperation. The ACU, which was set up precisely to anticipate and comprehend the kind of crisis developing countries face with regard to regional monetary and payments transactions, survived the existential dilemma that it faced when it became more attractive and viable to use the non ACU route to settle intra-regional transactions. Still, it could not go beyond the limited mandate that was given to it to foster greater monetary and financial cooperation in the region.

Today, there are growing voices on creating ACU of another kind (the ASEAN plus three have envisaged an Asian Currency Unit model, which is supposed to provide a regional band to stabilize movements of currencies in the region.), it becomes imperative to see how Asian countries in general and South Asian countries in particular were never really able to creatively define and interpret the mandate of an organization which perhaps could have provided a blueprint for pragmatic future regional monetary interaction. The present work therefore attempts a syncretic analysis of historical role and future directions of ACU if it has to figure a new role for itself.

Time and location however are major factors that judge the feasibility of any such work and it is precisely there that the author has experienced certain limitations in this study-not all of them totally avoidable. First, updating the works of this nature poses a challenge as not only the facts and figures change, but also the operating environment transforms. I have tried my level best to update the facts and figures and analyze them in the context of the changes that were being experienced in the ACU environment. Secondly at times there are new developments which may not be totally connected with the past events, but do show some future directions to the future growth and pace of the organization. I have tried to incorporate these additions by way of annexure and the postscripts which find a mention in the book.

Such limitations notwithstanding, I hope the essence of the work in formulating an approach to regional cooperation and integration in South Asia will certainly be of interest to those students, researchers and policymakers who remain inclined to bring our region together, irrespective of the obstacles that remain.

Acknowledgements

The present work, which is an updated version of my doctoral thesis submitted to the South Asian Studies Division, School of International Studies, Jawaharlal Nehru University owes its fruition to the numerous people and influences that have shaped my thinking on developing a 'Southern' perspective in general and a 'South Asian viewpoint' in particular. The initiation spans nearly a decade and a half's engagement with international relations and South Asia that began at JNU in early nineties and continues till date. I must emphasize that the present work is a mere beginning of what could be one of the key pillars of a future regional integration in South Asia and would generate further interest among those of us who are perennial optimists about regionalism in South Asia, its failings notwithstanding.

I would like to express my deep gratitude to my supervisor Prof. M.P. Lama who has been the guiding spirit behind the present endeavour. His insightful comments and constructive criticism enabled me to develop a wider perspective on the theme. It has been a privilege to be the first Ph.D scholar under a person who has himself been one of the foremost scholars and practitioners of the idea of regionalism in South Asia. He continues to inspire a new generation of South Asian scholars through his consistent application and tremendous outreach. Our numerous intense sessions (not always ending in agreement) during the final stages of the thesis did finally help in ensuring a better final output.

I am also thankful to Prof. I.N. Mukherjee, whose expertise on the area helped me in imparting a better focus to the study.

As one of the pioneers in the area of monetary and financial cooperation Studies in South Asia, he helped in filling some of the most important gaps in the work. I deeply acknowledge Prof. Muchkund Dubey, whose lectures on India's Foreign Economic Policy, while I was a student, and his constant guidance to me till date has enabled me to retain and refine the continuity in my thoughts on economic diplomacy and South Asia.

Relocating to Goa in the year 2000 immediately after submission of the thesis as faculty in Department of Political Science and taking up the cherished responsibility of Project Director, South Asia together at the International Centre, Goa enabled me to sustain my academic and professional engagement with South Asia. The Department, first under the headship of Prof. Peter deSouza who was perhaps among the first to introduce a course on South Asia in a non area-studies department and later under Dr. Aureliano Fernandes who made sure that the department maintains its focus on the emerging areas in the discipline provided me the right space to pursue my twin responsibilities despite all odds.

South Asia Together Project at the International Centre, Goa, an emerging hub of intellectual activity in the most beautiful part of India, provided me a unique opportunity to practice and experience the idea of bringing together young South Asians from diverse fields, and discuss with them the ways to create a peaceful and secure South Asia. Dr. V. A. Pai Panandikar, the eminent South Asian and visionary of the Project, helped me grow as an individual and a scholar, as he has done for an entire generation of South Asian scholars. He personifies a rare blend of intellectualism and institution building and remains one of the most penetrating and authoritative voices on good governance and constitutionalism in our region today. Ambassador Eric Gonsalves, a member of the esteemed Advisory Board and an active member of the Track II policy community, helped me update, through his numerous visits to Goa, on some of his key ideas on enlightened regionalism in South Asia. He remains perhaps the most accessible 'Diplomat' I have ever come across. Mr. Jayant

Chhaya the former Director of ICG has been an immense driving force for me.

A study of this magnitude would not have been possible without an interaction with a host of institutions and individuals who have been associated with the area. I thank Mr. Mohammad Firouzdor, the then Secretary General, Asian Clearing Union and the ACU Secretariat for providing me some valuable inputs on the structure and functioning of the ACU. I am also thankful to Mr. Purushottam Shreshta, Nepal Rashtra Bank for enabling me to interact with the delegates at the 28th Annual Meeting of Board of Governors at Kathmandu in April 1999. Discussions with Mr. M.B. Dissanayake and Dr. S.S. Colombage, from Central Bank of Sri Lanka helped me to understand the Sri Lankan perspective on the ACU. Visits to the SAARC Secretariat, first in 1997 and then in 2005 helped me to assess the institutions thinking on the area. Back home, Mr. AR. Appadurai, of the Reserve Bank of India was kind enough in responding to my persistent queries on the theme. I am also grateful to the Federation of Indian Chambers of Commerce and Industry, Federation of Sri Lankan Chamber of Commerce and Industry and the Federation of Nepalese Chamber of Commerce and Industry for providing me useful inputs on the industry perspective.

At a broader level visits to some of the 'North' based think tanks and institutions during my visit to the United States as part of the International Visitors Programme in 2002, which included among others Centre for Strategic and International Studies, Brookings Institution, Council for Foreign Relations and the World Bank, helped me to get the 'other' perspective on South-South Cooperation. My stint as a visiting faculty at College of International Relations, Nihon University enabled me to study from an Asian perspective the desirability of forging greater cooperation on monetary and financial issues in Asia.

I would also like to thank the members and the staff of the Jawaharlal Nehru University Library, Research and Information System for Non-Aligned and Other Developing Countries Library and the United Nations Information Centre at New Delhi.

My parents, friends and colleagues have been a constant source of encouragement and inspiration for me. My father, mother and sister Poonam were always a source of great strength and support. My grandfather Prof. Udai Narain Tewari has been one of the paramount influences in shaping my spiritual and academic being. As always, my friends Manish and Aparajita provided the best motivation and support when it mattered the most. At ICG, Arjun, Freda, Nandita and Joel wonderfully coped with my inconsistencies and aberrations. Last but not the least, Shilpa who has been my close confidant for the last three and a half years and little Tejas who joined her nearly two years back made sure that I was able to sustain my emotional strength when the chips were down and helped me to spring back to action in no time.

Needless to say, any shortcomings and demerits that remain in this work are mine alone.

January, 2009

RAHUL TRIPATHI
Goa

Content

List of Tables

List of Abbreviations

ACU	:	Asian Clearing Union
ADB	:	Asian Development Bank
ASEAN	:	Association of South East Asian Nations
BIS	:	Bank for International Settlements
CACH	:	Central American Clearing House
CAMU	:	Central African Monetary Union
CARICOM	:	Caribbean Community and Common Market
CMCF	:	CARICOM Multilateral Clearing Facility
ECAFE	:	Economic Commission for Asia and the Far East
ECO	:	Economic Cooperation Organisation
EPU	:	European Payments Union
ESCAP	:	Economic and Social Commission for Asia and the Pacific
IMF	:	International Monetary Fund
LAFTA	:	Latin American Free Trade Association
LAIA	:	Latin American Integration Association
LIBOR	:	London Inter-bank Offer Rate
LIMEAN	:	London Inter-bank Mean Rate
PTACH	:	Preferential Trade Area for Eastern and Southern African Clearing House
RPCS	:	Reciprocal Payments and Credit System
RCD	:	Regional Cooperation for Development
SAARC	:	South Asian Association for Regional Cooperation
SDR	:	Special Drawing Right
UNCTAD	:	United Nations Conference on Trade and Development
WACH	:	West African Clearing House
WAMU	:	West African Monetary Union

Chapter 1

Introduction

The developing nations face manifold challenges as they try to locate themselves in the contemporary global economic system. The rapidity with which events outpace the perceived plans makes it all the more difficult for them to draw a coherent plan of action. Caught in the basic dilemma of coping up with new processes without being able to do away with old institutions and structures, they are often found lacking in presenting a unified front even when issues at stake have a common bearing to all of them. As a result, the institutions and processes that had been evolved earlier—at a time when issues facing the developing world were no less critical, are being gradually eroded and emphasis is being given to a 'universal' set of principles that should guide the international economic relations. This poses some key questions before students of international political economy. Which are the dominant trends guiding the pattern of global economic interaction? In what way they are impinging on the manner in which developing countries interact among themselves and with rest of the world? Lastly and most importantly given the scope of the present study, to what extent are these developments affecting the institutions and processes established earlier that intended to address some of the collective concerns of the developing countries.

1.1 The Global Economic Setting

One needs to analyse the patterns that characterize the functioning of the contemporary global economic system in order to study its impact on the way developing countries interact among themselves and the rest of the world. The theme can be approached at various levels. First in terms of the processes that provide the conceptual domain in which global economic relations are defined—such as Globalisation and Regionalism. Secondly, in terms of the institutions through which these processes are being operationalised—such as the World Trade Organisation, International Monetary Fund and the World Bank. Thirdly, one can study the instruments which form the core of these processes and institutions aimed at redefining the linkages within and between the nations—namely through economic liberalisation and information revolution. For our purpose, we would focus on the first aspect as it encompasses elements of the other two while explaining the patterns in international economic relations.

Globalisation is a multifaceted process that impinges on the economic, social and political behaviour of nations in contemporary times. The three key tendencies driving globalisation have been described as technological change, liberalization and opening of markets and combination of technology and free market leading to transnationalisation of economic activity.[1] Impact of globalization on growth of per-capita incomes across the regions has however been varied [2]. These processes are sought to be reinforced with multilateralisation of rules and principles that govern the global economy. Consequently, there are limits to the extent to which national policy autonomy prevails over the multilateral setting. Although globalisation has generally been described as gradual process the roots of which go back to the late 19th century, yet the post-World War II period is seen as providing the adequate backdrop to the present wave of globalization.[3]

During the last five decades, there has been a major spurt in global trade. In fact, trade has far outpaced the growth in output thus showing a tendency for greater outward linkages among nations. The global merchandise exports, on an annual average basis grew by 6 per cent in real terms from 1948 to 1997, compared to an annual average output growth of 3.7 per cent. In other words, while trade for the period registered a 17 fold increase, the G.D.P. increased 6 fold. The annual foreign direct investment, another major indicator of transnationalisation of economic activity, increased 17 fold between 1973 and 1996 implying annual average growth of over 12 per cent. Besides, the average daily turnover in foreign exchange markets (symbol of the most recent wave of financial globalisation), increased from US $ 200 million in mid-eighties to US $1.2 trillion in 1996. There has been an increase in trade/GDP ratios for both developed as well as developing countries between 1985-1997, growing from 16.6 per cent to 24.1 per cent and 22.8 per cent to 38 per cent respectively.[4]

The nature and thrust of globalisation has necessitated a greater thrust towards building institutions and mechanisms aimed at maintaining steady growth in world trade and output. Also, given due importance are monetary and financial arrangements that not only help in sustaining global trade, but also maintain stability in the capital flows across markets. Besides, with growing financial linkages across the globe, there has also been a greater emphasis on pursuing standard norms for bank supervision and lending. These are to be reinforced with a smooth, technology driven payments system which could facilitate cross-border flow of funds. It is broadly under these categories, monetary and payments cooperation is sought specifically in response to the manner in which globalisation is sought to be pursued.

Accompanying the undercurrents of globalisation is an equally significant phenomenon of regionalism, which is becoming a major factor in shaping global economic realignments. In a way, regionalism seeks to provide a bridge between overarching globalised environment on one hand and the market led integration efforts by individual countries on the other. Regionalism aims at accomplishing a common set of goals by a group of countries which are often brought together by factors relating to geographical contiguity, economic complimentarily and collective well-being. As an instrument of policy, it seeks to harmonise the actions of member countries towards the attainment of a common objective such as a trading area (which can either be in a form of a preferential trade area, free trade area or a customs union), an investment area (encompassing special economic zones having common investment projects) or an economic union (having a complete harmonization of monetary and fiscal policy).

On the theoretical plain, attempts have been made to study regionalism in comparative terms more at the ideational rather than economic level.[5] It has been described as a centripetal process which leads to the movement of two or more societies towards deeper integration with greater pooling of their sovereignty.[6] Regionalism can be a political phenomenon, when driven by political imperatives, members pool in powers of the state and policy sovereignty; it can also be an economic phenomenon, driven by micro-economic forces towards greater trade and investment linkages[7]. Notwithstanding the different approaches at studying regionalism, the patterns in which it has manifested itself have been indicative of the nature of the global political economy prevailing. Attempts have been made to periodize the different phases in regional cooperation among developing countries that show that the process of regional cooperation evolved as a direct response to the change in global political economy as well as the changing emphasis of thinking about development policy.[8]

In the regional context, monetary and payment cooperation seeks to strengthen the on-going efforts at intra-regional trade and investment expansion. Depending on the nature and pattern of cooperation sought, monetary and payments arrangements may apart from strengthening intra-regional linkages, also provide a basis for global integration. For instance, a regional payments union may on one hand provide a financial facility to the members to meet intra-regional trade deficits; it may also prepare the participants for global convertibility by pursuing limited convertibility among the participants within the region.

The factors that lead to regionalism may be stated to be both endogenous and exogenous. The former relate to the inner logic of regional grouping which point to the benefits that can be derived out of expanded market opportunities, sharing of common resources and economies in production depending on the nature and orientation of the regional grouping.

Such factors essentially focus on the intrinsic capabilities existing within the region which can be best put to use by collaborative efforts at the regional level.[9] The other set of factors derive from the external impulses that the forces of the global economy generate. For instance, in an environment of multilateralisation of economic relations requiring uniformity in trade and investment policies globally, regionalism offers member countries an opportunity to take gradual steps towards global integration. It enables the member countries to experiment with regional mechanisms so that they may get attuned to the global forces when faced with. In a way, regionalism has been regarded as more manageable politically as domestic constituencies are likely to respond more favourably to regional issues than to the global issues that appear to be far removed from them at times.[10] There have been several other reasons put forward to explain the recent spurt in regionalism. One view seeks to relate the growth of regionalism to the inability of the multilateral mechanisms (such as erstwhile GATT) to achieve speedy results.[11] Multilateral negotiations, involving a large number of parties with varying levels of economic stakes are often likely to take longer time and the end result might not suit a particular group having a common interest.

There has been much discussion on whether regionalism complements or runs contrary to the spirit of multilateralism that is prevalent today. Fears have been expressed that regional trade agreements could lead to a fortress mentality, whereby a strengthened regional market could be used as an excuse to erect barriers to external competition. Besides, the trade diverting effects of regional agreements could be seen as increasing trade friction thus creating difficulties in freeing trade on a multilateral basis. It has been pointed out that preferential arrangements that are more trade diverting are more likely to be supported by the partner countries.[12] This is primarily because trade diversion out of a preferential arrangement tends to shift imports away from low cost non-member country to a higher cost member country. Such a move therefore, finds favour among the high cost producer members of a preferential arrangement. Some leading critics of preferential trading arrangements echo this sentiment by pointing out that trade creation, seen as affecting domestic producers would be opposed, whereas trade diversion would not arouse domestic sentiments.[13] This is because trade creation has greater impact on domestic producers as it replaces high cost domestic production by low cost imports from a member country.

At the same time, nevertheless, regional arrangements could foster faster liberalisation at the multilateral level by providing 'testing grounds' for countries which are yet unprepared for complete global integration. Besides, agreements between neighbours are stated to be less complicated to work out than at a multilateral forum consisting of more than 100 members.[14] At another level, regionalism may provide opportunities to the developing member countries to enhance their share in the global market place through coordinated efforts towards joint production and marketing (a point to be elaborated in the next section).

The WTO on its part permits the formation of regional arrangements and therefore acknowledges their compatibility with the multilateral trading system. As per Article XXIV of the WTO three criteria should be met (i) they must cover substantially all trade of member countries, (ii) they must avoid raising new barriers to non-members, and (iii) they must achieve free trade among members by a certain date. Thus WTO's acceptability of regional trading arrangements is based on the premise that these should be accompanied by parallel efforts at multilateral liberalisation.[15]

In sum, the debate on whether regionalism acts as a building block or a stumbling block towards globalisation has remained inconclusive. What has been generally agreed upon is the fact that regionalism, once accepted as part of the current international policy, must be carefully nurtured, through multilateral supervision and management to the broader goals of the world trading community. The role of the Committee on Regional Trade Agreements (CRTA) under the WTO has been seen as quite significant in this regard.[16] The attempt must be to see that regionalism must be structured so as to maximise the benefits of global free trade and liberalisation.

1.2 South-South Cooperation: The Recent Context

The manner in which global economic relations have shaped in the past two decades, there has been a gradual transformation in the linkages that hitherto characterised North-South as well as South-South relations. The 1960s and the 1970s saw the relations between the industrial, developed North and the impoverished, developing South as being unidirectional with the emphasis on aid and investment as a possible remedy to bridge the gap. At the same time, mutuality of interests between North and South were regarded as key to any programme of global economic restructuring that was sought.[17] This was also the period when South-South Cooperation (SSC) was seen as an effective strategy to not merely mitigate the dependence of the South on the North, but also to enable the developing countries to make best use of the opportunities that existed within. Third world bodies such as Group of 77 were seen as providing a common voice to the developing countries on the various multilateral fora. The fundamental premise shaping global economic linkages was based on the assumption that both the North and the South constituted two distinct groups, each having an inner homogeneity, thereby making a straightforward case for transfer of resources from one to the other.

Such logic however, got diluted in the 1990s as there was a sudden urge among most of the developing countries to embark on the path of economic reforms and liberalisation. South appeared to be more inclined to become part of the globalisation process rather than being seen as claiming its share in the seemingly inequitous order. This was seen as transforming the entire framework in which the North-South debate was being conducted. The following statement confirms to this school of thought:

> The developing countries are now too diverse in their economic and political circumstance and context to make generally possible a unified viewpoint as "theirs" (that is that of the South to). This changed reality surely played a principal role in the rapid demise in the 1970s of the global

negotiations that were predicated on the premise of North-South confrontation.[18]

Moreover, this view also seeks to emphasise on the universality of economic principles for both developing as well as developed nations, thereby discounting the differential treatment that was sought by former at various international fora. The implication is that global economic developments tend to have a similar impact on the nations and given a set of multilateral regimes which have a common binding, it is no longer pragmatic to identify South as a distinct group.

This view has been emphatically countered by emphasising the fact that with their per capita incomes way behind the levels prevailing in the North and many similar structural weaknesses hampering their development process, South continues to be a homogenous group. Moreover, with there being no sign of the income disparities narrowing down, it has become all the more necessary to identify South as a homogenous entity.[19] It is asserted that globalisation and liberalisation in fact offer new avenues for SSC not merely in terms of structuring the global economic relations but also providing an opportunity to learn from each others' experiences with regard to regional and sub-regional integration. Moreover, international economic scenario from the point of view of developing countries is still far too volatile and unpredictable for them to take a unanimous view on the benefits of globalisation and free trade. Some of the recent trends in the global economy confirm to this perception.

After witnessing a continuous growth since the early 1990s, the global output and trade growth deteriorated sharply in 1998 as imports of Japan and East Asia fell for the first time since 1974 (first oil crisis). The decline was spread across all regions and covered all broad product categories. More significantly, the share of developing countries in world trade dipped for the first time in more than one decade. Almost two-third of the world economy recorded decline in the export earnings which was worst performance in the 1990s.[20] The impact was more pronounced in the ESCAP region which recorded a growth rate of close to zero per cent in 1998 as against over 7 per cent in 1996 and 6 per cent in 1997.[21]

The reasons for this sudden fluctuation in global output and trade and the severity of its impact in Asia could largely be attributed to the financial crisis in South-East and East-Asian region. Till the crisis erupted, this region was seen as leading example of how developing countries could make themselves key partners in the globalisation process. The magnitude of the crisis was such that the leading practitioners and proponents of the global capitalist system were compelled to contemplate on the weaknesses inherent in the system that were to be guarded against so that the crisis did not replicate.[22] The crisis also brought to focus the need for greater efforts towards regional cooperation. This could both recognise the peculiar nature of the problems which had a regional dimension and enable the countries to establish regional mechanisms to face the crisis.[23] It would not be an exaggeration to say, that the issues of regional cooperation within the South have again been brought into focus in a new context, yet with same old urgency.

1.3 Monetary and Payments Arrangements and South-South Cooperation

Monetary and payments cooperation has been a significant theme in South-South Cooperation, although its form and content have varied depending on the context it was discussed. The early 1960s and the 1970s saw the growing emphasis on collective self-reliance and socio-economic progress among the developing countries. The institutional basis for such efforts had been provided by the groups such as G-77, Non-Aligned Movement and operationalised by bodies such as Economic Cooperation among Developing Countries (ECDC) under the auspices of United Nations Conference for Trade and Development (UNCTAD). The significance of multilateral efforts at monetary and payments cooperation was emphasised at some of the earliest initiatives on Asian-African Cooperation. The Afro-Asian Conference, held at Bandung in April 1955, accepted the principle of enlarging the scope of multilateral trade and payments arrangements. It recognised at the same time that some countries would have to take recourse to bilateral trade arrangements in view of their prevailing economic conditions[24]. The Third Non-Aligned Summit held at Lusaka in 1970, adopted the Programme of Action in the field of Trade Cooperation and Development which resolved, "to evolve payments arrangements to support expansion of trade exchanges among developing countries."[25] The ECDC programme under the auspices of G-77 further played a crucial role in outlining the agenda for monetary and payments cooperation among developing countries. The G-77 Conference on Economic Cooperation among Developing Countries held in Mexico in 1976 sought "establishment of a developing country payments union, through strengthening and improving existing clearing and payments arrangements, promoting new ones at sub-regional, regional and interregional level and establishing links among existing payment schemes."[26]

The subsequent meeting of the G-77 at Arusha in 1979, recommended with regard to the CPAs, "strengthening of the existing arrangements is considered to be a priority task". It recognised that the "establishment and development of subregional payments arrangement has shown that they constitute an important starting point to foster a gradual approach toward the creation of global network of multilateral schemes open to all developing countries, the expectation being that at a later stage an important element of reciprocal credits to support mutual trade flows will be incorporated. Fundamental importance is attached to the need for adopting all necessary steps aimed at promoting gradual but prompt linking up of multilateral payments arrangements within a global strategy for expansion of trade."[27] The emphasis on monetary and payments cooperation simultaneously developed as the inadequacy of the international economic system in taking care of the pressing concerns of developing countries such as declining share of trade, mounting debts, and adverse terms of trade was increasingly felt. Thus the importance of institutional arrangements within South that could not only assist in regional integration efforts but also provide them with autonomous support mechanisms to meet specific financial requirements, was realised.

In the more recent times, with the onset of globalisation and the moves towards global convertibility of currencies, scope of monetary and payments cooperation is still found to be valid. They have been seen as providing facilities for deferred payment, credit for intra-regional trade and through limited convertibility, a step towards global convertibility.[28] The G-77 and China meet held in San Jose in 1997 sought strengthening and enhancing South-South Cooperation to enable the developing countries to meet the challenges posed by globalisation and liberalisation. It also called for international and regional financial institutions to provide concrete support to the efforts of developing countries in this direction.[29]

By and large, the case for monetary and payments cooperation has been put forward primarily as making a positive contribution towards trade expansion effects. At the same time, there have been attempts to see it as providing an autonomous institutional basis for South to cover a wider domain. We shall briefly touch upon the proposals and actions that have been formulated time and again as part of South-South Cooperation. The main categories under which monetary and payments cooperation has been discussed are as under:

(a) Specific project/based financing.
(b) Multilateral or regional financial mechanisms.
(c) Broad based global institutional mechanisms.

(a) Specific Project/Based Financing

These have included a more localised initiative based on specific proposals relating to joint ventures and projects established under a mutual agreement by developing countries. The high level conference on Economic Cooperation among Developing Countries held in Caracas, Venezuela in 1981, discussed at length a set of proposals on financial cooperation among developing countries.[30] With specific reference to joint ventures and direct investments in a number of areas, it favoured establishment of regional and subregional banks. These could in turn establish facilities to undertake equity investments and promote co-financing of equity investments from other developing countries. It also discussed various investment incentives, joint venture agreements and other instruments to enhance intra-developing country capital flows. At the same time, additional measures have been suggested such as better exchange of information relating to development projects among the banks of developing countries.[31] Such exchange could enable the respective executive boards to design their future policy and be a useful source of information to the interested companies thinking of investing in other countries.

(b) Multilateral and Regional Financial Mechanisms

The regional financial initiatives have been regarded as the most effective and viable means of promoting South-South Cooperation. These have often been seen as complementing the regional cooperation and integration efforts that have been witnessed in developing countries. The various forms in which regional arrangements have been witnessed are as follows:

(i) *Multilateral Clearing and Payments Arrangements*—Such arrangements have been generally part of regional cooperation programmes among developing countries and their role in promoting trade has been seen as complementary to that of purely commercial instruments. Nevertheless, clearing arrangements, along with credit facilities for balance of payments support have been regarded as effective instruments of trade expansion.[32] The multilateral clearing arrangements tend to make use of the participants' currencies in the settlement of intra-regional trade, thereby economising on the use of hard currency among the member countries.

They are also important means of enhancing Central Bank interaction and promote greater linkages among the commercial banks of the region. The next chapter will deal at length with the various multilateral clearing and payments arrangement that have been in operation worldwide and discuss the peculiar characteristics that such arrangements exhibit.

(ii) *Regional Trade Financing Arrangements*—Promotion of schemes for export financing and guarantee facilities have been another major area where South-South Monetary Cooperation has been stressed. It has been pointed out that the growth of developing country exports depends to a large extent on their ability to succeed in the highly competitive world market where developed country exports are able to get extensive export credit on short-medium and long term basis, with guarantees and insurance provided by the government.[33] Emphasis has been laid therefore towards setting up of regional and interregional trade development banks and the establishment of Export Credit Guarantee facilities.

(iii) *Regional Reserve Funds*—Several regional arrangements providing their members with financial facilities to cover part of their balance of payments deficits have been another area where cooperation among developing countries has been stressed. At times these facilities have been established in addition to the payments arrangements. Such arrangements seek to address some of the fundamental concerns of the developing countries based on the likelihood of greater trade liberalisation leading to more balance of payments problems and drainage in their foreign exchange reserves.[34] As we shall see further, such arrangements have generally operated on the basis of a fund or pool of international monetary reserves contributed by the Central Banks of the member countries from their own available international reserves.

The regional financial initiatives as highlighted above have been the most effective instruments of South-South monetary interaction. Possibly, developing countries have found it much more convenient to participate in a regional facility where stakes are more immediate and common, unlike the global initiatives for South which have been mooted at times. This brings us to the final category under which Monetary and Payments Cooperation has figured under South-South Cooperation.

(c) Broad Based Global Institutional Mechanisms

These measures, to a certain extent an extension of regional initiatives, refer to the creation of global facilities for the South. This could provide an alternative support structure for developing countries, thereby reducing their dependence on the North. Some of these proposals have included.

(i) *A South Currency*—A common currency for developing countries had been mooted which could be used as part payment for goods and services traded among themselves. Such a currency would be expected to increase the purchasing power of each member country over the goods and services of every other member.[35] Besides, such scheme could operate irrespective of the system of trade or foreign exchange control of participating countries and they would be free to impose restrictions whenever economic conditions so required. The scheme could run for a period of possibly three years with provision for a subsequent review. Like the Special Drawing Right (SDR) the new currency could consist of book entries in ledgers and its allocation be based upon an agreed criteria. The proposal, however did not address the problem of possible accumulated arrears as some countries are likely to develop persistent surpluses with large amounts of accumulated new currency with others having persistent deficit.[36]

(ii) *A Third World Reserve Fund*—The proposal for a reserve fund managed by pooling in part of reserves of convertible currencies of developing countries was also seen as addressing balance of payments problems of member countries. Under such an arrangements, drawing rights could be determined according to global balance of payments deficits of members.[37] It was recognised that the general shortage of currencies among less developed countries could lead to difficulties in some member's contributions to such a facility. However, the members of the Organisation of Petroleum Exporting Countries making special contributions to the reserve fund was seen as a possible way out.[38]

(iii) *A South Bank*—There have also been proposals for a bank for developing countries which would be more like a commercial and merchant bank which could engage itself in all kind of banking activities. Such a bank, apart from pure banking activities, could also engage in training of banking professionals, commercial intelligence of particular interest in trade among developing countries, marketing research and identification, evaluation and formulation of projects. The initiative by the G-77 for the establishment of the G-77 development bank could be seen as a step in this regard.[39]

Thus we see that monetary and payments cooperation has been a major theme in South-South Cooperation. Its content and emphasis however, has varied depending on the parameters under which such cooperation has been sought. In the present context, one finds that the issues that were generally sought to be addressed have by and large still remained relevant. There has been, however, a gradual decline in emphasis on the role of such arrangements within the South in tackling these issues. This brings us to the subject matter of the present study which intends to study the changing patterns and context of Monetary and Payments Cooperation in South Asia by taking up the case study of Asian Clearing Union.

1.4 Scope and Objectives of the Present Study

The trends towards globalisation and liberalisation seem to be redefining the issues and priorities of the South away from collective efforts towards tackling common problems. This is more so in case of various mechanisms like monetary and payments arrangements designed and practiced under South-South Cooperation in the past. In such an environment a study of impact on regional monetary and payments mechanisms established during the time when South-South Cooperation had a definite, agenda gives us an important insight into the nature of crisis such initiatives face in the present context. There appears to be a two fold crises facing such arrangements. First, there is the moot question of redefining their role and agenda in a globalised world. Are such arrangements internally competent to be in tune with the nature of and pace of change that international monetary and financial system is witnessing? Secondly, are the countries which are part of these arrangements comfortable with the twin objectives of global integration and regional cooperation that are to be reconciled? In other words, are the member countries able to fulfil their obligations as members of a regional monetary arrangements, yet remain committed to the objectives of global convertibility, to raise a specific issue?

The case study of the Asian Clearing Union, the only clearing arrangement of its kind in Asia is an ideal example which may be taken up to analyse this dichotomy. Set up way back in 1975, the ACU is an example of a relatively successful clearing and payment arrangement across the globe without ever registering a default in its 32 years of operations. There are several reasons that make it an interesting theme of study. Firstly, it is the only existing mechanism of monetary and financial interaction in a region which is gradually responding to the imperatives of globalisation with continuous reforms in various institutional structures and policy framework. Secondly, it has periodically undergone changes which have at times raised fundamental questions about the viability of the mechanism *per se*. One is rather curious to know whether the adaptability has been a major reason for its continued function', Thirdly, unlike most other clearing arrangements, ACU has functioned in absence of any major regional integration initiative, its regular efforts to connect with the South Asian

Association for Regional Cooperation notwithstanding. Thus the ACU comes up as one of the important case studies which is relevant both because of their history and present.

The present state of literature on the ACU is rather limited both by its scope and coverage. First of all, there are very few independent studies on the ACU. In most of the literature ACU finds a mention as one of the many clearing arrangements across the developing world with the focus being merely on the objectives and operations of the Union. This strand of literature generally consists of the Reports by the UNCTAD, Independent Studies on South-South Cooperation etc. The other category of literature consists of the studies on Monetary and Payments Cooperation in South Asia where the role of the ACU is discussed as an instrument of promoting greater monetary interaction in South Asia.[40]

Such studies however, do not elaborate on the modifications needed in the mechanism to perform this role, barring an occasional mention. The third and the final stream of literature focuses on the ACU itself. It primarily consists of sponsored and independent studies conducted to review the functioning of the mechanism and suggest the possible changes needed to fine tune the functioning of the system.[41] Most of these studies are quite elaborate and deal extensively with both operational and procedural aspects. One of the common elements in these studies is that ACU has been analysed more at the macro level in terms of the organisation *per se*. Adequate analysis has not been done on the issues related to country specific perceptions and therein countries the instruments and procedures. Besides, adequate analysis of the trade patterns in tune with the ACU transactions is also not manifested.

The present study seeks to analyse the ACU from both the holistic as well as disaggregated point of view and attempts to link it up with the larger issue of monetary and financial cooperation in South Asia. At the broader level, it tries to judge ACU from patterns that are emerging at the global level particularly with regard to the issues of global convertibility and trade expansion. At the micro-level, it aims at analysing individual member states' perceptions and policies to shape the opinion on ACU. Simultaneously this study makes an effort to integrate these two levels of analysis to contribute to a better understanding of the problems and prospects of the ACU and how it could be adapted to meet the requirements of deeper monetary interaction in the region.

The specific objectives that the study shall seek to address would be to:

- put in perspective the significance of monetary and financial cooperation among developing countries as part of South-South Cooperation,
- explore the various elements of such cooperation in South Asia,
- study the origin of the Asian Clearing Union and the method of its operation,
- examine the trends and pattern of various transactions cleared through the mechanism,
- correlate these trends with the intra-regional and external trade pattern of the member countries,
- discuss the implications of various policy changes introduced in ACU at different stages,
- suggest the possible ways and means to modify the functioning of the ACU to make it more meaningful and useful to the cause of deeper monetary interaction in South Asia.

The present study shall put to test several hypotheses which would be as follows:

- The concept of Monetary and Payments Cooperation over the years has undergone a change in tune with global economic environment.
- At the regional level, Monetary and Payments Cooperation has so far been accorded only a limited role as a means to facilitate intra-regional trade and transit.
- The Asian Clearing Union, despite expanding its

activities has not been able to play a major promotional role in trade among member countries.

- The ACU has not been able to expand its role beyond that of a clearing facility to that of an agent of greater monetary cooperation.
- With the onset of economic reforms in most of the South Asian Countries, the prospects for ACU remain uncertain particularly in the absence of any major operational changes within it.

In line with the above objectives and hypotheses the study shall follow a thematic chapterisation. The second chapter shall deal with the conceptual and the theoretical issues relating to Monetary and Payments Cooperation. It would also analyse the levels and patterns in which such cooperation has been sought among various nations across the globe. While describing the patterns, it shall also seek to highlight the specific features and characteristics relevant to various clearing and payments arrangements. The third chapter would discuss the ACU in terms of its origin and evolution, particularly analysing the context in which it was set up. It would try to analyse the economic environment within and outside the ACU member countries which motivated the formation of the facility. It would then study the objectives that were laid out at the time of its inception, trying to place them in the immediate context. Subsequently it would also discuss the specific features through which this facility was to operate and try to see if these were in tune with the objectives that were laid out.

The fourth chapter examines the performance of the ACU in terms of its functioning over the years. It further assesses the institutional performance of the ACU alone (relating to transactions within ACU) and also tries to correlate these with the policies and performance of individual member countries. It also makes an effort to do a disaggregated analysis of the trade pattern of ACU member countries. The figures for the recent years have been added as annexure to the chapter to main continuity.

The fifth chapter would look into the critical issues facing the ACU today. The emphasis would be on placing the role of the ACU in the present context and try to redefine its agenda in the light of new priorities. It shall highlight the complexities that union faces in terms of administrative and procedural fronts as seen by the various constituents of the mechanism (bankers, traders etc.) and try to give some suggestions to address the present crisis.

The sixth chapter, that has been added as a post-script to the main thesis analyses the recent debates on monetary cooperation in South Asia and tries to explore how there appears to be a lack of convergence between the ideas propounded and the effective use of the mechanisms existing in the area. The final chapter would present concluding observations.

NOTES

1. World Trade Organisation, *Annual Report 1998*, p. 35.
2. See UNCTAD *Report on Globalization and Development, 2004* at http://www.unctad.org/en/docs/gdscsir20041c1_en.pdf. According to the Report, the per capita GDP for developing countries during 1980-2000 has increased from US $936 to US $1417, wheras for the developed world, it has risen by US $20397 to US $30557 for the same period.
3. V.R. Panchmukhi, *Contemporary International Economics* (Delhi, 1998), p. 5.
4. World Trade Organisation, n. 1, p. 33.
5. Richard Higgot, "*The International Political Economy of Regionalism*", in William D. Coleman and Geoffrey R.D. Underhill (eds.), Regionalism and Global Economic Integration: Europe. Asia and the Americas (London, 1998), p. 42.
6. Charles Oman, Globalisation and Regionalism: *The Challenge for Developing Countries* (Paris, 1994), p. 34.
7. *ibid.*
8. W. Andrew Axiline, The Political Economy of Regional Cooperation: *Comparative Case Studies* (London, 1994), p. 5.
9. Bela Balassa, *The Theory of Economic Integration* (London, 1961), p. 118.
10. Percy Mistry, *Regional Integration: Panacea and Pitfalls*. R.I.S Occasional Paper No. 47, p. 69.

11. Jaime Serra (*et al.*), Reflections on Regionalism, Report of the Study Group on International Trade, *Carnegie Endowment for International Peace* (Washington DC, 1997), p. 7.
12. Praveen Krishna, "Regionalism and Multilateralism: A Political Economy Approach", *Quarterly Journal of Economics*, February 1998, p. 229.
13. Jagdish Bhagwati and Anne A. Krueger, *The Dangerous Drift to Preferential Trade Agreements* (Washington DC, 1993), p. 29.
14. C. Fred Bergsten, "Globalising Free Trade", *Foreign Affairs*, Vol. 75, No.3, May-June 1996, p. 106.
15. Renato Ruggiero,"Multilateralism and Regionalism in Trade", *Reprinted from United States Information Agency's Electronic Journal*, November 1996.
16. *Ibid.*
17. See North-South: A Programme for Survival, *The Report of the Independent Commission on International Development Issues under the Chairmanship of Willy Brandt* (London,1980), p. 33. The Report was the first of its kind which came out with an exhaustive set of recommendations encompassing a gamut of North-South relations pertaining to poverty, food aid, trade, disarmament and the world monetary system. A few years later, it was followed by another report titled *Common Crisis, North-South: Cooperation for World Recovery*. The Brandt Commission 1983, which reflected on the impending crisis in the global economy and expressed dissatisfaction with the inadequate responses to tackle it.
18. Jagdish Bhagwati, 'The Global Age: From a Skeptical South to a Fearful North,' This paper was originally presented at the Raul Prebisch Lecture at UNCT-AD IX in Johannesburg, South Africa, on April 29, 1996. Reprinted in Jagdish Bhagwati, A Stream of Windows: *Unsettling Reflections on Trade, Immigration and Democracy* (New Delhi, 1999), p. 32.
19. V.R. Panchmukhi, *"South-South Cooperation: Possibilities and Challenges"* in Panchmukhi, n.2. 1998, p. 189. The author argues a case for a new rationale for South-South Cooperation deriving from the old rationale and arguments, many of which are still valid.
20. *WTO Annual Report* 1999, p. 8.
21. Economic and Social Survey of Asia and the Pacific (New York: United Nations, 1999), p. 23.
22. See the address by George Soros titled "Towards a Global Open Society: International Portfolio Investors", delivered to the World Bank Group-International Monetary Fund Annual Meeting, Hong

Kong SAR, China, September 21, 1997. Soros highlighted five main deficiencies of the global capitalist system, namely-uneven distribution of benefits, instability of the financial system, incipient threat of the global monopolies, role of the state and lastly, the question of values and social cohesion.

23. Issues of financial sector regulation, establishment of common prudential standards for the industry and development of early warning systems and establishment of a regional reserve fund were seen as possible areas for regional cooperation. See the Economic and Social Survey of Asia and the Pacific, n. 21, 1999, p. 71
24. Text of the Declaration of the Asian-African Conference, Bandung, 18-24 April, 1955 in ECDC Handbook/Documents of the Movement of Non-Aligned Countries and the Group of 77 (New Delhi: Ministry of External Affairs, 1983), p. 2.
25. Action Programme in the field of Trade, Cooperation and Development, adopted at the Third Non-Aligned Summit, Lusaka 8-10 September, 1970, in *ibid.* p. 9.
26. Resolution adopted at the G-77. *ECDC Programme/Mexico Conference on Economic Cooperation Among Developing Countries*, Mexico city 13-22, September, 1976 in *ibid.* p. 122.
27. G-77 ECDC Programme/Fourth, Meeting of G-77, *Arusha 12-16* February, 1979 in *ibid.*, p.138.
28. "Cooperation among Developing Countries in a Globalising Economy: Issues and Action Proposals", *RIS Digest,* Vo1. 14, No. 1-3, September 1997, p. 1.
29. See the San Jose Declaration of the G-77 and China meet at San Jose, 13-15 January 1997, in *ibid.*, p.166-170.
30. Dragoslav Avramovic (ed.), South-South Financial Cooperation: Approaches to the Current Crisis, *The Jamaica Papers.* (London, 1983), p. 2.
31. M. Marak "Exchange of Information among Developing Countries" Banks in the Field of Development Projects" in *South-South Banking Cooperation,* Regional Centre for Cooperation with Developing Countries (Ljubljana, 1983), p. 226.
32. Tomas Afonso Medina, "Monetary and Payments Agreements Among Developing Countries" in Breda Pavlic (*et al.*), *The Challenges of South-South Cooperation* (Colarado, 1983), p. 142.
33. Frances Stewart and Arjun Sengupta, International Financial Cooperation: *A Framework for Change* (Colarado, 1982), p. 173.
34. Tomas Afonso Medina, n.32, p.150.
35. *Ibid.* p. 185.

36. R. Stamenkovic, "*Proposals for Third World Financial Cooperation*" in Avramovic, n.30, p. 84.
37. F. Stewart, n.33, p.188.
38. Stamenkovic, n.36, p. 60. The proposal for an OPEC Fund was mooted first by Iraq in 1979. As per the proposal, the OPEC Special Fund could be converted into a development agency which could look after varied functions such as financing of balance of payments deficits, economic and social development projects and could underwrite loans floated by developing countries.
39. See the Draft Articles of Agreement of G-77 Development Bank, First Edition 1977.
40. S.S. Colomb age, *Monetary and Payments Cooperation* (Colombo, 1993); B.K. Madan, *Towards Monetary Cooperation in South Asia* (New Delhi, 1986); I.N. Mukherjee. "Towards Financial and Monetary Cooperation in South Asia", *South Asia Journal*, Vol.4, No. 2, 1990, I. N. Mukharjee. *Towards Economic Integration in Asia: An Evaluation of Trade Expansion Programme of Developing Countries in Asia and Pacific* (New Delhi, 1978); Committee on Studies for Cooperation in Development in South Asia: Regional Issues (New Delhi, 1984); K.M. Matin, *Monetary Cooperation in South Asia* (n. d.).
41. See M. Y. Khan, "Asian Clearing Union; An Assessment", *Reserve Bank of India Bulletin*, February 1991. Deepak Mohanty and Rajeev Ranjan, "Monetary Expansion and Inflation in Asian Clearing Union Countries", *RBI occasional papers*, Vo1. 14, No. 3, September 1993; Ercan Ugyar, *The Asian Clearing Union: An Assessment and Prospects, Paper for the UNCTAD Secretariat*, May 1994; R. Janakiraman, *Critical Study of the Procedure Regarding the Operations of the Asian Clearing Union, Study conducted for the ACU Secretariat*, 1995.

Chapter 2

Monetary and Payments Cooperation: Conceptual Issues

2.1 Introduction

The efforts towards regional cooperation across the world have been quite diverse in terms of both scope and content. Measures taken in this direction reflect the degree to which the member countries intend to explore the 'regional' option as compared to the bilateral or the multilateral one. Even within the regional arrangements, there are at times different patterns that emerge, showing the extent to which the regional choice prevails over national policy autonomy. For instance, while the European Monetary Union is gradually coming to terms with challenges and opportunities provided by the Euro, a fragile grouping like the South Asian Association for Regional Cooperation is still in the process of defining a critical agenda which would initiate a discussion on monetary and financial cooperation.

The present chapter is aimed at developing a conceptual framework for monetary and payments cooperation in order to trace the crucial nuances and functional matrices in existing arrangements. The attempt will be to first put the role of monetary and payments cooperation in the present global economic environment in a proper perspective. This would include highlighting the increasing significance of monetary arrangements in strengthening trade and capital flows across various regions. Subsequently, various forms of such cooperation would be analysed, giving at the same time the theoretical underpinnings of the issues involved. Attempts will also be made to correlate the theories with certain contemporary experiences where the role played by monetary and payments arrangements would be critically assessed particularly in terms of their ability to achieve broader objectives.

2.2 Monetary and Payments Issues

Monetary issues primarily relate to the flow of funds and its allocation across various sectors of the economy. They have a bearing on both the internal and the external components of the economy. For instance, at the domestic level are the issues relating to the money supply, the interest rates, inflation, the reserve ratios maintained with the banks etc. At the external level, the monetary issues deal with the impact of these policy measures on the balance of payments situation of a country. We shall elaborate on these issues one by one.

Money Supply

The supply of money in an economy is jointly determined by the monetary authority, banks and the public. It is the monetary authority which plays an active and dominant role in determination of the money supply. Any discussion on the determinants of the money supply depends crucially upon the definition of the money employed. The narrower the definition, the smaller will be the range of assets which are included and hence fewer will be the determinant factors.[1] In theoretical terms, money is measured as[2]—

$$M = C + DD$$

(Narrow measure of money = currency + demand deposits of banks held by the public).

The other measure of money known as high powered money, produced by the monetary authority is defined as—

$$H = C + R$$

(Reserve money = currency held by the public + cash reserves of the banks).

Furthermore, as per the H theory of money supply, it is the H (high powered money) that is the single most important and dominant factor that determines money supply. It is also called the money mutliplier theory of money supply. The equation is given by

$$M = mH$$

where,

m = money multiplier = $1 + c/[c + r(1 + t)]$,
r = bank's demand for reserves/total deposits,
t = time deposits/demand deposits, and
c = currency/deposit ratio of the public.

Interest Rates

Interest rate may be defined in general terms as the price established by the intersection of the supply of and the demand for future claims on resources.[3] It may also be termed as the price paid for borrowed funds. When this price is expressed as a rate per cent per unit time, such as per year or per month, it becomes a rate of interest. Since interest is cost to the borrower and return to the lender, it affects borrowing and lending, investment and saving, portfolio composition, selection of projects and their lives, capital intensity of production techniques chosen, international capital flows and distribution of income.

There are two main theories of determination of rate of interests. The first is Keynes' theory of liquidity preference, according to which rate of interest is a purely monetary phenomenon. Interest rate is in-fact a reward for parting with liquidity which is determined in the money market by the demand and supply of money. It is in sharp contrast to the classical theory in which interest rate is a real phenomenon which is determined in the commodity market by savings and investment at a level which equates the two. The loanable funds theory is an extension of the classical savings and investment theory of rate of interest and incorporates monetary factors with the non-monetary factors of savings and investment. According to this theory, the rate of interest is determined by the demand and supply of funds in the economy at that level at which the two are equated. At a more broader level the loanable funds market and the money market together play a critical role in determination of interest rests. Simultaneous equilibrium in these markets determines the rate of interest and aggregate income.[4]

Inflation

Inflation refers to a persistent rise in the general level of prices, usually measured as a rate per cent per unit, by forces operating on the demand side (demand pull) when aggregate demand has been pulled above what the economy is capable of producing in the short run. It may also be due to cost push, where autonomous increases in some important component or the other of cost is the true source of inflation. The three important ingredients of such theories are: (i) that the upward push in cost is autonomous of demand conditions in the concerned market, (ii) that the push forces operate through some important cost components such as wages, profits or material costs, and (iii) increase in costs is passed on to buyers of goods in the form of higher prices and not absorbed by producers.[5]

Reserve Ratios

These are primarily instruments of monetary control exercised by the Central Bank. Banks always keep a certain proportion of their total assets in from of cash, partly to meet the statutory reserve requirement and partly to meet their own day to day needs for making cash payments. Cash is held partly in the form of cash in hand and partly as balances with the Central Bank. All such cash is called cash reserve. They are usually divided under two heads: (a) required reserves, and (b) excess reserves. Required reserves are cash balances which a bank is statutorily required to hold with the Central Bank (for example, the Cash Reserve Ratio which is statutorily imposed by the Reserve Bank of India on the banks). Variations in the Required Reserve Ratios acts as an important instrument in controlling the supply of money by affecting the lending capacity of the banks. These have been regarded as better means of monetary control as compared to interest rate adjustments especially in times of severe inflationary pressures primarily because of lags in the adjustments of the latter.[6] Besides required reserves, banks also hold excess reserves which are reserves in excess of the required reserves. It is only these (excess) reserves which banks as a whole can use to meet their currency drains. The above mentioned variables constitute the key elements of the monetary policy in an economy. They are inter-linked with each other in a manner that the long-term objectives of growth and stability are maintained. For instance, an economy operating at below capacity is sought to be injected with an expansionary monetary policy. With increase in money supply the interest rate decreases, thereby leading to the spurt in private investment and inflationary pressure. This fuels excess demand in the economy as a result of which growth picks up. Monetary strategies, therefore, are concerned with determining the process of shock absorption in the economy in such a way that certain targets such as stabilization of output or the price level can be reached in an optimal way. This involves determining to what extent shocks should be contained by varying the money supply, interest rate or exchange rate in the economy.[7] This brings us to the external component of the monetary policy which affects the balance of payments equilibrium in the economy.

In a situation of domestic unemployment and external surplus expansionary monetary policy reduces interest rates and thereby stimulates private investment and income levels. With increase in income levels, imports of goods and services increases thereby increasing current account surpluses; and interest rate decreases would induce capital outflows, thereby eliminating current account surpluses. Similarly in case of domestic inflation and external deficit, a contractionary monetary policy increases the interest rate, thus reducing private investment and income levels. Imports of goods and services decreases thereby reducing current account deficits and interest rate increases leads to inflows of capital thus eliminating current account deficits. Such monetarist view, therefore, utilizes the monetary approach to the balance of payments in discussing the role of monetary policy in an open economy.[8]

Payments Issues

A payments system is the set of institutional arrangements through which purchasing power is transferred from one transactor to another. Thus an efficient organization of the monetary system is the *sin qua non* of an efficient payments system. The Central Bank is directly concerned with smooth functioning of the payment system. At the domestic level, the Central Bank supervises the banks and play key roles in the payment system and establishes appropriate public policy to govern the structure of private clearing and settlement arrangements. At the global level, the Central Bank adopts minimum standards to guide the design and operation of cross-border and multi-currency inter-bank netting arrangements.[9]

There are three key factors determining the effectiveness of the payment system. These are: range of usability, opportunity cost and riskiness. The value of a payments instruments increases with its usability, i.e. the volume, variety and significance of transactions for which it is acceptable. For instance, a universal means of payment would be regarded as the most effective instrument. The attractiveness of an asset as means of payment diminishes as the opportunity cost of holding the asset increases. This applies to cases where the resources tied up in holding a particular payment instrument could be invested in other assets having more returns. Lastly, the lesser the risk associated with holding a payment instrument, the greater is the attractiveness of that instrument. Such risks which could lead to decline in value of payment instrument could include depreciation risk—due to domestic inflation and external devaluation, default risk—when one participant in a transaction may default on his obligation leaving his counterpart to absorb the losses and systemic risk—which may deprive the agent of funds to settle his own obligations such as banking crises.[10]

Monetary and payments issues as discussed above combine to provide smooth functioning of the financial system. While the monetary variables ensure that the flow of funds is within the broad parameters of the monetary policy, the payments system ensures that transfer of funds takes place in a smooth and efficient manner. Together therefore, they play a crucial role in the national economic system. At the same time they have an equally significant role to play at the regional level. We shall elaborate this as we now discuss the role and rationale of monetary and payments cooperation.

2.3 Monetary and Payments Cooperation: Role and Rationale

The emerging pattern of international economic relations poses a certain paradoxical situation before the developing countries which seek greater integration in the global economy. On the one hand, they have to cope up with declining aid commitments which tends to put severe strains on their attempts to attain long-term growth. On the other hand, the compulsion to mobilize resources through other means makes them rely more on commercial capital flows, which adds to their vulnerability due to increasing volatility in the financial markets.[11] The private capital flows tend to sharply react whenever there are signs of decline in share prices. It is generally felt therefore, that a certain amount of policy coordination and regulation across the region is essential for nations to adjust to peculiar economic circumstances which might not always be conducive.

Monetary and payments issues have had a significant bearing on the way the global economy has evolved over a period of time. History of international monetary relations has shown that nations have been concerned with managing an ideal mix of exchange rate stability and concomitant monetary balance. While stability in exchange rates ensures an efficient price allocation in the tradable sector and gives positive signals to the foreign investors, monetary stability by way of keeping a check on money supply ensures domestic price stability. Steps in this direction have led nations to collaborate both at the global or the regional level by following a set of generally accepted rules.[12] For example, the post war reconstruction period saw the search for a transnational monetary system which could exude confidence and could withstand occasional disturbances such as balance of payment disequilibria and declining value of currencies. Besides, even as the search for an ideal international monetary system continued, regional initiatives were undertaken at the same time to foster monetary cooperation in tune with the growth of regionalism across the world.[13] As we shall elaborate later, these developments in the monetary sphere were in direct response to the distinct patterns that emerged in the global political economy, particularly so with regard to regional integration groupings such as European Union.

Monetary cooperation has a wider dimension as it entails a harmonization of variables such as interest rates and exchange rates having a bearing on monetary interaction among the nations. By its very nature it is generally part of a broader plan of economic integration of a region. It generally involves a certain amount of harmonization on monetary, fiscal and exchange rate policies to achieve macro-economic coordination with regard to money supply, taxation and exchange rate management respectively. Countries could go in for an adjustable pegged exchange rate system for instance, which fixes their exchange rates around a central rate and a band around these rates within which they can fluctuate freely. When the limits of this band are reached the Central Banks of the currencies involved are committed to maintain the exchange rate within the band.[14] This was done primarily to reduce exchange rate variability which could endanger the integration process. The other exchange rate systems include managed floating and the free floating.[15]

A system of fixed exchange rates inevitably incorporates in it other variables, such as money supply and interest rates as there is more pressure on the latter two with regard to balance of payment adjustment. This mechanism faces the problem of how to set the system wide level of money supply and interest rate. Under such a scenario, two possibilities exist. In the first case, one country takes the role of anchoring the money supply in the system, with the other countries adjusting their interest rates compatible to this level; or the countries could decide jointly about the level of money supply and interest rates. In the second case, cooperative monetary action can be sought in this regard through the system of intervention in foreign exchange markets. When the currencies hit their upper limits, the intervention would be in each other's currency so that the monetary effect in the two countries would be symmetrical.[16]

Payments cooperation has a rather specific and well defined role. Although it is generally discussed as part of broader monetary and financial arrangements that are undertaken among nations, there is nevertheless a need to delineate its definite role. It essentially deals with bilateral and multilateral payment mechanisms existing within nations and seeks to facilitate and harmonize the procedures that generally operate in settlement of mutual transactions. Payments cooperation at a specific level involves efficiency and economy in the settlement of transactions. At a broader level, it seeks to develop mechanisms that support the payment capabilities of the nations as the need arises.

There has been a quest for ideal payment mechanisms which could meet the challenges posed by ever expanding global economy. In the more recent times, the onset of financial iberalization, has led to opening of the capital markets to foreign institutional investors as well as local players raising funds from global equity markets. As a result, there has been a need for simultaneous reforms in payment system policies and operations. The international effort in this regard has aimed at ensuring a consistency between domestic objectives in payment system designing and its operational efficiency and competitiveness of international payments arrangements.[17] As in the monetary sphere, the payments arrangements too have been diversified ranging from a purely post war reconstruction arrangements such as the European Payments Union to a more reformist, technology driven Trans-European Automated Real-Time Gross Settlement Express Transfer System (Target).

Monetary and payment issues taken together, therefore form the core of any effort towards strengthening financial linkages across the region as well as the world. They seek to provide an adequate support mechanism to the existing institutional linkages in trade and investment by financing and facilitating intra-regional initiatives. They are therefore, likely to function more effectively where such linkages already sustain, rather than in isolation. The basic premise for cooperation in the field of international monetary relations is based on growing interdependence in the world economy. As stated previously, this is amply indicated by high average annual growth of both exports and foreign direct investment in the last 20 years. In recent times, linkages among countries have strengthened through the integration of markets for goods, services and capital.

Simultaneously, due to greater openness, a country's immunity from commercial and financial development elsewhere often tends to get reduced. In specific terms, a government's actions such as sudden devaluation could generate a variety of spillover effects, both regional and global. Depending upon the position of the country vis-a-vis others, it could influence its own ability and the ability of others to achieve preferred macro-economic or exchange rate objectives. The basic rationale for monetary cooperation has therefore, been stated as that of 'internalizing' these externalities, which are external costs arising out of growing burden on exporters for instance. This is done by giving each government partial control over the action of others, thereby preventing each one separately from reaching its own targets on its own,[18] by adopting a coordinated approach towards regional monetary and exchange rate policy.

Monetary cooperation at the global level has been however, regarded as a difficult proposition to sustain. The main reason behind this being that there is a certain intrinsic incompatibility of three key elements of government; exchange rate stability, capital mobility and national policy autonomy. These three elements have been stated as forming a kind of 'Unholy trinity' that operates regularly to erode efforts towards monetary cooperation.[19] This is because in a situation of pegged exchange rates and integrated financial markets, pursuit of independent monetary policy may lead to balance of payments disequilibrium and thus provoke outflow of speculative capital. The governments may therefore, in order to preserve exchange rate stability, either limit movement of capital or their own policy autonomy (through some joint decision) making. If any of these cannot be done, then exchange rate stability may have to be compromised. Thus the three goals may not be achieved simultaneously.[20] This must not however, prevent governments from undertaking suitable collaborative exercises aimed at exploring ways and means for greater monetary policy coordination. Given this desirability and rationale for such cooperation, it becomes imperative to go into certain theoretical issues outlining the various forms of cooperative monetary arrangements that have been entered into.

2.4 Theoretical Issues

The international monetary system as it evolved after the Second World War went through different phases of collaboration and discord. The agenda of post war reconstruction witnessed different agreements being entered into in order to maintain stability in exchange rates and payments. The setting up of Bretton Woods system of fixed exchange rates supported by a strong U.S. dollar reflected the ability of the U.S. to dominate the international monetary agenda. In 1971 however, Bretton Woods collapsed as the U.S. decided to suspend convertibility of dollar into gold as it ran into a huge fiscal deficit and decline in reserves. Attempts have been made to conceptualise these developments in terms of the theory of hegemonic stability. As per this theory, presence of a hegemonic power is crucial for continuance of strong international regimes. While fragmentation of power between competing countries leads to fragmentation of international economic regimes, the concentration of power is likely to lead to stability. The fact that the Bretton Woods regime collapsed only after the U.S. reserves had fallen sharply is seen as consistent with the theory of hegemonic stability. Apart from the presence of a hegemonic power, what is also needed is the existence of an international consensus on the objectives and formulation of monetary policy that allows central bank policies to be harmonized.[21]

The dominant role that U.S. played in the post war reconstruction particularly by providing the dollar liquidity enabled the weaker nations to build on the former's strength. The three major roles of the dollar—as a transactions currency, an intervention currency and a reserve currency were described as closely linked.[22] It was pointed out that elimination of either of these roles would seriously affect the other. International role of any currency was partly also seen as depending on the national dominance of their countries of issue, the cooperation extended by other countries and the attributes and national goals of the key currency country. Thus the international monetary system, backed by the gold dollar exchange functioned smoothly. But the moment the stability of the dollar and therefore, the ability of the U.S. to fund its obligations declined, the system took a severe beating.

This theory however, doesn't suggest the causal sequences adequately as the other factors which shaped the U.S. position during the period should also be taken into account. Thus while the theory does help to a certain extent in understanding the smooth operation of the classical gold standard and early Bretton Woods, much of the evidence needs a lot more clarification than the theory seeks, to answer. It has been stated rather, that 'Hegemonic Cooperation' that means cooperation existing even as a dominant player is present and encourages cooperative behaviour among others appears to be more directly applicable to international monetary relations.[23] This implies that the strength of the dollar may have acted as a key factor in evolving cooperative framework vis-a-vis other currencies.

The international monetary system in the more recent times has been characterized by a kind of iberalization of currencies[24] among blocs, with dollar exerting its influence in the western hemisphere, the yen in East Asia and the mark in Europe. There have been empiricial efforts at liberalization of currencies and its effect on trade. The idea of a currency bloc was reinforced with the tendency for nominal exchange rate variability to be lower within most of the groups than across the groups. The analysis showed that a higher volatility of exchange rates have negative effect on the volume of bilateral trade.[25] This all the more brings into focus the need for 'Cooperation' among major actors to maintain international trade and exchange rate stability.

Monetary and payments cooperation at the regional level, provides a slightly different context. Nations have been encouraged to enter into collaborative arrangements with a desire to make use of regional facilities for mutual gains even when the presence of a dominant partner may or may not be there. Such arrangements have been sought due to a variety of reasons both endogenous as well as exogenous. Firstly, they might be motivated by the desire to strengthen regional linkages by facilitating payments procedures, ensuring greater trade and investment flows and establishing regional support mechanisms. Secondly, they could be aimed at providing protection against external shocks and guard against 'contagion' effects coming from elsewhere. This would be more clearly stated as we now go into the patterns in which nations have sought to enter into cooperative monetary arrangements with each other.

The various forms of monetary and payments cooperation can be categorized as under:

(a) Clearing and Payments Arrangements
(b) Credit Arrangements
(c) Monetary Unions.

Clearing and Payments Arrangements (CPAs)

Clearing arrangements are useful instruments to facilitate payments and progressive liberalization of trade by creating conditions for intra-regional trade expansion. A multilateral clearing arrangement seeks to clear current transactions, primarily comprising of goods and services, without using convertible currencies except for settling the net balance (surplus or deficit) resulting from periodic settlements.[26] In other words, it uses the participants' own currencies for settling current transaction by setting off the claims against each other and it is only the net balances that have to be settled in hard currency.

A clearing arrangement operates under a centralized mechanism under which net outstanding balances of all transactions among member countries, multilaterally recorded by commercial banks of each country are settled through Central Banks. The Central Banks coordinate by extending credit to one another until settlement dates (depending on their net positions vis-a-vis others), when the creditor central bank settle claims in convertible currencies.[27] Such a mechanism reduces the use of scarce foreign exchange to the minimum by recording of debit and credit transactions in unit of accounts. The benefits of clearing arrangements have very aptly been described below:

> Currency fluctuations, trade barriers and foreign exchange restriction, each of these features of the international economy is crucial in understanding the welfare effects of clearing arrangements in an international payment system. The desire to avoid nominal exchange rate fluctuations combined with over expansionary macro-economic policies can generate real exchange rate overvaluation. Such over valutions in turn, causes a current account imbalance that drains the central banks of foreign exchange reserves and leads to demand for restriction on foreign trade and payments-restrictions which reduce overall economic welfare. The main benefits of international clearing arrangement derive from their impact on reducing restrictions on trade and on the use of foreign payments instruments in a situation of real overvaluation.[28]

It has been pointed out that with regard to the major role of clearing arrangements in promotion of trade, they are usually part of a more comprehensive programme of economic cooperation (such as a trade liberalization) among developing countries.[29] Their role in promoting trade expansion can be stated to be complementary to that of more active instruments of trade expansion such as tariff reduction. It cannot be denied however, that clearing arrangements along with other means aimed at providing credit facilities to refinance net debit balance can also be more effective instruments of trade promotion. In the long run, they can pave the way for monetary and economic integration of the developing regions.

There has been a considerable discussion on the role of clearing and payments arrangements in less developed countries which at times have minimal integration and policy coordination. It has been stated that considerable benefits can be derived by the less developed countries even in the absence of other forms of economic integration. At the same time, such benefits are not likely to have offsetting negative effects on LDC's trade with advanced countries, primarily because saving of hard currencies in intra-regional transaction could lead to greater demand for latter's export.[30] Same may not apply however, to the cases where economic disparities are not as widespread (for instance between developing member countries of a clearing union vis-a-vis hard currency non-members), soft currency members imports could increase at the cost of imports from non members.[31]

The benefits accruing out of CPAs may be categorized at various levels. At the broader level, it creates impulses for cooperation in a region which might not be integrated under a comprehensive programme. At the regional level it helps in taking further steps at strengthening monetary and financial linkages without compromising with national policy autonomy initially. It does not require any major policy shift while participating in a CPA. At more specific levels, a CPA economizes on the use of foreign currency and the transaction costs associated with currency conversions and bank margins. Besides speeding up intra-regional payments through the regional facility, it also provides particular guarantees to traders and commercial banks participating in each transaction against the risk of non-convertibility and or non-transferability of the value of transaction. In other words, the traders are assured that their payments will be honored. Lastly, it fosters, closer relationship among the central banks and monetary authorities in the region. It also strengthens the correspondent relationships among the commercial banks, thereby strengthening the regional banking community.

Before we go into the key operational features of the CPAs, it is essential to enlist some of the major arrangements which have functioned world-wide. Table 2.1 gives an account of the CPAs, their functional duration and membership.

Table 2.1: Post-1945 Regional Payments Arrangements

Name	*Abbr.*	*Period*	*Member Countries*
European Payments Union	EPU	1950-58	Austria, Belgium-Luxembourg, Denmark, France, West Germany, Greece, Iceland, Ireland, Italy, Netherlands, Norway, Portugal, Sweden, Switzerland, Turkey, UK
Central American Clearing House	CACH	1961-89	Costa Rica, El Salvador, Guatemala Honduras, Nicaragua
Reciprocal Payments and Credits System	RPCS	1966	Argentina, Bolivia, Brazil, Columbia, Chile, Dominican Republic, Ecuador Mexico, Paraguay, Peru, Uruguay, Venezuela.
Asian Clearing Union	ACU	1975	Bangladesh, India, Iran, Myanmar, Nepal, Pakistan, Sri Lanka, Bhutan.
West African Clearing House	WAC H	1976	Benin, Burkina Faso, Cape Verde, Cote, d'Ivoire, Gambia, Guinea, Guinea-Bissau, Liberia, Mali, Mauritania, Niger, Nigeria, Senegal, Sierra Leone, Togo.
Caribbean Community Multilateral Clearing Facility	CMCF	1977-83	Antigua, Barbados, Belize, Dominica Grenada, Guyana, Jamaica, Monsterrat, St. Kitts-Nevis, St. Lucia St. Vincent, Trinidad
Clearing House of Preferential Trade Area for Eastern and Southern Africa	PTAC H	1984	Burundi, Comoros, Djibouti, Ethiopia Kenya, Lesotho, Malawi, Mauritius, Rwanda, Somalia, Sudan, Swaziland Tanzania, Uganda, Zambia, Zimbab

Source: Byron Auguste (1998), p. 34.

We now come to the key operational characteristics of the CPAs which have varied from one arrangement to the other. The UNCTAD highlights the following as the key features prevalent in various clearing arrangements.[32]

- *Degree of Multilateralisation:* Multilateralisation is a crucial premise for any such arrangement. Through multilateralisation, the debits or credits are cumulatively added so as to reflect the position vis-a-vis the entire membership and not a single country alone. As a result, even if a country has a deficit with another country, it might still end up as net creditor as its surplus transactions with other countries are also added up. The net amount to be settled via central clearing therefore, automatically gets reduced in such circumstances. Different CPAs show different degrees of multilateral settlement of payments. For instance, clearing mechanisms in Asia, West Africa, Central Africa and the Caribbean exercised full multilateralisation with regard to clearing, settlement of net balances, and credit margins granted and received.[33] This implies that total credits or debits position and the net payments or credit margins granted or received, were calculated collectively with regard to the respective position of a member with other members taken together. The Latin American arrangements on the other hand, consisted of bilateral arrangements between pair of central banks which determine their level of reciprocal credit and the recording of eligible transaction. The multilateral clearing took place at the end of settlement period when individual net position of each participant was determined as a result of combined clearances of various bilateral arrangements.
- *Unit of Account*: The unit of account serves as the basis for valuation of clearing operations of outstanding balances in clearing arrangements where national currencies of participants for payments and transfers are used. It not only facilitates statistical and accounting

purposes, but also serves as means of enforcing the guarantee of maintaining the value of the creditors claim. A unit of account has to be carefully selected so as to reflect not merely the relevant exchange rate margins of member countries but also the international standard that is generally prevalent. This means that it should be based on realistic measure of the members' currencies. For this reason, different CPAs have adopted varied approaches as far as selecting unit of account. For instance, while the LAIA and the Caribbean facilities use the dollar for recording transactions, the ACU initially, and the African arrangements usually established units of account linked closely to the SDR allocated by the IMF.[34]

- *Interim Finance*: The provision of interim finance in the form of a short-term credit is another crucial component of CPAs as it provides a support mechanism to meet the temporary mismatches that emerge with regard to debits and credits of member countries. These mismatches occur when there is an imbalance in trade among the member countries. This leads to a situation where there is an imbalance in the payments and hence in the transactions credited (for exports) and transactions debited (for imports). The provision of interim finance in such cases helps by avoiding delays and interruption in settlement of payments among the member central banks. The modalities and provision of interim finance differs with regard to the period to be covered across various arrangements.

  While the CACH provided multilateral clearing facility in terms of six monthly uniform line of credit to each participant, CARICOM provided credit on the basis of reciprocal trade flows.[35] The difference between the two being that while the former was based on fixed amount, irrespective of the trading position of the country, the latter made the provision of credit conditional on reciprocal trade flows. The CACH limited the level of interim credit received by each participant to 1/6th of annual value of imports plus exports recorded with other partners. The LAIA, Reciprocal Payments and Credit System, under its 2-tiered Automatic Payments Programme, offered central banks automatic access to credit or debit positions of others and a short-term credit facility which extended the settlement period for Central Banks with difficult liquidity positions.[36]

- *Interest Rates:* Just as the unit of account, interest rates too are very crucial in determining the manner in which credit obligations are to be fulfilled. The interest rates are imposed on the countries which have to repay the amount resulting out of debits exceeding the credits. It has to be paid to the members which are offering credit. The interest rate has to be realistic enough to provide adequate incentive to the members offering credit. Different criteria have been adopted for determining the interest rates. The CARICOM adopted the concessional and preferential criteria where interest rates on amounts exceeding 20 per cent of the global credit margin were calculated at the average rate for Treasury bonds issued within the region. Members classified as LDCs were charged below the average rate. In the Asian Clearing Union SWAP facility, the interest rate is determined on the basis of London lnter-market Mean Rate.[37]
- *Settlement of Net Balances:* For a clearing arrangement to function in a smooth manner, the net balances i.e. surplus or deficit between participants have to be settled in a timely, mutually acceptable fashion. The participants in a clearing arrangement are committed to settle net balances in convertible currencies acceptable to the creditors. Different arrangements have generally fulfilled these functions in a consistent fashion. Several currencies have been used for settlement including the U.S. Dollar, Pound Sterling, Deutsch Mark and Swiss Franc. Besides, some clearing arrangements provide special clauses to facilitate the

settlement of outstanding balances, based on varying time periods and withdrawal facilities. For instance the CARICOM allowed debtors to pay a certain percentage of their net debits and to postpone payment of the balance to the next period of compensation, thus reducing the line of credit available. The LAIA offered a special facility under the multilateral arrangement to alleviate temporary liquidity shortages of members.

- *Eligibility of Transactions:* At times, several restrictions are imposed as far as eligibility of transactions through the facility is concerned. The reasons for this may vary ranging from economic relationships among member countries, foreign exchange regulations requirements, commitments arising out of other agreements and temporary foreign exchange policy. For instance, while in Latin America and Central American Clearing Arrangements, both capital and current transactions were eligible while in others the former were excluded. In ACU and WACH, payments for petrol and petrol products were excluded for some time primarily by virtue of being principle hard currency earners for some member countries. For instance Iran, for which oil was the principal foreign exchange earner, perceived inclusion of oil and petrol products under the ACU mechanism as depriving it of a major source of foreign exchange. Moreover, oil revenue had played a crucial role in alleviating the problem of insufficient domestic savings as a major constraining factor in growth besides easing up balance of payments difficulties.[38] Besides in ACU, transactions between India-Nepal and Iran-Pakistan were excluded as they were conducted under separate agreements.

Having discussed at length, certain key operational features of CPAs, we can see that these facilities play a crucial role broadly at two levels. Firstly, by laying down certain basic policy premises, they seek to strengthen the existing trade and financial linkages in a region without a country having to alter its national policy in a major way. Secondly, given a certain experience in the functioning of the arrangement, it enables the member countries to have bolder vision with regard to having a consensus on broader monetary issues such as exchange rates, interest rates, reserve funds etc. For the developing countries therefore, CPAs can be regarded as the essential first step towards greater monetary coordination.

We now turn to the next agenda in monetary and payments cooperation which pertains to the establishment of credit reserve funds.

Credit Arrangements

Developing countries, across various regions are often found to be confronted with severe problems on the balance of payments front, which may be triggered off by a combination of factors. For instance, a country may experience a run down on its reserve position due to declining export performance, jump in import requirements, capital outflows etc. While these developments need not be an outcome of a domestic policy environment alone, it all the more necessitates suitable policy measures to remedy the situation. Inability of a country to take the remedial steps often leads to aggravation of a sustaining payments crisis thereby making external assistance inevitable. The associated conditionalities with the external assistance have a number of adverse impacts. In this context, building up of regional reserve institutions to meet temporary contingency requirements of member countries has been suggested as one of the crucial areas of monetary cooperation. Besides, financial facilities aimed at covering part of member's balance of payment deficits have also been regarded as useful in strengthening the operation of clearing and payments arrangements.[39] Depending on the role and objectives laid out, the credit arrangements may be categorized as under:

(a) Payments Union
(b) Reserve Fund

Payments Union

A payments union is concerned with provision of automatic credit facilities which are closely connected with a mandatory clearing arrangement. These facilities are provided out of the surplus that exists within a clearing arrangement through which there is compulsory channeling of transactions. Thus the very notion of the credit is inbuilt in the nature of the payments union, without there being any external support. Under this mechanism, credits provided by countries having surplus in periodic clearings to the clearing house are in turn provided to the member country with a deficit. Normally, a ceiling exists for credit of and debit to a member country, depending on which the participants provide medium term balance of payment credit to each other, thus extending a small amount of interim credit within a clearing union. It generally has a broader scope of operation than a simple clearing arrangement.

It helps by providing medium term credit to finance imbalances in their mutual trade, thereby facilitating a more economical method of payment for their mutual trade transactions because it takes place within the ambit of the payment union. Besides, it also allows each member country more time to make the necessary balance of payments adjustments.[40] The theoretical premise for both a clearing union and a payment union is the same. That is, both these arrangements tend to reduce restrictions on trade and use of foreign payments instruments in a situation of real over valuation. In other words, countries which are part of such arrangements are less inclined to go in for trade and exchange restrictions. The only difference arises out of the nature of credit facility provided under each facility. Payment unions have been clearly distinguished from a clearing union in terms of the size and duration of credits made available for multilateral compensation of intra-regional trade. Besides, a discretionary credit—granting approach after the exhaustion of a certain maximum agreed level of automatic credit has been favoured.[41] While ACU is a simple clearing union, EPU was an example of a typical payments union.

There has been a considerable discussion on the role of payments union in facilitating intra-regional trade. Unlike a simple clearing mechanism which plays more of a facilitator, a payment union might be expected to play a more active promotional role in fostering intra-regional trade. It may encourage the member countries to go in for greater trade liberalisation measures as the fears regarding intra-regional payments deficits may get diminished.[42] A payment union, by fostering a keen relationship between creditors and debtors may also lead to some reciprocal measure between them on tariff and other trade barriers, thereby, laying the groundwork for larger plan of regional integration.[43] Attempts have also been made to measure the impact of payments unions on economic growth. By reducing the need to hold international reserves and permitting trade expansion, regional incomes are likely to go up. Due to a favourable impact on terms of trade, efficiency gains arising out of reduction in transaction costs are likely to lead to higher rate of investment, and faster capital accumulation, thereby leading to faster growth regional incomes than it otherwise would have been.[44]

The credit facilities offered under various Clearing and Payments Arrangements have varied in both scope and content. For instance, the Central American Monetary Stabilization Fund, established in 1969 was aimed at correcting temporary mal-adjustments in their balance of payments and to counteract trends harmful to the normal operation of exchange systems. The contributions were involuntary in nature and required equal contribution by the members with the credit limit extending upto 3 per cent. The Santo Domingo Accord in the Reciprocal Payments and Credit Scheme zone established in 1969 offered the balance of payments facility with a maximum credit extension limit of 12 per cent. Under this arrangement, a three-tier mechanism was set up, aimed at providing financial assistance to meet: (i) deficits in regional clearing and payments system, (ii) deficits in global balance of payments, and (iii) imbalances caused by natural disasters. The Association of South East Asian Nations (ASEAN) SWAP arrangement, introduced in 1977, provided automatic standby credit to the member countries for facing temporary, quickly reversible difficulties in their balance of payments.[45]

As per the SWAP, U.S. dollar was exchanged against the domestic currency of a requesting participant. The SWAP was undertaken through spot sale of U.S. dollar against the domestic currency of the requesting participant accompanied by a forward purchase of the same amount of domestic currency by that participant against U.S. dollar. The amount of U.S. dollar under SWAP was credited to the account of the requesting participant. The amount of domestic currency involved was credited to the respective non-interest bearing amount maintained with the Central Bank or Monetary Authority of the participant country and was not to be used except for the reversal of the SWAP.[46]

Reserve Fund

A reserve fund generally has a broader scope and context than a payment union which has a rather limited operational sphere. It provides a facility that enables the member countries to address their balance of payments deficits as generated by their extra-regional or global trade transactions rather than the intra-regional deficits. A reserve fund has a wider base, consisting of a capital fund of gold or reserve assets built from the monetary reserves of the member countries which are partly transferred to the fund. The reserve pooling approach has been regarded as superior to the payments union approach as the latter targets the uncompensable intra-regional deficits alone whereas the former tries to compensate for the total transactions of the member countries with world at large and could also help in conservation of reserves.[47] The modalities and the limits of providing financial assistance through such a fund to member countries differ across different arrangements depending on the nature of integration prevalent.

The theoretical rationale for reserve pooling is based on several premises. First and the foremost, assuming that countries hold international reserves to primarily finance their occasional balance of payments deficits, then the ability of these countries to hold such reserves is dependent on how often do they have to make these occasional payments. In other words, reserve pools are a function of variability of payments to be made whether they are to be made by one country or many countries.[48] The potential for reserve saving is greater if the membership of the scheme is larger, thereby reducing the variability of the payments to be made. In essence, pooling of reserves should be able to reduce the pooled standard deviation of the size of disturbance of the balance of payments which should be less than perfectly positively correlated with that of the other countries.[49] Thus some of the reserves held individually by the countries of a region for precautionary motive can be safely saved collectively. Each member can draw on the pool when it has to pay to others and deposit with the pool when it receives payments from others, thus keeping the pool solvent.

Besides, reserve pooling is also stated to lead to some direct benefits such as enhancing the bargaining strength of a regional reserve fund as compared to the bargaining strength of individual members vis-a-vis probable investment options. It could therefore, permit the members to earn higher rates of interest collectively than they could have earned individually by investing in requisite instruments. Besides, a regional reserve fund facility is likely to give a greater strength to the regional currencies collectively and could lead to their fuller convertibility and lesser probability of exchange rate depriciations. [50]

In the more recent times, the need for regional reserve institutions has been felt all the more, albeit for slightly different reasons. The East Asian economic crisis, which resulted in collapse of the financial system in most of the emerging Asian economies, in more ways than one has demonstrated the incapacity of the existing international financial system to safeguard against the volatility of capital flows and erratic exchange rate movements.

Since July 1997, there was a sharp plunge in the stock prices and exchange rate in East and South East Asia. Indonesia, Thailand and South Korea had the largest drops in exchange rates ranging from 36 per cent to 72 per cent by the end of March 1998.[51] There was a sharp pullout of funds by investors totaling $105 billion among the five most affected countries which also included Malaysia and Philippines. The vulnerability of both the real and financial sector was exposed as there was a decline in exports and most of the investments were found placed in non-tradable, speculative ventures including property and land. Once the property and stock market bubble burst, foreign lenders of short-term foreign exchange loans immediately rushed for withdrawals which led to running down of foreign exchange reserves of the South East Asian countries. When the region's currencies were floated, they all fell consistently along with domestic bankruptcies.

Although IMF had been warning the governments about financial sector weaknesses yet it had failed to force the virulence of the contagion effects produced by the crisis.[52] Moreover, its interventions were stated to have made things more complicated. For instance, increase in real interest rates, combined with other austerity measures (tax increases, cuts in government expenditure), only degressed firms' cash flows and raised their fixed payment obligations, making them more insolvent, accelerating capital outflows and reducing the inflows.[53]

The problem was compounded not merely by the absence of early monitoring system but also due to lack of financial mechanism which could contain the contagion effect of the regional crisis. In this regard, the proposal by Japan in September, 1997 of a new Asian Monetary Fund (AMF) with a reserve fund of about $100 billion sought to address the problems of liquidity to forestall speculative attacks on the region's currencies. Such a regional facility could be seen as a regional complement to the IMF and could provide forewarning of impending problems. The proposal however, could not take off due to objections by certain quarters that a financial support without any conditions attached could raise the risk of moral hazard and there could be a possible lack of coordination and potential conflict with the IMF.[54]

There have been instances of several reserve funds in operation among developing countries. The Arab Monetary

Fund, derived its financial resources from its capital which amounted to 750 million SDRs distributed among the shareholding countries according to their economic standing. The Andean Reserve Fund (ARF) was created through subscription of share by its member states for US $2.4 billion. The financial assistance available in both the cases was of short and medium term nature to correct the balance of payments. A common feature of such arrangements was that debtors were required to reimburse the loans in freely convertible currencies since credit was extended in international reserve assets.

We now finally turn to the most advanced form of monetary cooperation operationalised as monetary union.

Monetary Union

A monetary union differs from the monetary and payments arrangements discussed earlier with regard to the precedence it gives to the regional policy at the cost of national policy autonomy. The mechanism of monetary union has been aptly described as follows:

> "Monetary union requires the unification and management both of monetary policy and of external exchange rate policy of the union. Thus the rate of increase in money supply has to be determined jointly. Beyond an agreed amount of credit expansion, which is allowed to each member-state's central bank, a member-state has to finance any budget deficit in the union's capital market at the ruling rate of interest. Besides, the balance of payments of the entire union with the rest of the world has to be regulated at the union level. For this purpose, the monetary authority must dispose of a common pool of exchange reserves and the union exchange rates with other currencies must be regulated at the union level. Under such a system, it may not be possible for a member to calculate its balance of payments with its partners and the rest of the world."[55]

By seeking convergence on macro-economic targets such as inflation, fiscal deficit etc., a monetary union therefore sets regional goals that are to be pursued by the member countries rather than national ones. In other words, it reflects the highest degree of accommodation and integration of national policies into a regional one. It seeks coordination at both institutional and policy level, thereby leading to a complete harmonization of monetary and fiscal policies, encompassing money supply, interest rates, government expenditure and taxation between the member countries.

At the institutional level, it entails the creation of a common central bank which serves as the key arbiter in outlining the monetary agenda for the entire region, independent of the political authorities of the region at the same time. Such political independence is vital to ensure that budget deficits of the member government are not financed by measures such as printing money, no matter what the compulsions may be. At the national level, the domestic banking system has to adapt it self, in tune with the modified accounting standards and other procedural changes as necessitated by establishment of the common Central Bank.

At the core of a monetary union lies the policy switch to a common currency as the national currencies get eliminated. In fact, the system of common currency is equivalent to a system where national currencies become perfect substitutes. The common currency is expected to lead to efficiency gains at two different levels. Firstly, it leads to elimination of transaction costs associated with exchanging of national currencies. Secondly, it eliminates the risk involved in the uncertain future movements of the exchange rates vis-à-vis the individual national currencies[56]. Thirdly, depending on the relative weight the union enjoys in the global trade, a common currency thus formed has the potential to become a potent force in global financial markets. There are however, at the same time certain associated costs that are in built in a common currency situation. By relinquishing, the national currency, a country loses, at the same time, a key instrument of national economic policy. It implies that a country in such a situation no longer has the power to change the price of its currency or to determine the quantity of money in circulation.

The theoretical premise for a monetary union has been given by the theory of optimum currency areas as propounded by

Robert Mundell. As per this theory, labour or factor mobility has been regarded as the essential precondition for a region to have a common currency. It therefore, describes the operating environment in which such a union can function by stating that if the world can be divided into different regions within each of which there is factor mobility and between which there is factor immobility, then each of these regions should be assigned a separate currency which fluctuates relative to all other currencies.[57] Mobility of labour in this case enables achievement of both external and internal equilibrium within a region without the need to bring about monetary and fiscal adjustments among the member countries. It, therefore, provides suitable basis for the region to have a common monetary and fiscal policy. On the other hand, if wages are rigid and labour mobility is limited, then countries that form a monetary union will find it hard to adjust to demand shifts. In such cases, countries that have maintained their own national money would be in a better position to make policy adjustments by devaluing (revaluing) their currency.

Therefore, monetary union between two countries is optimal when one of the following conditions is satisfied.

(i) There is insufficient wage flexibility.
(ii) There is sufficient mobility of labour.

Mundell's theory however, has been criticized on several counts. It presupposes that there are differences existing within the countries with regard to production and employment that would generate free flow of labour and capital. Such differences at times are not important enough to ensure such free flows which could eventually restore internal and external balances. Besides as, a result of inflexibility of wages and prices in the downward direction due to pressure of labour unions, movement of labour from one country to another does not lead to narrowing down of cost differentials between the two. Therefore, the prerequisites for an optimal currency area are difficult to achieve. Moreover, the skills and abilities of all units of factors might not be identical; as a result, mobility of efficient factor from one country to another might hamper its productive potential. Thus a perpetual gap in their competitive position may remain. Lastly, production functions are often not the same as far as the two countries are concerned, which may lead to perpetuation of unemployment even if mobility of labour exists.

Taking Mundell's argument further, Ronald Mckinnon considers the factor immobility among industries. He states that it may not be feasible to consider slicing the world into currency areas along industrial groupings rather than geographical groupings. Given the case of factor immobility between regions A and B, each having specialized industries, he states that if it is possible to develop A type of industries in B then the need for factor mobility between the two is not great. The existing immobility can be accepted through monetary arrangements giving both regions their own currencies thus permitting more flexibility in enabling each area to pursue monetary and fiscal policy geared to internal stability. But if it is difficult for A type industries to be developed in B, then factor movements between the two is the only way to prevent a large fall in the unit incomes of potentially mobile factors. So a policy aimed at overcoming the immobility of factors is required and the two should be in a common currency area.[58]

The other criteria identified as being significant for currency unions have been the openness of the economies and greater regional interdependence among countries.

This premise is based on the fact that open economies must rely on monetary and fiscal policies rather than exchange rate changes to achieve external and internal balance. Exchange rate flexibility is regarded as more useful instrument to achieve external balance when the economy is relatively closed. In the event of a decline in real demand for a country's exports, exchange rate adjustment can be made depending on the share of traded goods sector. The larger the exchange rate change, larger is the movements in internal prices that result. Given the objectives of price stability therefore, more liberal economies having relatively large tradable sector have been regarded as good candidates for fixed exchange rates vis-à-vis their trading partners. This includes the possibility of joining them in currency union, provided that the policies of their neighbours are consistent with price stability.[59]

Besides industrial and portfolio diversification in an economy also to a certain extent determines whether a currency union is feasible or not.[60] The more diversified the industrial structure, the less is the likelihood of supply and demand shocks affecting the output of the whole economy. A diversified economy therefore, has less need to retain exchange rate flexibility to mitigate the effect of shocks. Similarly, adverse shocks to incomes in particular regions can be cushioned by holding assets that generate incomes from external sources.[61] Not much is known however, about prevalence of such portfolio diversification in practice.

Given the theoretical premise for formation of monetary union through common currency areas, it is essential to analyse where such schemes have been operationalised. Monetary unions have been in operation under various arrangements such as the East Caribbean Authority, the Rand Monetary Area, the Central African Monetary Union (CAMU), the West African Union (WAMU) and the more recently launched European Monetary Union. These arrangements have varied in terms of both criteria and the policy followed as part of the broader plan of monetary integration. The WAMU has been succeeded by the West African Economic and Monetary Union (UEMOA) which came into being in August 1994. Its objective is to deepen monetary cooperation pursued over two decades under WAMU and supplement it with deeper economic integration involving convergence in economic policies and performance, creation of a common market, coordination of national sectoral policies.

The WAMU which was signed in November 1973, encompassed the issue of a single monetary unit, the issue and management of which was entrusted to a joint institution of issue, namely the Central Bank of West African States (BCEAO) and assistance in the effective use of the monetary resources of members. The CAMU is also part of the Economic and Monetary Community of Central Africa (CEMAC) which is based on strengthening of the common currency, the coordination of macro-economic policies, the establishment of a legal framework conducive to the revival of investment and growth and the attainment of a single market. The CAMU operates under the single currency issued by the Bank of Central African States (BEAC).[62] Both CAMU and WAMU are part of the CFA franc arrangements. Each area has a central bank that sets and coordination monetary policy. The extent of intra-union trade in the CFA zone depends heavily on whether and how trade of the African countries with France is treated in calculations. While the intra-union trade among the African country is low, they all have an important trading partner in France.

Due to the very nature of CFA franc zone however, sub-regional integration has been hampered in two respects. First, high value of the CFA franc in the past and its convertibility favoured imports from France and encouraged black-market trade between CFA and non-CFA franc zone countries. This acted as a disincentive to intra-subregional trade flows and cooperation. The devaluation of the CFA franc in 1994 brought some realignment with other subregional currencies in West Africa which led to more trade with other countries of the subregion. Secondly, the existence of the CFA franc zone was at variance with the objective of setting up a single monetary zone in West Africa with a single currency and a Central Bank. Since the CFA franc zone countries with their single currency and subregional central banks have already attained this objective, they were unlikely to consider an alternative mechanism.[63]

The currency unions among eastern Caribbean countries also exhibit only a small amount of intra-regional trade, exports to the rest of the world. Thus for both CFA franc zone and East Caribbean Union, volume of intra-regional trade has not been the main motivation for currency unions. More important has been the objective of monetary stability through a supra-national monetary institution.

The EMU launched on 1st January 1999 has been the most comprehensive and substantive effort at monetary integration in the recent times. The European Union accounting for about

31 per cent of world output and 20 per cent of world trade is seen as a major economic bloc. As a result, the Euro (single currency of the EMU) is likely to emerge as the strongest contender for dollar. Estimates have shown that there is likely to be a portfolio diversification of $500 billion to $1 trillion into euros as the creation of the euro will narrow and eventually close the monetary gap between United States and Europe.[64]

The primary motivation behind the EMU derives from the integration efforts that had been initiated well in past. With the formation of the Common Market in 1992, the urge for having a complete harmonization of monetary and fiscal policy grew even more. The Maastricht Treaty signed in 1992 established the convergence criteria which were to determine Member-States which would participate in the EMU at the time of its inception in 1999. The criteria laid down were: (a) inflation rates, observed over a period of one year would not be more than 15 per cent above the best three performing countries, (b) long-term interest rates similarly must not be above 2 per cent, (c) Budget deficits should not exceed 3 per cent of GDP unless they are exceptional, and (d) public debt should not exceed 60 per cent of GDP.

The countdown to Euro has been a careful and gradual one. EMU was preceded by long drawn discussions on the desirability and the eligibility for the membership before eleven out of the fifteen members of the EU finally joined. The EMU process is likely to be completed in different phases as the members and the enterprises are to be given sufficient time to adopt to the new guidelines. The launch of euro was preceded by the formation of the European Central Bank which is at the institutional core of the EMU process. The role of the ECB has been clearly spelt out in the Maastricht Treaty according to which its primary objective would be to maintain price stability. Besides, the treaty prohibits overdraft facilities or any other type of credit facility with the ECB or with the national central banks to community institutions or bodies, Central Government, regional or local authorities, public authorities. Thus attempts have been made to give political independence to the ECB.[65] Subsequent to the formation of the ECB, the conversion rates of the member countries currencies into the euro were to be fixed. The euro notes and coins were to be introduced in early 2002, following which national notes and coins were to cease to be legal tender.[66] According to an OECD Survey, "The early years of monetary union have shown that less flexible economies can have a rough ride, missing out on the full benefits of the single currency. Structural rigidities tend to reduce growth, make inflation more persistent and reduce the economy's ability to absorb shocks. Some countries are more flexible than others, and this matters because it implies that the common monetary policy will often be too loose for some and too tight for others. For that reason, the single currency would be more beneficial for everyone if structural reforms were put in place so that economies became more flexible and more tightly integrated."[67]

Thus the EMU has been regarded as one of the major developments of the post war international monetary system. Starting from the European Payments Union in the early fifties, European countries gradually responded to the growing impulses for regional integration in a series of steps which led to the single market in1992 and to the EMU eventually in 1999. The economic cooperation among developing countries, despite having a slightly different rationale, may draw significant lessons from the European experience.

NOTES

1. David L. Goacher, An Introduction to *Monetary Economics* (London, 1986), p. 53.
2. S.B. Gupta, *Monetary Economics: Institutions, Theory and Policy* (New Delhi, 1988), p. 286.
3. Goacher, n. 1, p. 71.
4. Christopher J. Green, "The Determination of Interest Rates and Asset Price: A Survey of Theory and Evidence" in Christopher J. Green and David T. Llewellyn (eds.), *Surveys in Monetary Economics*, Vol. (Oxford, 1991), p. 76.
5. *Ibid.*, p. 272.

6. C. Goodhart, "*The Conduct of Monetary Policy*" in Christopher J. Green and David T. Llewellyn, n.4, p. 292. During inflationary pressures, lags in the process of interest rate adjustments would induce the authorities to temporarily accommodate each inflationary shock to the demand for money until they managed both to observe it and to come to a decision to offset it. Thus the need for an alternative method of monetary control is sought.
7. Rudiger Pohl, "Money Supply, Interest Rate and Exchange Rate Targets: Conflicting Issues in an Open Economy" in Stephen F. Frown (ed.), *Monetary Theory and Monetary Policy: New Tracks for the 1990s* (New York, 1993), p. 171.
8. Paul Davidson, "*Monetary Theory and Policy in a Global Context with a Large International Debt*", *ibid.*
9. Andrew Splinder and Bruce I. Summers, "The Central Bank and the Payment System" in Bruce I. Summers (00.) The Payment System: Design, *Management and Supervision* (Washington D.C., 1994); p. 164.
10. Byron Auguste, *The Economics of International Payments Unions and Clearing Houses: Theory and Measurement* (London, 1997), p. 14
11. *Asian Development Outlook 1999* (Manila, 1999), p. 4. It notes that the net private capital flows to developing economies declined to $29 billion in 1998 from a peak of $177 billion in 1996.
12. David T. Llewellyn and John R. Presley, "The Role of Hegemonic Arrangements in the Evolution of International Monetary System" in Jaime Reis (ed.), *International Monetary System in Historical Perspectives* (London, 1995), p. 259.
13. For instance, the European Union consistently experimented a coordinated monetary and exchange rate policy with diverse strategies, in line with its efforts towards economic integration.
14. The Exchange Rate Mechanism (ERM) which was part of the European Monetary System (EMS) instituted in 1979 was an example of such adjustable peg. In this case, the band was set at +2.25% and –2.25% around the central rate for most member countries.
15. Under a managed floating exchange rate system, the exchange rates are allowed to be freely determined by the foreign exchange market, subject to intervention by the Central Bank if the exchange rate goes beyond a certain limit. In a free floating exchange rate system, the exchange rates are determined solely by the forces of demand and supply of foreign exchange. These forces are influenced by factors such as a nation's economic health, trade performance, balance of payment position, interest rates, etc.

16. Paul De Gruawe, *The Economics of Monetary Integration* (New York, 1992), p. 115. 39
17. E.G Johnson (*et al.*), *Payment Systems, Monetary Policy and the Role of the Central Bank* (Washington D.C., 1998), p. 11.
18. Benjamin Cohen, "The Triad and the Unholy Trinity: Problems of International Monetary Cooperation," in Jeffrey A Frieden and David A. Lake (eds.) *International Political Economy: Perspectives on Global Power and Wealth* (London, 1995), p. 257.
19. *Ibid.*, p. 256.
20. *Ibid.*, p. 261.
21 Robert O. Keohane, International Institutions and State Power: *Essays in International Relations Theory* (Westview, 1989), p. 90.
22. As a transaction currency, dollar was used as the medium for settlement of global trade transactions. As an intervention currency, dollar was used to prop up the currencies which were facing a steep decline in their values. While in its role as a reserve currency, dollar was used as a reserve asset by most of the countries to bolster their foreign exchange reserves.
23. Barry Eichengreen, "*Hegemonic Stability Theories in International Monetary System*" in Frieden and Lake, n.18, p. 254.
24. Regionalisation in this context implies the relative strength a particular currency enjoys in a particular regional trading environment. In such cases movements of currencies are linked to the relative position of the dominant currency in their respective areas. The strength of the currency depends on a number of factors such as the share of the country in the total output, trade of the region, level of inflation, growth rate etc.
25. Jeffrey A. Frenkel and Shang Jin Wei, "Regionalisation of World Trade and Currencies" in Jeffrey A. Frenkel (ed.) *The Regionalisation of the World Economy* (Chicago, 1998), p. 200.
26. UNCTAD, A Review of the Main Features of Clearing Arrangements of Developing Countries (UNCTAD/ECDCI/128), 22 November, 1982, p. 2.
27. B.K. Madan, *Towards Monetary Cooperation in South Asia* (New Delhi, 1986), p. 65.
28. Auguste, n. 10, p. 18.
29. UNCTAD, n. 26, p. 2.
30. Jaroslav Vanek, "Payments Unions Among the Less Developed Countries and their Economic Integration", *Journal of Common Market Studies*, Vol.5, No.2, 1966, p.187. Vanek sees the payments unions among less developed countries as reducing the relative price and cost between them, thereby leading to an improvement

in resource allocation and growth. As a result of a payment union, the bilateral claims are settled in member's own currencies and the residual through either short-term credit arrangements or by hard currencies. As a result, the divergences in relative prices and costs imputable to overvaluation with respect to hard currencies will be eliminated and trade will expand due to correct price signals.

31. Auguste, n. 1, p. 67. The author develops a benchmark model to assess the impact of a clearing union and regards a clearing union as having both a substitution effect which tends to increase intra-regional imports at the expense of extra-regional imports and income effect which tends to increase imports from all sources.
32. UNCTAD, n. 26, p. 23.
33. *Ibid.*
34. The Asian Clearing Union switched over to US dollar denominated transactions since January, 1996.
35. Madan, n. 27, p. 66.
36. UNCTAD, Clearing and Payments Arrangements Among Developing Countries: Recent Developments, Long-term Policy Considerations (UNCTAD/ECDC/238), 4 February 1994, p. 12.
37. London Inter-market Mean Rate is equivalent to mean of London Inter Bank Interest Rate (LIBIR) and London Inter-bank Offer Rate (LIBOR). The LIBOR is an average of the interest rates at which leading international banks are prepared to offer term Euro-dollar deposits to each other. The interest rate differs according to the deposit maturity and the soundness of the borrowing banks.
38. Jahangir Amuzegar and M. Ali Fekrat, *Iran: Economic Conditions tender Dualistic Conditions* (Chicago, 1979), p. 111.
39. Tomas Alfonso Medina, "Monetary and Payments Arrangements Among Developing Countries" in Breda Pavlic (*et al.*) *The Challenges of South—South Cooperation* (Boulder, 1983), p.150.
40. Francis Stewart & Arjun Sengupta, *International Financial Cooperation: A Framework for Change* (Colorado, 1982), p.182.
41. Charan.D. Wadhwa, "Regional Payments Arrangements: An Application to Asia and the Far East", *Yale Economic Essays*, Vol. 10. No.1, 1976, p. 168
42. *ibid.*
43. J.R. Gunn, "'Payments Unions Among the Less Developed Countries and their Economic Integration: A Comment", *Journal of Common Market Studies*, Vol. 6, No. 1, 1967, p. 57. He asserts that a certain amount of coordinated trade liberalisation and payment

measures, a customs union might logically evolve out of a simple payments union.

44. Auguste, n. 10, p. 102.
45. UNCTAD, Strengthening the Weakest Link: A Review of Certain Aspects of South-South Trade and Finance (UNCTAD/ST/ECDC/28), October 1985, p. 16.
46. Article 3 of the ASEAN SWAP arrangement in Michael T. Skully, ASEAN Financial Cooperation: Developments in Banking, Finance and Insurance (London, 1985).
47. Wadhwa, n. 41.
48. J.R. Dodsworth and J Diamon, "Monetary Cooperation as a Source of Development Finance: The ASEAN Case", *Journal of Development Economics,* Vol. 7, 1980, p. 410
49. Charan D. Wadhwa," Reserve Pooling in Asia and the Far—East", *The Pakistan Development Review,* Vol. IX, No. 3, Autumn, 1969, p. 310.
50. *Ibid.,* p. 312
51. Robert Wade, "The Asian Crisis and the Global Economy: Causes, Consequences and Cure", Current History, November 1998, p. 361. Also see Linda Y.C. Lim, "Whose 'Model Failed?" *Implications of the Asian Economic Crisis, Washington Quarterly,* Vol. 21, No. 3, Summer 1998, pp. 25-36. Ethan B. Kapstein, "Global Rules for Global Finance, Current History, November 1998, pp. 355-60.
52. Stanley Fischer, "The Asian Crisis and the Changing Role of the IMF", *Finance and Development,* Vol. 35, No.2, June 1998, p. 5.
53. Robert Wade, n. 51, p. 366.
54. *Asian Development Outlook,* 1999, p. 44.
55. P. Robson, The Economics of International Integration (London, 1985), as quoted in Ali M. El-Agraa, *The Theory and Measurement of International Economic Integration* (London, 1989), p. 76.
56. Paul De Grauwe, *The Economics of Monetary Integration* (New York, 1992), p. 11
57. Robert Mundell, "A Theory of Optimum Currency Areas", *American Economic Review,* September 1961, p. 664.
58. Ronald I. Mckinnon, "Optimum Currency Areas", *American Economic Review,* September 1963, p. 724.
59. Paul R. Masson and Mark P. Taylor," Issues in Operation of Monetary Unions and Optimum Currency Areas" in Morris Goldstein and Peter Issard (eds.) Policy Issues in the Evolving International Monetary Systems, I.M.F. *Occassional Paper, 1996,* June 1992, p. 45.

60. The product diversification approach as propounded by Peter Kenen, as opposed to Mckinnon regarded closed economies as ideal candidates for fixed exchange rates as they are likely to be more diversified and their domestic price and income level are more insulated from foreign disturbances.
61. Masson and Taylor, n. 59, p. 46.
62. UNCTAD, State of South-South Cooperation (New York, 1995), pp. 4-5. UNCTAD, *Handbook of Economic Integration and Cooperation Groupings of Developing Countries*, Vol.1. (New York, 1996), p. 32.
63. UNCTAD, Regional Experiences in the Economic Integration Process of Developing Countries, Report by the UNCTAD Secretariat, UNCTAD/ITCD/TSB/1, 25 June 1997, p. 23.
64. C. Fred Bergston, *"The Dollar and the Euro"*, Foreign Affairs (Washington), Vo1.76, No.4, p. 84.
65. Paul De Grauwe, n. 16, p. 161.
66. "The European Monetary Union Survey", *The Economist* (London), April, 11th-17th, 1998.
67. http://www.oecd.org/document/62/0,3343,en_2649_201185_37849918_1_1_1_1,00.html.

Chapter 3

Asian Clearing Union: Origin, Objectives and Features

3.1 Introduction

The Asian Clearing Union (ACU), which is the only clearing facility of its kind in the whole of Asia, stands apart as one of the relatively successful examples of regional cooperation in Asia. It came up at a time when regionalism in Asia was still at a nascent stage. The erstwhile Economic and Social Commission for Asia and the Far East (ECAFE) and other agencies led ambitious programmes of regional trade liberalization and industrial joint ventures could not really make any major impact. The ACU on its part, stuck to its specific agenda and continued to respond albeit in a limited sense to the changes that were taking place in the global monetary and financial environment. Its successes or failures, therefore, have to be seen in the light of the specific objectives that were assigned to it and the operational mechanisms that it sought to put into practice to achieve those objectives.

This chapter is aimed at analyzing the ACU with regard to its evolution, objectives and characteristics. It would begin by taking note of the critical developments taking place in the international economic environment when the ACU was envisaged as a small step towards monetary and payments cooperation. It would, at the same time take note of the economic developments within the member countries as they decided to become part of the multilateral facility. This chapter also traces the larger institutional and academic exercises that finally prepared the ground for the launch of the ACU. Finally, it would highlight the major objectives that were laid out and the key features that characterized the operational mechanisms. We would also highlight the key changes that were introduced in its operations in the light of the changing requirements. The chapter therefore, in essence, would provide us an analytical framework which would help us in studying the trends in its operations in the following chapters.

3.2 Evolution of the Asian Clearing Union

Global/Regional Economic Environment

The decades of 1960s and 1970s which preceded the establishment of ACU in 1974 were shaped by certain parallel trends in the global economy over a period of time. On the one hand, as we shall elaborate further, the international economic environment was marked by growing fluctuation and disparity in the world trade. This was accompanied by declining terms of trade for developing countries with steep hike in prices of several essential commodities such as oil. At the same time, realising the need for collective action, several regional economic arrangements among developing countries were gradually coming up to tackle the growing pressures on them. The situation was best summarised by U. Nyun, Executive Secretary of the ECAFE at the first Ministerial Conference on Asian Economic Cooperation at Manila. He stated:

> "Recent international economic developments have perhaps brought home one lesson more vividly than any others; singly and separately, the developing nations of the ECAFE region cannot hope to attain reasonably satisfactory rates of economic growth which will support their fast growing populations at decent levels of living .... All the prognostications and projections made of the future international trade of ECAFE developing countries point to the large and growing trade gap, with which the region will be confronted in the coming years. On the one hand, the prospective increase in export earnings from

traditional export commodities is fairly limited and on the other, their import requirements for the minimum living needs of their peoples and for executing their programmes of economic development are growing steeply."[1]

A study of the trade pattern of the ECAFE region in the 1960s and the 1970s confirms that the performance of the Asian trade growth relative to the total world trade development was far from satisfactory. During the period 1958-64, the export trade of the developing ECAFE countries registered a growth rate of 5 per cent per year (in value terms), far below the world total growth rate of 8 per cent per year, and still farther below the rate of developed ECAFE countries which registered 12.8 per cent growth. In 1965-66, the developing ECAFE countries exports increased by 5.3 per cent over 1964, while their imports increased by about 9 per cent and their trade deficit increased from $2,068 million to $7,600 million.[2] The global trade pattern in the 1970s recorded an erratic trend. While in value terms, rates of changes were much higher as compared to the 1960s, yet in real terms the situation varied. The rate of growth of world trade declined gradually in early 1970s, registering a negative growth in 1975 in both exports and imports in industrial and other developed countries.

These developments had subsequent impact on the export of ESCAP economies (ECAFE was changed into Economic and Social Commission for Asia and Pacific in 1974) which responded in a volatile manner to the changes in the level and rate of growth in aggregate demand and the increasing incidence of protectionism in advanced industrial countries.[3] The trends of protectionism in 1970s and 1980s were more visible with regard to manufactured goods in which a number of developing countries had successfully been able to expand their exports. In 1980, for instance among the product categories, 40.8 per cent of food items were found to be subject to non-tariff measures. The incidence of quantitative restrictions was also as high as 27.5 per cent.[4] Besides, they were also affected by sharp changes in international commodity markets apart from domestic price fluctuations. The level and composition of imports, on the other hand, were affected by the steep rise in price of oil and by the world food crisis of the early

1970s. There was a steady growth in the share of fuels and food in the total import bill. For the developing ESCAP region as a whole, the performance was satisfactory as the developing market economies registered in real terms a growth of 9.8 per cent per annum on the average during 1970-75. Coming down to the sub-regional level, the situation was however, quite different.

Table 3.1: Developing ESCAP Economies: Export Growth 1960-77
Annual Percentage Change

	1960-65	*1965-70*	*1970-75*	*1971*	*1972*	*1973*	*1974*	*1975*	*1976*	*1977*
Developing ESCAP (selected)	5.3	8.3	9.8	9.1	14.6	17.4	6.7	1.3	20.4	8.8
South-East Asia	4.4	7.6	12.3	14.2	17.4	24	4.8	1.2	19.4	11.2
East-Asia	11.8	16.1	17.4	13.2	23.5	36	1.7	12.4	32	14.7
South-Asia	4.6	3	1.4	1.9	4.4	-1.5	0.2	2	14.8	-6.8
ACU Countries										
Bangladesh	—	—	-4.9	—	—	1.6	-8.3	-8	36.7	-4
Burma	0.3	-16	-11	26.8	-11.7	-2.5	-45.8	-21.9	26	1.6
India	4.2	4.4	2.9	-1.6	7.5	-1.2	7.9	1.7	17.3	-5.1
Iran	9.3	14.6	5.0	9.7	3.2	-2.1	46.6	-13.7	4.4	-6.1
Nepal	—	—	—	—	—	—	—	—	—	-
Pakistan	9.3	5.4	-15.4	-7.9	-45.8	-19.4	-11	6.9	1.4	-1.6
Sri Lanka	2.5	0.1	-0.1	-3.5	2.4	4.4	-18.1	14.2	-15.4	-2.1

Source: Compiled from *Economic and Social Survey of Asia and the Pacific* 1978. United Nations, Bangkok.

As Table 3.1 shows, while the period 1970-75 saw high export growth in the South East Asian and the East Asian region South Asia on the other hand, recorded a consistent decline from the 1960s with exports growing only by 1.4 per cent for the period 1970-75. The trends in the countries which later formed the Asian Clearing Union were more pronounced with four countries viz. Bangladesh, Burma, Pakistan and Sri Lanka experiencing negative growth in exports during 1970-75. India and Iran registered a small growth of 2.9 per cent and 5.0 per cent respectively, which was way below the developing ESCAP standards.

The low income economies belonging to the sub-region of South Asia were affected by economic volatility to a greater extent than the remaining parts. In South Asia, export growth in real terms dropped alarmingly from 1971 and 1977 from 1.9 per cent to -6.8 per cent. This was mainly because South Asia's share of total non-oil exports of developing ESCAP region fell from 27.5 per cent in 1970 to 17.9 per cent in 1977.[5]

Table 3.2: Developing ESCAP Region: Major Capital Account Components of the Balance of Payments 1972-77 (by sub-region)

South Asia	*1972*	*1973*	*1974*	*1975*	*1976*	*1977*
Official Capital and Transfers	762	1346	2666	3079	2944	1696
Private Long Term Capital	20	-16	-1	25	2	15
Change in Reserves	14	5	-202	96	2416	212
South-East and East Asia						
Official Capital and Transfers	941	902	1694	2199	2718	2607
Private Long Term Capital	533	774	1478	1474	1391	1470
Change in Reserves	969	1814	1385	790	2455	1959

Source: *Economic and Social Survey of Asia and the Pacific* 1978, United Nations, Bangkok.

The situation with regard to external resource flows equally varied within the developing ESCAP region with differing patterns of changing international financial reserves among countries over a period of time. While there was a decline in the reserve position as far as Bangladesh, Pakistan and Burma, differing fluctuations were witnessed for India and Sri Lanka. The private long-term capital flows were primarily concentrated in East and South East Asian sub-region. South Asia, on the other hand, accounted for a major chunk of official capital flows which registered steady growth in the 1970s, there being an exception in the 1976.

As Table 3.2 shows, for South Asia while the official capital and transfers had a steady growth, the private long terms capital flows were erratic and often declining. The reserves also showed a marginal increase in the early 1970s before rising significantly in the later years. South-East and East Asia combined on the other hand, had steady inflow of both official capital and private long term capital with reserves changing by significant levels. The South Asian countries however, registered a collective outflow of over $273 million in private debt, implying that on balance, they acted as private international creditors.[6] The South East Asian countries on the other hand, were major private international borrowers with an aggregate private debt inflow.

The debt burden for South Asian economies was further compounded by high debt servicing ratios as compared to the other sub-regions in Asia. The average annual debt service ratio for 1971-73 amounted to around 15 per cent for South Asia as compared to around 5 per cent for South East Asia. Another major problem area pertained to the persistent retardation in the absorption of substantial inflow of financial resources. Nearly one-fourth of the total foreign debt outstanding remained undisbursed in South Asia at the end of 1976 which suggests increasing inefficiency in the use of financial resources. This has been more manifest in case of project lending where implementation suffered because of a number of administrative reasons such as delays in finalising bid specifications, evaluations of offers and placing of contracts. At times, the problem has been compounded by non-availability of domestic funds needed at times for expansion of projects, thus contributing to lags in utilization.[7]

The above developments in the global and regional economic environment were at the same time accompanied by greater efforts within Asia at exploring ways to further regional economic cooperation. However, unlike in West Europe and Latin America where such efforts focused at closer regional economic integration, in Asia this could not be envisaged because of the diversity and disparity in socio-economic structures among countries. In fact in Asia, the problem of regional cooperation and integration were largely seen from a political angle. As a result, this, in fact, stood as a major impediment to any major collective action.[8] Since Asian countries were characterised by diverse political systems with differing political values, there was a lack of political and ideological convergence of interests. While India, Japan, Ceylon and Malaysia had representative political systems, there were traditional monarchies such as in Afghanistan, Iran and Nepal. On the other hand, countries like China, North Korea, North

Vietnam had communist regimes. Besides smaller and less, developed countries of the region were apprehensive of their interests not being taken care of in the intra-regional economic cooperation schemes. Even under these circumstances, the ECAFE had been constantly monitoring international economic developments and their subsequent implications on the member economies. Although the initial focus of its efforts was primarily aimed at exploring schemes on intra-regional trade liberalization and development of joint industrial and infrastructure projects, the thrust on monetary and payments cooperation was to come only in the late 1960s.

Possibly, the ECAFE sought to build up gradually on the experiences of modest schemes of regional cooperation before venturing into more ambitious areas. Besides, within Asia, there were differences among countries in terms of relative importance that these countries attached to the role of monetary and financial cooperation. On the one hand, the South East Asian countries had already initiated such efforts under the auspices of ASEAN Special Committee of Central Banks and Monetary Authorities.[9] On the other hand, in South Asia, there was near absence of regional coordination as different countries sought to pursue independent policies to tackle even those problems which affected them collectively.[10] The basic stimulus for establishing a regional monetary and payments facility was therefore, to come from sustained efforts that had been initiated well in the past under the auspices of ECAFE and related bodies. This would be elaborated further as we now trace the developments at the institutional level that preceded the formation of the ACU.

Institutional Exercises Preceding ACU

The UN ECAFE had been from the beginning a key actor in the efforts to explore means at regional monetary and payments arrangement in Asia. In 1948 it authorized its Secretariat to undertake studies on the subject. The report of the study group submitted later that year recognized the necessity of special trade and clearing arrangements as long as production and trade difficulties persisted. At the same time, it regarded such measures as temporary substitutes for the more desirable system of universal multilateral trade and exchange. Due to limitation in terms of availability of data, however, it could not lay down definite conclusions regarding the practicability of regional multilateral clearing. Subsequently, the IMF, was entrusted with the task of undertaking a detailed study with ECAFE on the issue. It concluded on the basis of inadequate evidence that a regional clearing union was impractical.[11]

The feasibility of establishing a regional clearing and payments facility continued to be explored subsequently at the official level but the problems and constraints of such a facility at the regional level continued to be the inhibiting factors. The expert group constituted in 1954, consisting of Central Banks of nine Asian countries, IMF and the ECAFE Secretariat for studying the payments problems, highlighted the shortage of foreign exchange and inconvertibility of currency as two major problems facing the region. The utility and desirability of regional payments union was regarded as limited due to predominant use of sterling, franc and guilder for a multilateral compensation. Besides it also highlighted the existence of persistent debtors and creditors within the union as a possible problem area. Under such circumstances the creditor countries might not have been willing to extend credit to deficit member countries even for shorter periods.[12] In fact, persistence of debtor and creditor position within a multilateral clearing facility poses a major challenge to the successful functioning of any such mechanism. By its very nature, any deficit or surplus position on part of a country acquires a multilateral character. Therefore, a country which is running a persistent deficit passes it on to the other members too because of the multilateral nature of compensation. It was precisely this fear that appeared to bear on the minds of the expert group.

Continuing its efforts at accelerating regional economic cooperation in the region, ECAFE at its 19th Session held in Manila in March 1963 convened a group of experts to recommend practical measures at regional cooperation. The report submitted by the panel saw limited need of formal payment arrangements in presence of safeguard arrangements in the form of reciprocity and escape clauses to prevent possibility of serious imbalances in intra-regional trade. This indicates that a payments union was conventionally seen merely as addressing the problem of trade imbalances. Its role as facility which could cut down the need for restrictions on intra-regional trade by deficit countries was hardly discussed.

First Ministerial Conference on Asian Economic Cooperation 1963

The first conference of cabinet ministers and high ranking officials on Asian Economic Cooperation was organised under the auspices of ECAFE at Manila in December 1963. The meeting was attended by representatives of nineteen member countries and two associate members, namely: Afghanistan, Australia, Burma, Ceylon, China, India, Indonesia, Iran, Japan, the Republic of Korea, Laos, the Mongolian People's Republic, Nepal, New Zealand, Pakistan, Philippines, the Republic of Vietnam, Thailand, Western Samoa, Brunei and Hong Kong.

The conference recognized the need for closer economic cooperation among the member countries of the ECAFE region and suggested the formation of adhoc committees to look into specific institutional arrangements such as a programme of trade liberalisation, removal of quota restriction and tariff reduction and also the establishment of an Asian Development Bank.[13] The conference had taken note of the regional trade groupings and their effectiveness in Europe and South America. It, therefore, saw intra-regional trade expansion as a key to counter the growing protectionist tendencies in the developed markets. At the same time, establishment of the Asian Development Bank was seen as essential in financing the development projects being undertaken.

The conference thus set out an explicit agenda for collective action on part of the ECAFE region which appeared to be lagging behind the other regions. However, such efforts were to be taken keeping in mind the specific needs and environment in the ECAFE Region. As U Nyun, the Executive Secretary of ECAFE noted:

> "By comparison with other continents, progress in regional economic cooperation in Asia has been slow and rather limited and has failed to take bold and ambitions forms. I do not mean to suggest that the policies and institutions which are appropriate to and successful in other regions of the world can be transplanted or copied in the Asian region. We have necessarily to take into consideration our own political and economic conditions .... Asian countries have to forge policies and institutions according to our own conditions and genius."[14]

More significantly, the meeting set into motion an institutionalised mechanism at the ministerial level which would henceforth, meet regularly to review the progress in the implementation of the programme of regional economic cooperation outlined at the conference.

Expert Group on Trade Liberalisation 1964

The Working Group of Experts on Trade Liberalisation was convened by the Executive Secretary of the ECAFE pursuant to the 1963 Ministerial Conference. The Group suggested a series of measures on trade liberalisation under: (a) bilateral trade agreements, (b) free lists of imports of selected commodities, and (c) regional quotas for selected commodities. Such measures, it stated however, were unlikely to result in a significant growth of intra-regional trade unless they were accompanied by some form of a payment arrangement.[15] Besides, it considered the provision of credit facilities to member countries experiencing imbalances as paving the way for fast trade liberalisation.

For the first time, it carefully dealt with both forms of payments arrangements *viz.*, a clearing union as well as a payment union. It emphasised that a clearing union would neither be a precondition nor conditional upon the initiation of trade liberalisation measures. It could also be supplemented by a payments union which would provide for credit beyond the accounting period. It considered two alternative forms which a payment union could take (i) one in which credit facilities would cover the deficits and surpluses in total intra-regional trade, and (ii) the other in which only deficits and surplus arising from supplementary trade region would be covered. The former type was considered unsuitable for the ECAFE region as fairly sizable and persisting deficits and surpluses realised in intra-regional trade would put too much strain on the resources of creditor countries. This would be regardless of their overall balance of payments position unless a significant proportion of the resources required by the union were to come from outside the region.

The latter form of arrangement on the other hand, could be expected to overcome these difficulties with respect to the existing structural imbalances in intra-regional trade. The Group also touched upon the scope and methods of finance and operation of the union. The deficit country could be entitled to partial settlement of the deficit by borrowing from the union, the remainder could be settled in convertible currency. The sources of funds it stated, could come from both the member countries contribution and external resources raised from institutions from governments of developed countries. With regard to supplementing the reserve position of the union, the Report noted:

> "The foreign exchange resources of the union could be significantly augumented and the strain on the member countries alleviated by specific aid funds from developed countries as in the case of EPU which obtained funds under the European Recovery Programme. The channeling of funds through the proposed Asian Development Bank would be a possible method of augmenting the resources of the union."[16]

The next ECAFE Ministerial Conference on Asian Economic Cooperation held in Manila in 1965 specifically called for a study group in order to examine the financial aspects of trade expansion and the need for payments arrangements to counter the imbalances arising out of expanded intra-regional trade. The ECAFE's Committee on Trade at its tenth session held at Bangkok in February 1967 considered the Secretariat proposal to convene a seminar on financial aspects of trade expansion in 1967 and to prepare a study on regional payments arrangement for examination by experts at the seminar. The committee recommended that the study should contain several alternative schemes covering such facilities such as simple clearing arrangement, a reserve fund and various types of credit arrangements on both regional and subregional basis.

Seminar on Financial Aspects of Trade Expansion 1967

The seminar was jointly organised at Bangkok, in August 1967 by ECAFE and the United Nations Office of Technical Cooperation. Experts from Afghanistan, Australia, Ceylon, India, Indonesia, Iran, Japan, Republic of Korea, Laos, Nepal, New Zealand, Philippines, Thailand and Republic of Vietnam participated in it in their personal capacity and not as government representatives. Representatives from the IMF and the Asian Development Bank attended the Seminar in a consultative capacity.

The seminar, undertook a comprehensive analysis of possible scenarios and the operational details of payments arrangement within the ECAFE. It recognized that a clearing union would bring about a closer degree of consultation and cooperation on trade and financial matters among member countries. Regarding the types of transactions that could be channeled, it was generally agreed that all international payments including current and capital could be covered by the clearing union, although specific types of capital transaction might be excluded by general agreement. The matter of the scheme being mandatory or optional was left for the countries to decide. It also favoured a clearing union consisting of a larger group involving a greater amount of compensable trade.[17]

The seminar also examined the subject of payments and reserve arrangements which provided for extension of credit beyond the settlement dates as provided for in the clearing scheme. In this regard, a scheme of credits geared to a programme of trade liberalisation was seen as more acceptable to countries which had made most progress towards trade liberalization and currency convertibility since it would help other countries accelerate their own progress in the same direction. In fact, it also proposed a linkage between intra-regional trade liberalization and the provision of credit facility by making provision of credit facilities subject to acceptance and implementation of trade liberalisation commitments. Such facilities would also be geared to the overall balances of payments and reserve positions of members, rather than to intra-regional debit and surplus as such.

The IMF representative however, took a very cautious line. He did not see the system of automatic regional credit as bringing any kind of harmonization. This was because "such schemes would lead to commitments or provide incentives towards a purely regional balances of payments at the expense of the requirements of overall balance. They might thus, create a strong incentive for the member countries to institute or intensify discriminatory systems."[18] He also ruled out any Fund assistance to clearing or payment union as its Articles of Agreement would not allow it to furnish working capital, or to offer stand by facilities in support of any regional organisation. In fact the main utility of the clearing union was seen less as a cost saving device, but more as an institution which brought together monetary authorities of member countries together and gradually coordinate monetary and fiscal policies of the region.

Nevertheless, with several concrete suggestions coming out of the seminar, stage was set for greater thrust for monetary and financial cooperation. By this time, there appeared to be a definite realization, on part of the member countries to give a serious thought to the formation of a regional clearing and payment facilities to assist the trade expansion programme.

Third Ministerial Conference on Asian Economic Cooperation 1968

The Third Ministerial Conference in Asian Economic Cooperation held in December 1968 further enjoined the member countries to give serious consideration to the proposals and studies for the establishment of payments and clearing arrangements. These were meant to provide the necessary support for schemes of trade expansion. This was followed by informal discussions in Brussels in March 1970 among international experts to give technical guidance to the Secretariat in formulating concrete proposals for trade expansion linked with a supporting clearing and payments arrangement. At its 26th session in April 1970, the ECAFE Commission recognized that consultation had constituted concrete step forward towards regional trade expansion and monetary cooperation. Based on the above discussions, the ECAFE Secretariat prepared preliminary papers, namely considerations and proposals for trade and monetary cooperation in the ECAFE region with expert assistance of the staff of International Monetary Fund and UNCTAD as well as other international and regional bodies.

These took note of the existing practices in international payments and the existing efforts towards sub-regional clearing mechanisms. It was pointed out that most of the countries of the ECAFE had exchange system involving fixed and unitary exchange rate and conducted exchange transactions on the basis of par values agreed with the IMF.[19] Besides, the regulations regarding authorized currencies for the making of international settlements varied considerably from country to country. The international banking relationships of the region were characterized by the existence of a network of branch relationships (mostly of British and United States Banks) and a much larger network of correspondent relationships. (involving banks in the region as well as correspondent relationships with banks in London and New York). The correspondent and branch relationships with other banks in the region basically served the purpose of enabling payment orders to be issued directly between two countries in the region as well as correspondent relationships with banks in London and New York.

There was also a predominant use of sterling and United States dollar (almost 90%) while making intra-regional payments.[20] Keeping in view the fact that regional payments arrangements could be considered as an adjunct to trade expansion and liberalisation, the proposals suggested that a clearing scheme could constitute the first step towards monetary cooperation on a regional level.

Expert Mission

These papers were circulated to the Governments of member countries of the region for consideration. This was followed by visit of ECAFE high level expert mission to a large number of countries of the region in August/September 1970 for consultations with policy makers and experts on the subject. The Mission reported a favourable response from most of the countries for creation of an Asian Payments Union both as a necessary framework for the progress of any trade expansion programme and as a way to decrease excessive dependence of the region's trade settlements and monetary reserves on non-member currencies, particularly sterling and the dollar.[21] The Mission's Report was followed by an informal consultation on monetary cooperation organised by the ECAFE Secretariat with the cooperation of the IMF during the course of the annual Bank/Fund Meeting at Copenhagen in 1970. It was felt that the member countries could go ahead with a full discussion on monetary arrangements even in advance of the full conclusion of trade negotiations if the latter were to last for long.[22]

Meeting of Government and Central Bank Officials on Trade and Monetary Cooperation

Subsequently, a meeting of Government and Central Bank officials was organised at Bangkok in November 1970 to consider the Missions' report in conjunction with the draft proposals for trade and monetary cooperation in the ECAFE region. The meeting after taking due note of the efforts of ECAFE in finalising the studies on trade and monetary cooperation adopted the draft guidelines for the establishment of the Asian Clearing Union. The draft guidelines dealt with the specific issues of purposes, participation, unit of account , methods of payment, guarantees and organisation etc., of the arrangement. It was felt that the Executive Secretary should, under his responsibility, be authorized to transmit these documents for consideration by the Council of Ministers.[23] The Council of Ministers at its fourth session at Kabul from

16-19 December 1970 decided to establish a preparatory committee to examine the given guidelines and to negotiate among themselves an agreement on terms and conditions acceptable to them for early establishment of the union. This comprised of representatives of regional member and associate member countries of ECAFE interested in the establishment of an Asian Clearing Union.[24]

The Kabul Ministerial Conference therefore was a significant step in the in the formation of ACU in the sense that it gave the mandate at the highest level for initiating the process. Till then proposals for a clearing union were being considered in a routine way in the various official and semi-official channels and that too as part of wider plans for intra-regional trade expansion. The Kabul meet realised that plans for monetary cooperation in Asia and the Far East had not really moved in the desired direction and thus gave the go ahead for an early launch of the process. The Kabul Declaration was adopted after much debate between the participating countries on the feasibility of the Union. A summary of the responses of the participating countries is given below:

Individual Country Responses to ACU

- *Australia*—It felt that benefits of ACU were being overstated and likely costs in terms of real resources could be high and out of proportion to the likely benefits. It shared an earlier view of the IMF that such an arrangement by itself could hardly be expected to give any substantial stimulus to intra-regional trade. Besides it could also limit developing countries access to existing source of finance if by getting influenced by ACU, they turned their backs on the major financial centres of the world.[25]
- *Burma*—Burma initially sought a more careful approach towards monetary cooperation. It emphasised on searching for a lowest common denominator of understanding upon which a sizable number of countries could agree to act.[26]

- *Ceylon*—Fully supported the proposal to set up the ACU and regarded it as a concrete step towards establishment of closer relations among the countries of the ECAFE region and specifically as an important move towards more effective cooperation in monetary and financial matters.[27]
- *China*—China was hesitant in fully supporting the ACU. It asserted that it was not clear as to how much efficiency and economy would the establishment of ACU bring. It saw ACU as offering only a limited and indirect help in overcoming obstacles to trade expansion and made its joining subject to others going ahead.[28]
- *India*—Favoured joining the ACU and was willing to subscribe to the principles for trade expansion among the developing countries of the ECAFE region.[29]
- *Iran*—Iran was in agreement with the estabishment of the ACU. It emphasised on the exclusion of petroleum and petroleum products from the scope of the ACU and wanted separate attention being given to it.[30]
- *Laos*—Despite being convinced with the value of the scheme, could not join the ACU because it had to follow complete convertibility as directed by I.M.F. because of its precarious balance of payment position.[31]
- *Malaysia*—Its obligations as per Article 8 did not permit it to have restrictions on payments and felt there were adequate banking facilities for trade transactions existing in the region. Besides it felt that an ACU encompassing the whole of Asia would be unwieldy.[32]
- *Nepal*—While pointing out the special position of countries having bilateral payments arrangements, it was willing to be part of the ACU and even offered to host the facility.[33]
- *Pakistan*—Supported the scheme for clearing union but stated that implementation of such schemes would depend on a broad based agreement on cooperation in trade and monetary matters.[34]

The adoption of the draft guidelines at the Meeting of Government and Central Bank officials at Bangkok and its subsequent follow-up at the Fourth Ministerial meet at Kabul, thus, set into motion the process of formal launch of the ACU. The draft guidelines explicitly laid out the purposes of the proposed union as facilitating the expansion of intra-regional trade and promoting monetary cooperation among the member countries of the ECAFE. It sought to provide a clearing mechanism for the multilateral settlement of intra-regional payments by promoting use of regional currencies and closer relations between banking systems of the region.[35] The guidelines also sought to make the use of the mechanism optional to banks, firms and individuals, without prejudice to the right of the monetary authority of any country to make it mandatory. It appears that a cautious approach was preferred with regard to the option of using of facility initially. The guidelines defined the specific terms relating to methods and duration of payment and left the eligibility of instruments and the actual accounting and settlement periods to be determined at a later stage.[36]

The first meeting of the preparatory committee as mooted by the Kabul Ministerial meet was held at Bangkok in March 1971 which evolved a Draft Agreement for setting up the ACU. It also agreed to take opinion of the UN legal office and the IMF on some legal questions before the final endorsement.[37] Thereafter, in February 1973, the ECAFE Secretariat convened a meeting of senior officials of governments and Central Banks of nine Asian countries including Burma, India, Iran, Khmer Republic, Laos, Nepal, Pakistan, Republic of Vietnam and Sri Lanka. The meeting examined the revised draft which had been reshaped into a simple operational agreement by the IMF staff with UNCTAD's cooperation. This draft comprehensively laid down the specific provisions of the agreement detailing various articles relating to the purposes, participation, unit of account, settlement of balances, organization and administration of the ACU. It also laid down the procedures for amendment and provisions for the entry into force of the agreement.[38]

After making the necessary changes, the meeting finally adopted the final draft agreement for the establishment of the

ACU. It also discussed the criteria for a suitable location of the union and felt that adequacy of communication supporting services in terms of personnel data processing, accounting machines etc., would be essential for the efficient functioning of the union.

The agreement was finally opened for signature at the annual session of ECAFE held at Tokyo in April 1973. While Iran and Sri Lanka signed the agreement at the session itself, India, Bangladesh, Nepal and Pakistan signed it subsequently. The agreement entered into force on 9th December 1974 and became operational from 1 November 1975. Burma was the seventh country to join the ACU on 13th January 1977.[39] The latest entrant has been Bhutan which joined the grouping in September 2000.

An analysis of the background of the formation of ACU, therefore, shows that it was a gradual process that finally gained momentum due to a variety off actors both extrinsic and intrinsic. At broader level was the growing realization that the developing countries of the Asian region were lagging far behind *vis-a-vis* other parts in terms of economic growth and trade. The intra-regional trade within the ECAFE region accounted for approximately a third of its total trade, while trade among developing countries accounted for approximately one quarter of total intra-regional trade. A significant feature was the tendency for trade among the developing countries of the region (with the exception of the trade in oil), to decline from 15.6 per cent of global trade in 1960 to only 6.4 per cent in 1968. The attainment of a greater level of self-sufficiency in a number of primary products, similarity in production patterns and an intensification of restrictive trade policies, contributed to the declining volume of trade among developing countries of the region. The substitution of regional imports for imports from non-regional sources, particularly in the case of aid imports, could have been an additional factor.[40] Besides intra-regional trade within the ECAFE at times showed declining trends, there were growing protectionist tendencies in the developed countries leading to a substantial burden on the balance of trade front. It was against this backdrop that the need was felt for greater economic cooperation among the Asian countries.

The need for a regional payments arrangement, therefore, was considered adjunct to the plan of trade expansion and liberalisation. At a more specific level, efforts at establishing a regional payment facility were focused not only on providing a facilitating mechanism but also on overcoming the limitations posed by the existing payment mechanisms. Nearly all of the internal as well as the external trade of the ECAFE region was conducted in hard currencies, with sterling and the US dollars playing the most important roles. An importer, therefore, had to effect payment for an international transaction by converting local currency into internationally acceptable currency through the central bank or commercial banking institution and settlements had to be done through the correspondent banks located in London or New York. The effective control which the governments of the region exercised over the use of the countries' foreign exchange occurred through the techniques of trade licences and/or multiple exchange rates applicable to different transactions or commodities and/or foreign exchange rationing schemes. Such direct controls were designed to serve the multiple purpose of keeping a restraint on the total amount of foreign exchange expenditures, protecting domestic manufacturers and inducing increased production or export.[41]

As stated earlier dependence on a few currencies for mutual trade which had to be transacted through financial centres located in the West made any programme of trade liberalisation dependent on the way these currencies fluctuated. Besides, transaction costs associated with currency conversions and bank margins added to the overall burden on trade. There was also an urgent need for conservation of foreign exchange resources which could help in meeting contingent needs of the member countries. Lastly unlike in the West Europe or Latin America where regional integration efforts complemented monetary and financial schemes, there wasn't any forum in Asia which could promote monetary and financial interaction. It was primarily this specific background which eventually led to the establishment of the Asian Clearing Union.

3.3 Objectives

The main objectives of the ACU as laid out in the Agreement are as follows:

(i) To provide a facility to settle on a multilateral basis, payments for current international transactions among the territories of the participants;
(ii) To promote the use of participants' currencies in current transaction between their respective territories and thereby effect economies in the use of participants exchange reserves;
(iii) To promote monetary cooperation among participants and closer relations among the banking system in their territories and thereby, contribute to the expansion of trade and economic activity among the countries of the ESCAP region; and
(iv) To provide for currency swap arrangement among the participants so as to make Asian Monetary Units available to them temporarily.[42]

The key emphasis in these objectives was on the provision of a multilateral facility which could be used to settle the payments arising out of intra-regional transactions. The benefits of such a facility would be two fold. Firstly, it would enable multilateralisation of payment obligations. It meant that a country's obligations or entitlements (regarding payments) would not be decided by bilateral positions but by multilateral positions *vis-a-vis* all other countries taken together. This led to an easing of the burden depending on what the net positions may be after taking into account the positions of other countries. Secondly, by developing a regional facility for clearing current transactions, unnecessary costs and delays accruing due to conventional channels could be avoided. With the resulting ease in the payment settlement, more traders could be expected to make use of the facility, thereby leading to a possible expansion in intra-regional trade.

The next significant objective related to the use of participants' currencies in the current transactions which would lead to conservation of foreign exchange reserves of the member countries.

As mentioned earlier, the early 1970s was a period of extreme vulnerability to some of the member countries as they experienced declining exports, high indebtedness and fluctuating exchange rates which further constrained their foreign exchange positions.[43] As a result, economizing on the use of foreign exchange reserves was considered as vital for meeting essential import requirements and repayment obligations. By making use of participants' currencies at least an initial step towards saving foreign exchange' could be taken. The benefits arising out of this however, would be significant only if there was expansion in the membership of the union and corresponding increase in the volume of transactions covered. As we shall later see, due to lack of further increase in the membership of the union, the foreign exchange saved was confined to the transactions settled within the member countries and could hardly be expected to add to existing reserves in a major way.

Finally but significantly, ACU was intended to be a mechanism which would lead to greater monetary cooperation among the member countries and foster greater relations among the banking systems. This was a broader objective which could be seen as strengthening the regional monetary and financial system which could be a prerequisite for greater economic interaction within the region. Given a regular interaction of the Central Banks and monetary authorities of the member countries under the ACU, a forum would be available where issues relating to monetary and exchange rate policies could be discussed and attempts could be made to harmonize these policies so that larger integration efforts could be assisted. Although, given the operational nature of the ACU, the nature of interaction was limited to that of clearing, yet in the long run greater coordination in payments, credit and trade could be considered. However, the role of the ACU as a mode of financial cooperation was to remain limited as we shall elaborate later, and it continued to focus on the clearing part with only small steps being taken to look after the financing part.[44]

3.4 Operational Features

The establishment of the ACU sought to change the existing mechanism of intra-regional payments. Previously, all the transactions got channeled through bilateral mechanism whereby two countries settled mutual payments in hard currencies through correspondent banking relationships held in New York and London. In such cases, the commercial banks operating the accounts of both the exporters and importers had dollar/sterling accounts maintained with correspondent banks in New York/London. Payments to be made in dollars in lieu of imports for example were therefore made by the importer's correspondent bank in to the exporter's correspondent bank in New York. With the initiation of the ACU mechanism, bilateral compensations were transformed into multilateral ones and a country's obligations were calculated in terms of its combined net position vis-a-vis the other members.

In other words, a country's net payment position was determined not on the basis of what it owed to other countries individually but after taking all credits and debits combined. Its obligations were therefore based on the net total amount that was owed to other members taken together. Besides correspondent banking relationships were now confined to the banks operating within the region as the settlement was done through participants' own currencies. The operational mechanism through which the ACU was put into practice shall become clear when we discuss separately the various modalities that were devised for the mechanism to function. We would simultaneously analyse the modifications that were made at the procedural level and their underlying significance and implications.

1. *Unit of account*—The unit of account serves as the key unit in terms of which the transactions cleared through

the clearing union. Article IV of the Agreement which provides for the unit of account states that:

"(a) The Accounts of the Asian Clearing Union shall be kept in a common unit of account hereby designated as the 'Asian Monetary Unit,' which may be referred to in the abbreviated form as "AMU".

(b) The value of one Asian Monetary Unit shall, with effect from 1-1-1996 and until such time as it is changed by the Board in terms of sub clause (c) of the article, be equivalent in value to one US dollar. The Asian Monetary Unit may also be termed as 'ACU' dollar.

(c) The Board of Directors may change the value of Asian Monetary Unit at any time by a unanimous vote of all the Directors."[45]

The value of one AMU had initially been kept equivalent to one Special Drawing Right (SDR) allocated by the IMF. The designated value continued for almost two decades before it was changed as equivalent in value to one US dollar with effect from 1-1-1996. The switch over to dollar denominated transactions was preceded by a number of developments relating to exchange rate management in respective member countries as part of their broader reform programmes which would be elaborated further. As per the traditional role assigned to it, the ACU was intended to be a mechanism whereby use of participants' own currencies was encouraged to settle mutual payments for eligible transactions. As per Article II Section 6, among the purposes of the Agreement was to "promote the use of participants' currencies in current transactions between their respective territories and thereby effect economies in the use of participants' exchange reserves." Since it was only the net amount remaining that was to be settled in hard currencies, the mechanism served as an instrument of foreign exchange conservation among the member countries. Given the record of ACU's functioning over time, it does appear that this basic objective was fulfilled satisfactorily to a great extent.[46]

The exchange rates of the member currencies in terms of the AMU were announced for a fortnight initially. The ACU would arrive at the middle rates of participants' currencies on the basis of the latest S.D.R. rates *vis-a-vis* the intervention currency and convey them to the central banks. These central banks would thus announce their buying and selling rates for each member's currency simultaneously. This was done twice a month with the rates remaining in force for a fortnight. However, due to rapid changes in the international currency rates, the ACU rates could not hold as initially intended for 15 days and had often to be changed during this period. In order to remove this time lag, the ACU, started announcing the rates three times a month at 10-day intervals. Even this involved considerable lags in the rates and ACU started announcing the rates everyday. Due to rapid changes in international currency rates, these ACU rates could not hold for a fortnight and often had to be changed. As a result, the rates were then announced for ten days and finally for everyday to make up for the time lag that was created. Even the daily rates so computed were communicated to all participants by cable and telex and became applicable only from the third day from the day to which they pertained.[47]

Studies conducted at this point of time pointed to the possibility of some traders' unwillingness to make or receive currencies quotations in regional currencies or AMUs because of difficulty of converting these into hard currencies used in international markets.[48] The Board of Directors at their meeting in Colombo in May 1995 recognized the difficulties faced by exporters and importers while using the clearing facilities which eventually hindered the growth of clearing volumes. It therefore, decided to initiate a study to critically analyse the procedures and operations of the union and to remove the difficulties to enable smooth and effective functioning of the mechanism.

The study took note of the changing scenario such as rapidly changing international currency rates, adoption of current account convertibility by most countries in which the ACU had to cope up with a situation with members moving towards full convertibility and the major problem areas that had emerged, requiring immediate attention. It highlighted the following as major difficulties that had come up in using the ACU.[49]

(i) The lag in the announcement of the rates (as mentioned earlier) which became operative only on the third day to which they pertain put the traders at a disadvantage as they had to deal with rates which were three days old. The ACU rate system was therefore, felt to be rigid and inflexible to move in tune with other fast changing rates in international currencies like the US dollar. This time lag often made it unattractive to quote prices or draw documents in local currencies in view of the exchange risks involved.

(ii) Absence of forward cover to counter exchange risk in ACU currencies often put the traders in a tight spot. A forward cover ensures that local currency proceeds of exports realised some months after the dispatch of goods do not result in a loss on account of exchange rate fluctuations of the currency of payment. While such forward cover was easily available for an international currency, it was not available for the ACU currencies in the absence of a well developed market for them.

(iii) Besides, the exporters under the ACU mechanism were also not able to avail the pre-shipment credit facilities denominated in foreign currencies. Preshipment credit is generally in the form of packing credit, advance against cash incentives and others. Packing credit is offered to an exporter for packing and shipment and also manufacture of goods, which may be in form of loan, cash credit or overdraft facility. ACU traders could not avail these because such credits were generally required to be repaid back in US dollars on maturity while the ACU exports were realised only in local currency.

(iv) The ACU currencies lacked a well developed forward market thereby making it impossible for the ACU traders to avail of exchange risk management instruments such as 'put' and 'call' options. An option contract is an agreement between two parties in which one grants the other the right to buy (call option) or sell (put option) an asset under specified conditions and assumes the obligation to sell or buy it. Since ACU currencies could not be used for trading, the ACU traders were deprived of a potential tool in managing foreign currency exposure.

The study therefore, concluded that most of the ills afflicting the ACU were related to the disadvantageous position in which traders were being placed *vis-a-vis* non-ACU traders primarily because of their inability to get their proceeds in convertible currencies. In order to remove these difficulties, it suggested that the traders should be allowed not only to invoice the trade in international currencies such as the US dollar but also make and receive actual payments in the same currency as was the practice in international trade.

2. *Settlement of Balance among Participants*—Initially, the settlement of net positions and accrued interests were to be made at the end of each four week settlement period and to the extent required by section 3 of Article VI (pertaining to net credit and debit limits of each participant) at the end of each two week accounting period. In 1977, the settlement period was extended from one month to two months and the accounting

period from two weeks to one month. As per section 3 Article VI, the Secretary General of the ACU shall notify each participant of its net position, including "accrued interest, and of the amounts it shall pay to, or receive from, other participants at the end of each settlement period. Each debtor participant, within four working days of the receipt from the General Manager of the notice of the amounts to be paid, shall make the payments in international reserve assets specified by the Board of Directors for the purpose. Payments may also be made in the currency of the creditor subject to its specific consent."[50]

The two monthly period given for settlement of net balances gives an automatic credit to the deficit participants for about two months which gives them crucial time to make suitable arrangements. Besides, initially there was a limit on the net credit or debit position that could be held by participant countries.[51] These limits were however, removed from 1981 onwards and subsequently any level of mutual trade could be reached at without having to transfer convertible currency during settlement period.

3. *Interest Rates*—The interest rate has to be paid by net debtors and transferred to net creditors on daily balances outstanding between settlement dates. The accrued interest has to be included in the calculation of the net amounts to be paid and received at the end of each settlement period along with the net position of each participant.[52] As per the ACU Procedure Rule No. 9, "the rate of interest on net debit and credit balance will be the closing rate on the first working day of the last week of the previous calender month offered by the Bank for International Settlement for one month Euro-dollar deposits. In the event that the Bank for International Settlements does not quote rates for such deposits, the last available rates will apply until such rates become available.[53]
4. *Clearing Operations*—The clearing operations form the core of the functioning of the ACU which provide for

settlement of mutual payments and net balances arising out of these settlements. The clearing operations under the union have undergone significant changes over a period of time. Between 1974 and 1980, all the transactions were routed through the respective Central Banks with exporters being required to present appropriate documents to his bank for collection or for sale. This procedure was however, dispensed with in 1980 as the Central Banks found it difficult to handle the growing load of transactions and subsequently commercial banks were incorporated within the mechanism. Henceforth, the exporters were required to deal with commercial banks as far as documentation and repatriation is concerned. The commercial banks were allowed to maintain ACU account in the correspondent bank in other countries in their own currencies. All payments other than ineligible payments such as capital account transactions, travel etc. were to be settled by the banks concerned through these accounts.

Following changes in the ACU operating mechanism into dollar denominated transactions, the banks subsequently were to maintain ACU dollar accounts with their corresponding banks in other participating countries under this dispensation. If a commercial bank, desires to fund its ACU dollar account owing to obligations arising out of imports, with its correspondent bank in another participating country, then it may purchase the required ACU dollar either from a local commercial bank having surplus in that participating country or from its Central Bank. For this, it has to surrender the equivalent amount of US dollar or at the option of the Central Bank, the equivalent in the local currency to its own Central Bank for remittance through the ACU mechanism. The participant receiving the amount advises the participant in the country concerned to make available the amount in US dollars to the concerned

Bank in that country. After making the payment, the second participant will advise the General Manager of the ACU to credit its account by debit to the fist participant's account. (See Figure No.3.1 at the end of the chapter).

For example, let us assume an Indian Commercial Bank opens an ACU dollar account with a Sri Lankan commercial bank. This account would be used for both making payments to Sri Lankan exporters, surplus dollar funds remitted to the Indian Commercial Bank through the Central Bank of Sri Lanka and interests on overdrafts and commissions paid by the Indian Bank (Debits) and for receiving US dollar amounts from Sri Lankan importers, dollar remittances received and interest and commission payable to Indian commercial banks (credits).[54]

Now in case there is a surplus of $1 million in the Indian commercial bank's account with Sri Lankan commercial bank it has to be remitted to India. Sri Lankan commercial bank will pay $1 million to Central Bank of Sri Lanka (CBSL), by debit to Indian commercial bank's account. The CBSL will retain the dollar fund with it as part of the credit received by Sri Lanka under ACU arrangement. It will advise the Reserve Bank of India (RBI) to pay $1 million to the Indian Commercial Bank and inform the ACU to afford credit to India in ACU accounts by debit to Sri Lanka on the value date. The RBI in turn will make $1 million available out of its foreign balances to the Indian Bank and confirm from ACU that its account in the ACU books have been credited on value date. [55]

Similarly, repatriation of funds from the ACU dollar account entails selling of the desired ACU dollar to either a local commercial bank desiring to fund its ACU dollar account or the Central Bank which in turn requests the bank to effect the remittance through the ACU mechanism. For instance, to keep the ACU transactions distinct the Reserve Bank of India gives a direction for the payments to be made through ACU dollar denominated accounts maintained with authorized dealers in India and banks in participating countries. The RBI would arrange for funding of such ACU dollar accounts or absorb surplus liquidity as the situation may be. Funding of an ACU dollar account maintained in corresponding bank in another ACU nation would come into effect only on intimation that equivalent amount of US dollar was being credited to its account with Federal Reserve Bank of New York.[56]

5. *Eligibility of Transactions*—ACU has gone through periodic changes as far as eligibility of transactions to be channeled is concerned. As per the initial agreement, payments between India and Nepal and Pakistan and Iran were not eligible for inclusion in the clearing facility.[57] They have now been included since November 1990. Besides, until 1985, trade in petrol and petroleum products were considered ineligible for clearing purposes and were therefore, not channeled through the facility. However, this prevented a major portion of trade from being covered under the facility, especially with regard to Iran's export to other countries. Oil was the only source of foreign exchange revenue for Iran. Therefore, making oil payments eligible under the ACU system would have deprived Iran of its main source of hard currency. It was precisely for this reason that keeping in mind Iranian interests; the above mentioned categories were not included under the mechanism. The removal of these restrictions in 1985 has been seen as a significant achievement as payments for oil and oil products at times accounted for more than 50 per cent of total intra-trade transactions of ACU member countries.[58]

   A participant may require residents to make payments through the clearing facility, but such a requirement should not restrict or delay the payments for international transactions or create a discriminatory currency arrangement. The use of the facility otherwise has been kept optional.[59] This implies that the use of the facility is mandatory only to the extent that it does not affect the smooth functioning of international payments and doesn't give rise to discriminatory practices. While five of the seven participant countries excluding India and Myanmar made channeling of eligible transactions through the ACU compulsory in 1983, the remaining two followed suit in 1984. This shows that the member countries were essentially careful in the initial years in not making the use facility mandatory. However, following the introduction of Liberalised Exchange Rate Management System (LERMS), India again made it optional by relaxing compulsory routing through the ACU in 1993.

6. *Currency Swap Agreement*—In one of the most significant developments in ACU operations since its inception, an arrangement aimed at providing short term credit for member countries in deficit positions at the end of settlement period was started since 1989. As per this arrangement, every eligible participant shall be entitled to the facility from every other participant upto 20 per cent of the gross payments made by it through the ACU mechanism to the other participants during the three previous calendar years. This implies that the amount that a participant is entitled to receive is linked to the amount that it has paid to others previously. A participant however, shall not draw more than its overall deficit at the end of settlement period. The drawal by each participant from each other participant shall be in the same proportion as its overall deficit bears to its maximum entitlement. The rate of interest chargeable on each drawal would be equal to LIMEAN (London Interbank Mean Rate) on US dollar for the period of two months. The reference LIMEAN will be Barclay's Bank London at 11:00 a.m. applicable for the concerned value date.[60]

An overview of the key operational features of the ACU therefore gives us an idea of the manner in which the functioning of the Union has been put into practice. A striking feature of the entire operational mechanism has been the tendency to take corrective modifications in the procedures/ operations as per the needs whether it pertains to the eligibility of payments, calculations of exchange rates, unit of account or introduction of a new scheme altogether such as a currency Swap. While the feasibility and viability of the ACU has been put to severe test because of dynamic changes in the external environment, its ability to take corrective measures have nevertheless enabled it to perform more or less smoothly.

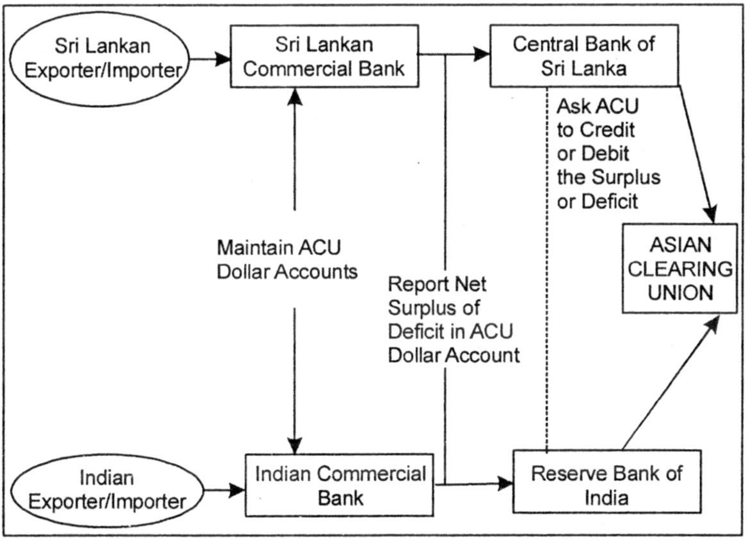

Fig. 3.1: ACU Transactions-Flow Chart

NOTES

1. Statement by U. Nyun, Executive Secretary of the United Nations Economic Commission for Asia and the Far-East, *Report of the Ministerial Conference on Asian Economic Cooperation, Manila,* 3-6 December 1963, United Nations, New York 1964, p. II.
2. Figures cited in the Report and Recommendations of the Seminar on Financial Aspects of Trade Expansion, *Regional Economic*

Cooperation (REC) Series No.6, United Nations, New York, 1968, p. 13.
3. *Economic and Social Survey of Asia and the Pacific, United Nations*, 1978, p. 57.
4. Gary P. Sampson, "Structural Change: Accommodating Imports from Developing Countries" in John Black and AlasdairI; MacBean, (ed.), *Causes of Changes in the Structure of International Trade* (London, 1989), p. 176
5. *Ibid.* For the same period, while the share of South East Asia remained stable at 40 per cent, that of East-Asia increased from 28.4 per cent to 39.1 per cent.
6. *Ibid.*, p. 74.
7. S. Guharr, "The World Bank's Lending in South Asia," Brookings Occasional Paper, *The Brookings Institution*, Washington D.C., 1995, p. 23
8. L.P. Singh, *The Politics of Economic Cooperation in Asia* (Columbia, 1966), pp. 232.
9. Michael T. Skully, *ASEAN Financial Cooperation* (London, 1985), p. 4
10. T.K. Jayraman, *Economic Cooperation in the Indian Subcontinent* (Bombay, 1978), p. 48.
11. I.N. Mukherjee, *Towards Economic Integration in Asia: An Evaluation of Trade Expansion Programme of Developing Countries in Asia and Pacific* (New Delhi, 1978), p. 2.
12. *Ibid.*, p. 4.
13. Report of the Ministerial Conference on Asian Economic Cooperation, n. I, p. 385.
14. *Ibid.* p. 13.
15. United Nations, "The Asian Development Bank and Trade Liberalization", *REC Series No. 2. ECAFE* (New York,1965), p. 90.
16. *Ibid.* p. 91
17. United Nations, "Report and Recommendation of the Seminar on Financial Aspects of Trade Expansion", *REC Series No. 6, ECAFE* (New York, 1968), p. 2.
18. See the statement of IMF representative, S. Mookherjee in *ibid.*, p. 85
19. United Nations, "Considerations and Proposals for Monetary Cooperation in ECAFE Region", *REC Series No.7 ECAFE* (New York, 1971), p. 51.
20. *Ibid.*, p. 52.
21. See "An outline of proposed agreement for an Asian Payments Union" in *Report of the Expert Mission, ibid.*, p. 75.
22. A Summary of the Informal Consultation on Monetary

Cooperation in the ECAFE Region, Copenhagen, 24th September 1970 in No.19, p. 81.

23. "Report of the Meeting of Government and Central Bank Officials on Trade and Monetary Cooperation", in n.19, p. 1.
24. See the "Kabul Declaration on Asian Economic Cooperation and Development" in the Report of Council of Ministers for Asian Economic Cooperation, 4th Session, *REC Series No.8, ECAFE,* United Nations, (New York, 1971), p. 4.
25. Statement by the Representative of Australia, *ibid.,* p. 23.
26. Statement by the Representative of Burma, *ibid.,* p. 24.
27. Statement by the Representative of Ceylon, *ibid.,* p. 25.
28. Statement by the Representative of China, *ibid.,* p. 27.
29. Statement by the Representative of India, *ibid.,* pp. 28, 95.
30. Statement by the Representative of Iran, in the Report of the Meeting of the Council of Ministers for Asian Economic Cooperation, 4th Session, *REC Series No.8, ECAFE,* United Nations (New York, 1971), p. 34.
31. Statement by the Representative of Laos, *ibid.,* p. 41.
32. Statement by the Representative of Malaysia, *ibid.,* p. 42.
33. Statement by the Representative of Nepal, *ibid.,* p. 46.
34. Statement by the Representative of Pakistan, *ibid.,* p. 48.
35. See, the Draft Guidelines for the Establishment of the Asian Clearing Union, n.19, p. 13.
36. *Ibid.*
37. I.N. Mukherjee. n.11, p. 11.
38. Report of the Meeting of Senior Officials of Governments and Central Banks for the Establishment of an Asian Clearing Union, Trade/ACU/MOGCB/6, 12 March 1973.
39. I.N. Mukherjee, n. 11, p. 12.
40. United Nations, n. 19, p. 24.
41. United Nations, n. 17, p. 18.
42. See Article II of the Agreement Establishing the Asian Clearing Union, ACU Secretariat, Teheran, 1996.
43. For instance in 1973, devaluation of the dollars by the United States of around 10 per cent and appreciation of other currencies was estimated to lead to a loss in real value of foreign exchange reserves of around 1 billion US dollar. See Extracts from a Statement by U. Nyun, Executive Secretary of ECAFE, in n. 38, p. 21.
44. M.Y. Khan, "Asian Clearing Union: An Assessment", *RBI Bulletin,* February,1991, pp. 120.
45. See Article IV, n. 42.

46. M.Y. Khan, n.44, p. 124.
47. This was because S.D.R. rates announced by the I.M.F on the basis of exchange rates as quoted by the Bank of England at 12:00 noon in London could only be communicated to the ACU Headquarters the next day. The calculation of the individual currency rates and their communication to their purchase and sale rates to their operating offices took another day.
48. R. Janakiraman, Critical Study of the Procedures Regarding the Operation of the Asian Clearing Union (Bombay, 1995), p. 3.
49. *Ibid.*, p. 10.
50. See Article IV, Section III, n. 42.
51. Net Credit granted by each member was limited to 1/12th of annual visible exports to other members excluding petroleum, petro-products, natural gas and natural gas products. Net Debit limits were put to 1/24th of its visible imports excluding the above products.
52. See Article, VI Section 2, n. 42.
53. See Article, VI Section 2, n. 42. ACU Procedure Rule No. 9(a), n. 42.
54. Example cited from R. Janakiraman, n. 48, p. 11.
55. *Ibid.*, p. 12.
56. See Article V, Section 2(b), n. 42.
57. See Rule n. 4, ACU Procedure Rules, n. 42. While between India and Nepal, trade used to take place in rupee, Iran and Pakistan had their own payment arrangement under the RCD, which was wound up later.
58. M.Y. Khan, n. 44, p. 120.
59. See Article, V Section 4 a, n. 42.
60. See ACU Procedure Rules No. 7, n. 42.

Chapter 4

Asian Clearing Union: Trends and Performance

4.1 Introduction

Given the background of its origin, evolution and features of the ACU since inception in 1975, we now come to the mechanisms of ACU operations. The present chapter analyses the trends within the ACU member countries with regard to the broad macro-economic aggregates and tries to correlate them with the performance of the ACU system. It also analyses at the same time the policy environment prevailing within the ACU member countries which has had a bearing on their participation within the ACU system. The time period under consideration has been generally taken as between 1975-1998.[1](The figures for the recent years have been analysed in the annexure to the chapter). There are three levels at which data have been analyzed. First at the broad, aggregate level where the ACU countries' performance at the macro-level are analyzed. Secondly, an analysis of the intra-ACU transactions and their linkages with the trade pattern among the ACU member countries and lastly, the member countries' participation and policies at the country level have been analysed.

4.2 Macro-economic Aggregates of ACU Member Countries

As an organisation consisting of the central banks of the member countries, the ACU is a body where macro-economic policies and targets have a crucial role in shaping the pattern of interaction among them. They not merely reflect the nature of changes taking place within, but also refer to the pattern of member countries interaction with the rest of the world. This would now be further elaborated as we analyse the trends with regard to (i) exports and imports, (ii) exports and imports as per centage of GDP, (iii) balance of trade, and (iv) total reserves.

Exports/Imports

By and large, almost all the ACU countries have registered an increase in exports during the period 1975-1998. As Table 4.1 shows, the period 1975-80 registered the highest average annual growth in exports for all the member countries except Nepal. Myanmar registered the highest growth (34.57%) followed by Pakistan (29.77%), Bangladesh (28.50%), Iran (22.97%), India (19.43%) and Sri Lanka (15.39%). Nepal on the other hand experienced a negative growth of -4 per cent.

Table 4.1: ACU Countries Total Exports 1975-1998

(Billions of US Dollars)

Countries	*1975*	*1980*	*1985*	*1990*	*1995*	*1996*	*1997*	*1998*
Bangladesh	0.33	0.79	1.00	1.67	3.17	3.30	3.78	3.83
		28.50	**5.20**	**13.45**	**17.98**	(0.78)	(2.92)	(0.28)
India	4.36	8.59	9.14	18.00	30.76	33.05	34.25	32.88
		19.43	**1.29**	**19.38**	**14.19**	(1.49)	(0.72)	(-0.80)
Iran	7.96	17.11	13.33	19.31	18.36	22.39	NA	NA
		22.97	**-4.42**	**8.97**	**-0.98**	(4.39)		
Myanmar	0.17	0.47	0.30	0.33	0.85	0.73	0.87	1.07
		34.57	**-7.16**	**1.45**	**32.06**	(-2.70)	(3.66)	(4.64)
Nepal	0.10	0.08	0.16	0.20	0.35	0.39	0.40	0.47
		-4.00	**20.00**	**5.50**	**13.82**	(2.32)	(0.88)	(3.58)
Pakistan	1.05	2.62	2.74	5.60	8.01	9.34	8.73	8.50
		29.77	**0.92**	**20.80**	**8.60**	(3.33)	(-1.30)	(-0.53)
Sri Lanka	0.60	1.07	1.97	1.98	3.80	4.10	4.63	4.73
		15.39	**16.98**	**0.10**	**18.31**	(1.56)	(2.63)	(0.43)

Source: International Financial Statistics Yearbook 1999.

Note: Figures in bold are the average annual growth rate for the period. Figures in parenthesis are the annual growth rates NA—Not Available.

For most of the other countries, this spectacular growth in exports may be attributed to the post-1973 oil shock recovery period. Although exports continued to grow in the subsequent periods *i.e.* from 1980-85, 1985-90 and 1990-95, the rate of growth was not as pronounced. The average annual growth in the late 1990s has slowed down. In 1998, in fact both India and Pakistan experienced negative growth rates of -0.80 per cent and -0.53 per cent respectively.

Table 4.2: ACU Countries Total Imports 1975-1998

(Billion US Dollars)

Countries	*1975*	*1980*	*1985*	*1990*	*1995*	*1996*	*1997*	*1998*
Bangladesh	1.32	2.60	2.77	3.60	6.50	6.62	6.71	7.04
		19.35	**1.33**	**5.96**	**16.11**	(1.83)	(1.44)	(4.93)
India	6.38	14.86	15.93	23.64	34.52	37.38	41.02	42.20
		26.59	**1.43**	**9.69**	**9.20**	(8.26)	(9.74)	(2.89)
Iran	10.34	12.25	11.64	20.32	13.88	16.27	NA	NA
		3.68	**-1.00**	**14.93**	**-6.34**	(17.23)		
Myanmar	0.20	0.35	0.28	0.27	1.34	1.36	2.05	2.67
		15.84	**-3.97**	**-0.92**	**78.89**	(1.72)	(51.18)	(29.86)
Nepal	0.17	0.34	0.45	0.67	1.33	1.44	1.72	1.24
		20.00	**6.49**	**9.67**	**19.58**	(8.42)	(19.00)	(-27.80)
Pakistan	2.16	5.36	5.90	7.39	11.48	12.15	11.62	9.32
		29.60	**2.02**	**5.04**	**11.08**	(5.84)	(-4.41)	(-19.80)
Sri Lanka	0.82	2.04	1.84	2.69	5.19	5.42	5.84	5.92
		29.93	**-1.90**	**9.14**	**18.62**	(4.46)	(7.81)	(1.34)

Source: International Financial Statistics Yearbook 1999, pp. 132-36.

Note: Figures in bold are the average annual growth rate for the period. Figures in parenthesis are the annual growth rate NA—Not Available.

The trends with regard to imports in ACU countries are somewhat similar. As Table 4.2 shows, the 1975-80 period was marked by high average annual growth of imports. With the exception of Iran all the ACU countries experienced average growth of more than 15 per cent with Sri Lanka leading by experiencing growth of 29.93 per cent, followed by Pakistan (29.60 %), India (26.59%), Nepal (20%), Bangladesh (19.35%) and Iran (3.68%). The period 1980-85 registered a steep decline in import growth with only Nepal (20%) and Sri Lanka (16.98%)

registering growth in double digits with Iran and Myanmar recording negative growth. After a brief recovery, during the period 1985-90 and 1990-95, the annual growth of imports in 1995-98 has generally been sluggish with Pakistan and Nepal even registering negative growth (-19.80% and -27.80% respectively) in 1998.

The 1990s therefore have been symbolic of greater outward orientation among the ACU countries, there being a significant increase in export as well as imports compared to the eighties. The latter however have increased at a faster rate compared to the former. Besides there have been variations within as far as patterns of export and import growth are concerned. We shall also examine the impact on the respective balance of payments positions as a result of these trends but before that we analyze the relative shares of export/import in the respective national incomes of ACU countries as that would indicate to a certain extent the significance of the trade sector in the respective economies.

Exports/Imports as Percentage of GDP

Table 4.3 shows that exports as a percentage of GDP have increased for all the ACU countries except Pakistan. In case of Bangladesh, Nepal and Iran it has been quite pronounced while India and Sri Lanka have shown an increasing trend.

Table 4.3: ACU Countries Exports of Goods and Services: 1991-1997 as Percentage of GDP

Countries	*1991*	*1992*	*1993*	*1994*	*1995*	*1996*	*1997*
Bangladesh	9.3	11.1	12.8	13.8	15.3	14.8	17.3
India	8.5	9.2	9.4	9.5	10.1	10.3	10.3
Iran	2.6	2	26	27.1	18.5	17.3	17
Myanmar	1.3	2.1	—	—	—	—	—
Nepal	15.9	18.6	22.7	23.5	24.4	26.1	26.4
Pakistan	18.4	17.5	17.4	17.2	17.1	17.4	17
Sri Lanka	28.3	30.1	33.1	33.8	35.4	35	36.5

Source: IMF, International Financial Statistics Yearbook 1999, pp.154-55.

Nepal and Sri Lanka have had a relatively higher export/GDP ratio in the late nineties (more than 25%) compared to India, Pakistan and Bangladesh (which have rarely crossed 20%).

The pattern with regard to imports of goods and services as percentage of GDP are somewhat varied. While Bangladesh, Nepal and India have witnessed an increase in import/GDP ratio in the 1990s, Pakistan, Sri Lanka and Iran have registered declining trends (Table 4.4). Nevertheless, the import/GDP ratio in all these countries have been higher than the corresponding export/GDP ratios (around 25% or more for Bangladesh, Nepal, Sri Lanka and 13-25% for India and Pakistan).

Table 4.4: ACU Imports of Goods and Services 1991-1997 as Percentage of GDP

Countries	*1991*	*1992*	*1993*	*1994*	*1995*	*1996*	*1997*
Bangladesh	16.5	17.8	19.2	21	26.1	23.9	24.6
India	10	10.9	10.6	11.4	12.8	13.8	13.5
Iran	4.2	2.9	33.7	21.6	14.8	13.5	10.9
Myanmar	1.5	2.2	—	—	—	—	—
Nepal	29.1	27.9	31.5	36.1	38.5	39.6	40.2
Pakistan	25.5	25.6	25.1	23	23.7	25.9	22.8
Sri Lanka	39.7	39.6	42.6	45.6	45.9	43.9	43.6

Source: IMF, International Financial Statistics Yearbook 1999, pp.156-57.

Trade Balance

Thus it is clear that there has been a gradual increase in the outward orientation within which imports have generally constituted a greater share of the GDP as compared to the exports. This reflected in a consistent pattern the balance of trade has recorded in the ACU countries (Table 4.5). We can clearly see that almost all the ACU countries (with the exception of Iran) have had negative balance of trade position in the 1990s. After experiencing a favourable current account balance in the early nineties, Bangladesh has recorded a declining trend in the same in the later years. India's balance of trade position has consistently been on the negative with there being periods of high current account imbalance in the early 1990s, a declining trend in the mid 1990s before again showing increasing signs in the later years. Nepal, Pakistan and Sri Lanka have shown similar trends of high trade imbalance in the mid 1990s to a relatively better position in the end. Iran has been the only exception with there being high current account imbalance in 1991 and 1992, followed by continuously increasing balance of trade surplus in the following years.

Table 4.5: ACU Countries Trade Balance 1991-1998

(Millions of US Dollars)

Countries	*1991*	*1992*	*1993*	*1994*	*1995*	*1996*	*1997*	*1998*
Bangladesh	-1386	-1256	-1113	-1416	-2324	-2275	-1748	—
India	-2992	-2911	-2093	-4150	-6719	-10052	-10349	-10973
Iran	-6529	-3406	-1207	6817	5586	7402	4258	—
Myanmar	-53	-105	—	—	—	—	—	—
Nepal	-482	-376	-462	-790	961	-1106	-1308	-748
Pakistan	-2265	-2795	-2578	-2231	-2882	-3645	-2392	—
Sri Lanka	-805	-715	-742	-1085	-985	-800	-640	-567

Source: IMF, International Financial Statistics Yearbook 1999, p.143.

Total Reserves

Reserve assets refer to the external assets readily available to and controlled by monetary authorities primarily for direct financing of payments imbalances and for indirect regulating of the magnitude of such imbalances through exchange rate market intervention. With regard to the total reserves position, the ACU countries experienced a quantum increase in the 1990s compared to the 1980s. Yet this increase was not evenly distributed among the member countries (Table 4.6). India had a continuously growing reserve position between 1975-1998 with there being a sudden dip in 1990 at the peak of the balance of payment crisis. It registered nearly ten fold increase between 1990 and 1998. Bangladesh, Nepal and Myanmar registered a moderate increase during the same period. For the entire period, Pakistan experienced intermittent phases of declining and increasing , foreign exchange revenues. Sri Lanka, on the other hand, had a steady growth in total reserves.

Table 4.6: ACU Countries Total Reserves: 1975-1998
Million of SDRS

(with Gold at SDR 35 per ounce)

	1975	*1980*	*1985*	*1990*	*1995*	*1996*	*1997*	*1998*
Bangladesh	127	325	308	445	1577	1279	1176	—
India	1174	5745	6174	1443	12504	14474	18744	19820
Iran	7600	8188	—	—	—	—	—	—
Myanmar	120	213	40	229	386	167	193	232
Nepal	86	149	56	213	400	403	469	542
Pakistan	346	452	802	276	1238	453	958	803
Sri Lanka	50	195	413	299	1407	1366	1502	1408

Source: IMF, International Financial Statistics Yearbook (various issues).

Thus the macro-economic performance of the ACU member countries in the nineties exhibits certain peculiar trends. With most of the countries fully entrenched on the road to economic liberalisation and reforms, there has been a clear evidence of a growing linkage with the rest of the world through expansion in exports as well as imports. However, this pace has not been uniform among the member countries primarily due to different policy approaches followed by them (as we shall examine in the next section). Besides, in most of these countries imports have outpaced the growth in exports leading to an adverse balance of payments position which at times limits the members abilities for greater outward expansion. However, whether these broad macro economic trends have had any bearing in the pattern of economic interaction within the member countries is something that we later examine by studying each country individually in terms of the policies and the patterns of trade with the other member countries.

Having discussed the aggregate macro-economic performance and policies of the ACU countries, we now come to the intra-ACU transactions. The level of analysis in this section will be three folds. First the aggregated level of transactions routed through ACU. Secondly, country wise participation in the ACU with transactions credited and debited in each case. There would be a comparison of the clearing transaction along with the level of country wise trade. Lastly there would be an attempt to compare the levels of cleared trade with total intra ACU trade and the global trade of the ACU countries. This would enable us to analyze the relative significance that the ACU system occupies in the broader trade patterns of the member countries.

4.3 Intra-ACU Transactions

Total Transactions Routed through the ACU

As indicated in Table 4.7a(1) there has been a steady growth in the transactions channeled through the ACU in its 30 years of operation. From a mere 25.6 million dollars in 1976, the transactions routed through the facility have increased to a record 3161.1 million US dollar in 1996 before coming down to 2842 MN US dollar in 1998. Significantly, the value of transactions have grown every year except for four years in 1985,1987,1993 and 1997 which registered a negative growth compared to the previous year.

Taking into account the first twenty years of the ACU, the first quarter registered the highest average rate of growth of 72.7 per cent, probably on account of the initial thrust towards making use of the facility in its formative years. The average rate of change declined drastically to 14.2 per cent in the second quarter before rising to 27.3 per cent in the 3rd quarter. The last quarter of this period has maintained an average growth of 23.7 per cent which is commendable keeping in mind that it coincided with the reform process in most of the member countries, especially when currency convertibility was seen as diminishing the utility of such clearing arrangement.

It is quite interesting to note that the value of transactions channeled actually declined for the first time in 1985, the year when channeling of oil payments was started. The largest decline was seen in 1993, probably an outcome of the tendency of the traders to settle the transactions outside the ACU mechanism as LERMS was introduced and settlement within ACU was made optional. Nevertheless, the transactions channeled since 1996 continued to grow albeit at a lower rate, implying that the switch over to dollar as the mode of settlement within the union did not have a negative impact contrary to the fears expressed in certain quarters. The ACU therefore continued to attract additional players. The year 2004 witnessed the highest growth in transactions in the last decade and a half (47%).

Table 4.7a(1): Asian Clearing Union Total Transactions Channeled Through the ACU Mechanism (1975-2005)

(In Million US Dollars)

Year	*Yearly Transactions*		*Cleared in the System*		*Settled in Hard Currency*	
	*Amount**	*(%)*	*Amount*	*(%)*	*Amount*	*(%)*
1975	0.44	—	0.09	20	0.35	80
1976	25.72	5745	4.12	16	21.60	84
1977	79.36	209	16.67	21	62.69	79
1978	137.60	73	39.90	29	97.70	71
1979	161.31	17	83.88	52	77.43	48
1980	182.94	13	98.79	54	84.15	46
1981	269.39	47	166.92	62	102.47	38
1982	300.41	12	196.63	65	103.78	35
1983	498.66	66	192.32	39	306.34	61
1984	662.84	33	322.24	49	340.60	51
1985	605.20	-9	373.50	62	231.70	38
1986	690.62	14	851.12	84	109.50	16
1987	625.34	-9	396.97	64	228.37	36
1988	940.84	50	698.52	74	242.32	26
1989	104.78	11	832.39	80	209.39	20
1990	1366.54	31	947.79	69	418.75	31
1991	1851.44	35	1424.35	77	427.09	23
1992	1928.32	4	1172.46	61	755.86	39
1993	1448.88	-25	1018.00	70	430.88	30
1994	1965.38	36	1110.71	57	854.67	43
1995	2702.90	38	1353.42	50	1349.48	50
1996	3161.10	17	1448.30	46	1712.80	54
1997	2654.95	-16	1251.60	47	1403.35	53
1998	2842.77	7	1130.61	40	1712.16	60
1999	2630.74	-7	1057.39	40	1573.35	60
2000	3383.54	29	1634.36	48	1748.88	52
2001	3553.67	5	1643.56	46	1990.11	54
2002	3448.40	-3	1446.40	42	2002.00	58
2003	4546.30	32	1877.95	41	2668.35	59
2004	6679.79	47	3163.25	47	3516.54	53
2005	8199.62	23	4512.15	55	3687.47	45
Total	**58586.79**	**—**	**30196.66**	**52**	**28390.13**	**48**

* Amount relevant to year 1975 to 1995 converted from SDRs to US Dollars.

Source: ACU Annual Report, 2005.

Transactions Credited and Debited

Transactions credited refer to the entry that is made in the ACU accounts in lieu of the payments received for exports of the member countries through the ACU dollar account. As Table 4.7 shows member countries showed varied results as far as transactions are concerned.

India has experienced continuous growth in transaction's credited over the period 1976-1998 (except 1997). Bangladesh, too, has exhibited similar pattern, although experiencing periods of decline in the mid-nineties. Iran, which had very limited credited transactions in the 1980s (primarily due to exclusion of oil payments) exhibited a sharp increase after 1985. There has been a net decline in transactions credited for most of the countries between 1992 and 1998 with the exception of Bangladesh and India. India and Iran accounted for a major share of transactions credited during this period.

Transactions debited refer to the entry that is made in the ACU accounts in lieu of the payments made for imports of the member countries through the ACU dollar account. The pattern of transactions debited for the period was much more varied. For the period 1976-85, the transactions debited increased for all the countries. In the 1990 however, there were differing trends.

While India and Myanmar showed a net decline in debited transactions during this period, all the other countries showed a net increase. However none of the countries registered a continuous increase. Unlike the case of credited transactions, the debited transactions were evenly spread among the member countries. While India accounted for the largest share of debited transactions for 1992 and 1993 it was replaced by Bangladesh for subsequent period.

Transactions Credited and Exports

A comparison of the trends for transactions credited and exports for individual countries gives an indication of the direction in which two have proceeded. As Table 4.8 indicates

Table 4.7: ACU Transactions Credited and Debited to Participant Central Banks (1976-1998)

		Bangladesh	*India*	*Iran*	*Myanmar*	*Nepal*	*Pakistan*	*Sri Lanka*	*Total*
1976	Credited	0.04	15.89	0.74	0.00	0.00	0.42	2.09	16.57
	Debited	0.01	0.06	2.68	0.00	0.00	0.28	16.06	19.11
1980	Credited	0.65	60.81	0.03	0.48	0.31	5.09	40.85	83.42
	Debited	0.11	7.25	10.41	0.17	0.34	24.28	65.67	108.22
1985	Credited	0.98	2.07	3.72	14.71	0.07	66.04	69.72	121.78
	Debited	68.90	73.78	145.39	1.70	3.33	73.01	95.07	451.18
1992	Credited	74.21	425.48	883.43	46.94	24.73	282.60	190.92	1928.29
	Debited	282.82	813.07	241.23	0.19	3.14	237.28	350.56	1928.29
1993	Credited	61.98	449.31	505.03	64.95	16.25	167.46	183.94	1448.92
	Debited	274.12	438.34	164.37	0.11	1.83	221.89	348.26	1448.92
1994	Credited	60.65	987.72	542.82	35.96	1.22	188267	148.35	1965.38
	Debited	589.66	464.86	245.72	1.25	6.02	231.55	426.32	1965.38
1995	Credited	45.13	1517.24	639.33	33.03	6.70	264.88	196.51	2702.80
	Debited	1050.61	555.92	293.10	0.44	2.90	259.88	540.46	2702.80
1996	Credited	93.83	1778.88	931.76	10.74	7.07	227.03	111.79	3161.10
	Debited	1132.90	697.38	303.97	9.39	4.90	397.12	615.43	3161.10
1997	Credited	113.24	1480.26	796.36	7.98	15.77	155.77	85.58	2654.95
	Debited	860.32	598.66	290.60	0.01	7.74	349.13	548.50	2654.95
1998	Credited	119.44	1875.58	485.15	8.04	15.86	244.70	94.00	2842.77
	Debited	1301.73	453.79	252.05	0.01	18.05	195.46	621.69	2842.77

Source: ACU Annual Reports (various issues).

Table 4.8: Transactions Credited and Exports 1976-1997

			Bangladesh	*India*	*Iran*	*Myanmar*	*Nepal**	*Pakistan*	*Sri Lanka*	*Total*
1976	Credited	(a)	0.04	15.89	0.74	0.00	0.00	0.42	2.07	19.17
	Exports	(b)	23.90	129.30	594.00		2.00	981.10	57.59	1787.89
	(a) as percent of	(b)	0.17	12.29	0.13	0.00	0	0.04	3.60	1.07
1980	Credited	(a)	0.65	60.64	0.03	0.48	0.31	5.07	40.73	107.91
	Exports	(b)	122.40	439.00	1367.00		00.31	365.50	101.20	2401.70
	(a) as percent of	(b)	0.53	13.81	0.00	0	6.60	1.39	40.25	4.49
1985	Credited	(a)	1.25	263.97	4.73	18.71	4.72	84.02	88.65	461.41
	Exports	(b)	160.30	458.00	2088.00	31.39	0.09	181.60	64.20	2998.27
	(a) as percent of	(b)	0.78	57.64	0.23	59.62	5.78	46.26	138.08	15.44
1991	Credited	(a)	53.20	277.48	365.91	18.64	1.53	161.21	109.47	988.70
	Exports	(b)	125.00	667.00	793.00	52.00	2.78	389.00	128.00	2158.00
	(a) as percent of	(b)	42.56	41.60	46.14	35.84	4.00	41.44	85.53	45.82
1992	Credited	(a)	74.20	425.40	883.40	46.90	69.43	282.50	190.90	1928.00
	Exports	(b)	96.00	770.00	628.00	728.00	24.70	450.00	98.00	2795.00
	(a) as percent of	(b)	77.29	55.25	140.67	6.44	25.00	62.78	194.80	68.98
1993	Credited	(a)	61.90	449.30	505	64.90	98.80	167.40	183.98	1448.68
	Exports	(b)	97.00	899.00	608.00	142.00	16.20	236.00	82.00	2065.00
	(a) as percent of	(b)	63.81	49.98	83.06	45.70	1.00	70.93	224.37	70.15
1994	Credited	(a)	60.60	987.70	542.80	35.90	1620.0	188.60	148.30	1965.10
	Exports	(b)	107.00	10.80	740.00	133.00	1.00	269.00	93.00	2423.00
	(a) as percent of	(b)	56.64	91.45	73.35	26.99	120.00	70.11	159.46	81.11
1995	Credited	(a)	45.10	1517.2	639.30	33.00	6.60	264.80	196.50	2702.00
	Exports	(b)	119.00	1594.0	834.00	179.00	5.00	376.00	112.00	3219.00
	(a) as percent of	(b)	37.90	95.18	76.65	18.44	132.00	70.43	175.45	83.95

(Contd.)

Table 4.8: (*Contd.*)

			Bangladesh	India	Iran	Myanmar	Nepal*	Pakistan	Sri Lanka	Total
1996	Credited	(a)	93.80	1778.8	931.70	10.70	7.00	227.00	111.70	3160.70
	Exports	(b)	119.00	1673.0	771.00	164.00	5.00	307.00	130.00	3137.00
	(a) as percent of	(b)	107.82	106.32	120.84	6.52	140.00	73.94	85.92	100.76
1997	Credited	(a)	113.20	1480.2	796.30	7.90	15.70	155.70	85.50	2654.50
	Exports	(b)	136.00	1460.0	935.00	168.00	16.00	254.00	126.00	3095.00
	(a) as percent of	(b)	83.24	101.38	85.17	4.70	98.13	61.30	67.86	85.77

Note: *Figures for India and Nepal do not include bilateral trade as it is conducted out side ACU.

Source: Credited transactions-ACU Annual Report (various issues).

Exports–IMF Directions of Trade Statistics (various issues).

that the period 1976-85 saw growth in transactions credited along with exports in case of most of the ACU countries with the exception of Pakistan which registered decline in export as the transactions credited increased. For the 1990s, the ACU countries may be divided into two broad categories. The first belonging to the one whose credited transactions have changed consistently along with total exports to ACU at the aggregate level for the period 1991-1996. India, Pakistan and Nepal belong to this category. The other group including Sri Lanka, Bangladesh and Myanmar shows an inconsistent pattern value of exports and transactions credited for the same period.

The year 1997 was fairly consistent in this regard as for most of the countries except (Iran and Myanmar), transactions credited increased with increase in exports and *vice versa* relative to 1996. It can be clearly seen that credits as proportion of exports have generally increased for the period 1976-97. This trend has been more pronounced for India, Bangaldesh, Pakistan and Iran. Myanmar on the other hand, has shown a declining trend. At the aggregate level, the total transactions credited as proportion of intra ACU exports has remained at around 80 per cent in the 1990s.

Transactions Debited and Imports

During the initial years of ACU's formation, the transactions debited remained quite low despite there being significant growth between the member countries' imports (Table 4.9). As a result, the years 1976 and 1980 show the debits as a negligible percentage of the total imports of most of the countries. By 1985, debits as a per cent of imports picked up with Bangladesh and Myanmar routing more than 70 per cent of their imports through the ACU. A comparison of the values of transactions debited along with total imports from 1991-1997 shows that the individual countries broadly exhibit a uniform pattern for 1991-1997. Most of the countries show a consistent pattern between the transactions credited and total imports for the period.

Table 4.9: Transactions Debited and Imports 1976-1997

			Bangladesh	India	Iran	Myanmar	Nepal*	Pakistan	Sri Lanka	Total
1976	Debited	(a)	0	0	3	0	0	0	16	19
	Imports	(b)	68	602	475		0	68	81	1295
	(a) as percent of	(b)	0	0	1	0	0	24	65	108
1980	Debited	(a)	0	7	10	0	0	24	65	108
	Imports	(b)	147	1491	458		1	142	266	2504
	(a) as percent of	(b)	0	0	2	0	37	17	25	4
1985	Debited	(a)	88	94	185	2	4	93	121	587
	Imports	(b)	116	2222	380	3	6	216	281	3224
	(a) as percent of	(b)	76	4	49	68	73	43	43	18
1991	Debited	(a)	155	290	187	0	4	130	222	989
	Imports	(b)	256	712	341	6	14	237	443	2009
	(a) as percent of	(b)	61	41	55	3	30	55	50	49
1992	Debited	(a)	283	813	241	0	3	237	351	1928
	Imports	(b)	386	798	430	10	2	313	535	2474
	(a) as percent of	(b)	73	102	56	2	155	76	66	78
1993	Debited	(a)	275	438	164	0	2	222	348	1449
	Imports	(b)	386	798	430	10	2	313	535	2474
	(a) as percent of	(b)	56	84	47	0	23	75	69	66
1994	Debited	(a)	590	465	246	1	6	232	426	1965
	Imports	(b)	599	708	330	39	20	266	556	2518
	(a) as percent of	(b)	91	63	65	2	16	71	88	77
1995	Debited	(a)	1051	556	293	0	2	260	540	2703
	Imports	(b)	1159	889	448	28	14	366	615	3519
	(a) as percent of	(b)	91	63	65	2	16	71	88	77

(Contd.)

(*Contd.*)

			Bangladesh	*India*	*Iran*	*Myanmar*	*Nepal**	*Pakistan*	*Sri Lanka*	*Total*
1996	Debited	(a)	1133	697	304	9	5	397	615	3161
	Imports	(b)	1137	1090	379	65	7	568	697	3943
	(a) as percent of	(b)	100	64	80	14	70	70	88	80
1997	Debited	(a)	860	599	291	1	8	349	548	2655
	Imports	(b)	894	952	296	72	5	439	710	3368
	(a) as percent of	(b)	96	63	98	1	154	80	77	79

Note: Figures for India and Nepal do not include bilateral trade as it is conducted out side ACU.

Source: Credited transactions-ACU Annual Report (various issues).

Imports: IMF Directions of Trade (various issues).

For India and Sri Lanka, the debited transactions increased as imports increased and *vice versa*. Iran, Bangladesh and Pakistan followed the same pattern with exceptions in one or two years. Myanmar and Nepal on the other hand showed an inconsistent pattern between transactions debited and imports. For instance, while Myanmar registered decrease in its transactions debited while its imports increased for the period 1991-93, Nepal on the other hand intermittently experienced periods with increasing imports and declining debit transactions. There was a continuous increase in transactions debited as a percentage of imports for most of the countries.

Cleared Trade as a Proportion of Total Trade

Finally we analyse the transactions cleared through the ACU in relation to total ACU trade and its global trade. This would give us an indication of the extent to which the facility has been made use of.

As Table 4.10 shows, there has been a steady increase of trade cleared through the ACU along with the total intra-ACU exports for 1976-1996, with there being a decline in 1997 in both. ACU countries' global trade, on the other hand, has consistently risen over the entire period. The cleared trade as a proportion of total intra-ACU trade has been quite high going up to 94 per cent in 1996. However there have been periods of rapid decline in 1993 and 1997 when it went down to 67 per cent and 79 per cent respectively. As a proportion of its global trade, the cleared trade has shown a rapid decline in the 1990s as compared to the 1980s. While it was as high as 2.27 in 1985, it came down to abysmally low 0.03 in 1997, However, this was in tune with decline in total intra-ACU trade as a proportion of its global trade which came down from 9.04 per cent in 1980 to 4.31 in 1997. Thus there has been a clear shift in trade away from the ACU in the 1990s.

Table 4.10: Cleared Trade as a Proportion of Total Trade

(Million of US Dollars)

Year	*Cleared Trade*	*Intra-ACU Exports*	*Global Trade*	*I as% of II*	*I as % of III*	*II as% of III*
	I	*II*	*III*	*IV*	*V*	*VI*
1976	0.4	853	26736	0.05	0.00	3.19
1980	181	2477	27403	7.31	0.66	9.04
1985	603	1875	26549	32.16	2.27	7.06
1991	1851.4	2252	47286	82.2	0.03	4.76
1992	1928.4	2289	51198	84.2	0.03	4.47
1993	1449.5	2157	51394	67.1	0.02	4.20
1994	1965.4	2521	58089	77.9	0.03	4.34
1995	2702.7	3351	61521	80	0.04	5.45
1996	3161.1	3340	72956	94	0.04	4.58
1997	2655	3325	77222	79	0.03	4.31

Source: I. ACU Annual Report (various issues).
II. and III. IMF, Directions of Trade Statistics Yearbook (various issues).

4.4 Country-Wise Analysis

Bangladesh

General Economic Outlook

In the recent years, Bangladesh has been able to achieve an improved GDP growth rate. This growth has been in sharp contrast to the 1980s which was marked by consistently low rates of growth, While in 1970s, the GD P growth rate was more than 4.4 per cent on average, between 1982-83 it came down to 3.1 per cent.[2] The economic growth in the mid nineties (1996-98) was able to break the 4 per cent barrier that persisted during the 1970s and 1980s. In 1998, GDP grew at a rate of 5.7 per cent, slightly less than the 5.9 rate achieved in 1997. The industrial growth had a strong recovery from its disappointing performance in 1997 partly because of the improving energy supply, Since the early 1990s, improvements in saving and investment have been impressive. The savings rate as a percentage of GDP more than doubled from 1990 to 1997, the investment rate however, was about one percentage point of GDP lower than in 1997 due to decline in foreign savings, particularly in foreign aid disbursement.[3]

Bangladesh had been since the 1970s under pressure by the donors to restructure its trade and industrial policy. The principal recommendations included privatisation of the economy, import liberalisation, elimination of subsidies and exchange rate reforms. The New Industrial Policy of 1982, addressed to most of the issues by undertaking privatisation, liberalisation of import regime, simplification of licensing procedure etc. However, the impact of these reforms was not too encouraging as there was stagnation in industrial investment and industrial production. During the Fiscal Year 1982-Fiscal Year 1989, manufacturing sector grew at a mere 2.69 per cent as against 12.83 per cent during FY1977-FY1981.[4]

Trade liberalisation and export promotion policies initiated in the early 1990s resulted in sharp expansion of external trade. Export performance improved substantially with a growth rate of 16.8 per cent in 1998, which was one of the highest in Asia. The garments and the knitwear sub-sectors accounted for almost the entire increase in exports. By contrast, export of jute, leather and frozen foods fell. The growth rate of imports like wise increased in 1998. The impact of the Asian crisis on Bangladesh's economy was generally limited.[5] The pace of reforms was generally slow although the government tried to address some of the structural problems relating to the banking system, capital markets, administered pricing and infrastructure. The 5th five-year plan (1997-2002) approved in March 1998 has set the average annual growth target at 7 per cent, essential to make any significant impact on poverty.

Trade Policy

Bangladesh has sought to pursue a liberal trade policy over the years. The emphasis has been on liberalisation of imports through significant reduction of tariff and non-tariff barriers and simplification of procedures. Besides, tariff structures have been rationalized to remove disincentives to domestic production. This has included lowering duties on industrial inputs and machinery. Besides exports have been promoted through the simplification of procedures for import duty free inputs, providing fast duty drawback and making the Taka convertible on the current account. As a result, the import of most commodities into Bangladesh is permitted freely, except for items mentioned in the Import Policy Order (IPO) which consisted of around 100 items. (The restricted category included certain textiles, factory rejects, goods of substandard quality, used items and materials inimical to public order or religious beliefs.) The rate of customs duty was gradually brought down in successive budgets. The items exempted from customs duty included certain types of textile machinery inputs to fishing, poultry, cattle and dairy farming, agricultural irrigation equipment, diesel engines upto 45 HP etc. The import tariff structure is designed to strengthen domestic production, discourage import of luxury goods and to ensure supply of essential goods.

Payments and Exchange Arrangements

During the initial years after Bangladesh's independence, it entered into a number of trade and payments agreements with India.[6] The main objective of the arrangement was primarily to enable larger exports from Bangladesh and at the same time enable exports from India of essential commodities required by India. India agreed to give a line of credit up to 100 million rupees (Indian) to Bangladesh for importing from India goods produced in India.[7] All repayments of principal and payments of interest were to be made in Indian rupees through sale of convertible currencies to authorized foreign exchange banks in India.[8]

Bangladesh has a unitary exchange rate structure with its currency taka pegged to a weighted currency basket of the major trading partners. Since January 1,1996, Bangladesh Bank ceased to deal in the currencies of other ACU countries and now deals with authorized domestic banks only in dollars, the intervention currency. Authorized banks are free to set their own buying and selling rates for the dollar and the rates for other currencies, based on cross rates in international markets.

Settlements normally take place in convertible currencies and in some cases, through non-resident taka accounts. Settlements with ACU countries are required to be effected through the ACU in terms of the AMU (Asian Monetary Unit, equivalent in value to the dollar w.e.f. January 1, 1996). Settlements for trade under bilateral commodity exchange agreements are effected through special non-convertible dollar accounts. Payments for imports may be made to any country (with the exception of countries from which importation is prohibited). They may be made (1) in taka for credit in Bangladesh to a non-resident bank account of the country concerned, (2) in the currency of the country concerned or, (3) in any freely convertible currency. Export proceeds must be received in freely convertible foreign exchange or in taka from a non-resident taka account.[9]

Bangladesh has generally followed flexible exchange rate management with a view to maintaining the competitiveness of Bangladesh's products abroad and encouraging inward wage earners remittances. While pursuing this policy, implications of changes in balance of payments position were taken into consideration. The taka dollar exchange rate was continuously readjusted. As a result, the taka-dollar exchange rate stood at Taka 43.65 as on June 30,1997 as against Taka. 41.75 as on June 30,1996 indicating a 4.4 per cent depreciation of Taka against the US dollar during the year.[10] In the early 2000, Bangladesh was apparently under pressure from international agencies to convert to free floating, but certain policy studies recommended a cautious approach.[11]

Trade with ACU Countries

As per Table 4.11, Bangladesh has witnessed a gradual growth in its trade with the ACU countries. For the period 1975-85, Bangladesh's exports to ACU increased at a faster rate compared to its global trade, with India, Iran and Pakistan being the major partners. Its imports from ACU however declined relative to its global imports. While the growth on export front for the period 1991-97 is less pronounced (from 125 mn. US dollar in 1991 to 136 mn. US dollar in 1997), imports have grown more than three fold (form 256 mn US dollar to 894 mn US dollar) for the same period. There have been country-wise variations. Bangladesh's imports from India have shown a sharp upturn in the late 1990's. While exports have remained relatively stable. With regard to Pakistan both exports and imports have been relatively balanced over the years. Both Sri Lanka and Myanmar have registered declining trade with Bangladesh in the late 1990s. With Iran, the situation has been rather peculiar, as the exports from Bangladesh, which have fluctuated in the mid 1990's, have far outweighed the imports which have remained fairly stable.

One can clearly see that there has been a sharp decline in Bangladesh's trade with ACU countries in relation to both its trade with Asia as a whole and global trade (Table 4.12). Its ACU exports as a percentage of Asian exports have declined from a high of 74.3 per cent to 38.9 per cent for the period 1975-97. Similarly, the imports to ACU as a proportion of imports from Asia declined from 84.3 per cent to 26.2 per cent. The import liberalisation policies followed in Bangladesh in the 1990s have enabled the other Asian countries to make inroads in a better way. Significantly Bangladesh's ACU exports as a proportion to exports to Asia declined from 7.5 per cent to 4.7 per cent whereas its imports from ACU as a proportion to its global imports actually increased from 8.8 per cent to 10.3 per cent for the same period.

Table 4.11: Bangladesh's Trade with ACU Countries (1975-1997)

(Millions of US Dollars)

Year		*India*	*Iran*	*Myanm-ar*	*Nep-al*	*Paki-stan*	*Sri Lanka*	*Total*	*Asia*	*World*
1975	Exports	5.3	15.6	0.8	—	—	2.9	24.6	17.5	326.5
	Imports	83.3	12.8	—	—	24.0	3.5	123.6	133.8	1400.3
1980	Exports	8.0	47.8	6.0	0.5	55.3	4.8	122.4	206.3	790.2
	Imports	55.6	39.9	10.9	1.0	34.9	91.4	233.7	428.3	2610.6
1985	Exports	29.6	77.9	6.0	5.1	41.5	0.2	160.3	146.0	998.8
	Imports	61.9	—	10.2	—	35.3	8.4	115.8	76.5	2697.1
1990	Exports	22.0	31.0	—	7.0	23.0	8.0	91.0	169.0	1672.0
	Imports	170.0	5.0	—	2.0	70.0	8.0	255.0	1242.0	3656.0
1991	Exports	23.0	45.0	—	12.0	39.0	6.0	125.0	177.0	1487.0
	Imports	189.0	5.0	—	—	57.0	5.0	256.0	1147.0	3421.0
1992	Exports	4.0	49.0	2.0	—	30.0	11.0	96.0	198.0	2037.0
	Imports	284.0	7.0	1.0	—	88.0	6.0	386.0	1465.0	3731.0
1993	Exports	13.0	29.0	13.0	7.0	26.0	9.0	97.0	239.0	2277.0
	Imports	380.0	6.0	7.0	—	90.0	7.0	490.0	1635.0	4015.0
1994	Exports	24.0	39.0	7.0	14.0	19.0	4.0	107.0	274.0	2650.0
	Imports	467.0	6.0	8.0	1.0	110.0	7.0	599.0	2025.0	4584.0
1995	Exports	36.0	34.0	2.0	10.0	26.0	11.0	119.0	281.0	3129.0
	Imports	994.0	7.0	5.0	4.0	138.0	11.0	1159.0	3382.0	6496.0
1996	Exports	21.0	26.0	1.0	—	37.0	2.0	87.0	254.0	3297.0
	Imports	1018.0	9.0	4.0	6.0	90.0	10.0	1137.0	3378.0	6898.0
1997	Exports	41.0	50.0	—	1.0	40.0	4.0	136.0	322.0	4076.0
	Imports	796.0	6.0	3.0	11.0	69.0	9.0	894.0	3552.0	6857.0

Source: IMF Directions of Trade Statistics Yearbook (various issues).

Table 4.12: Bangladesh's Trade with ACU Countries as a Proportion of its Trade with Asian Countries and World (1975-97)

Year	*Exports to ACU Exports to Asia*	*Imports to ACU: Imports to Asia*	*Exports to ACU: Total Global Exports*	*Imports to ACU: Total Global Imports*
1975	74.3	84.3	7.5	8.8
1980	84.3	48.2	8.8	15.5
1985	48.2	49.9	15.5	9.0
1990	49.9	71.6	9.0	16.0
1991	71.6	22.2	16.0	4.3
1992	NA	45.5	4.3	5.4
1993	45.5	20.4	56.3	7.0
1994	20.4	56.3	7.0	8.4
1995	56.3	22.2	8.4	7.5
1996	22.2	38.9	26.2	4.7
1997	38.9	26.2	4.7	10.3

Note: Since IMF statistics separates Iran's figures from that of Asia, Iran's figures have been added to derive the percentage for Asia.

India

General Economic Outlook

The Indian economy has completed nearly two decades since the economic reforms were initiated in 1991.[12] After growing successively for three years averaging more than seven per cent during 1994-96, growth slowed to about 5 per cent in 1997. The growth recorded increased during 1998 due to better agriculture performance and was expected to grow by 5.9 per cent in 1999-2000. There were prospects for industrial recovery as the growth of GDP from manufacturing was likely to double to 7 per cent in 1999-2000 from 3.6 per cent in 1998-1999. The inflation rate dropped to international levels of 2 to 3 per cent for the first time in decades. The exports recorded strongly in 1999 growing by 12.9 per cent in April-December 1999 as the overall import growth remained at manageable 9 per cent. The balance of payment situation was relatively stable with continuing rise in foreign exchange reserves by over US $2.4 billion during the year with a stable exchange rate.[13]

Trade Policy

India's trade policy reforms have aimed at achieving rapid increase in exports through significant changes in the Exim policy. These have included country specific and commodity specific measures to promote export along with creating the institutional structure for export policy environment. Some of the recent measures have included removal of qualitative restrictions with import 894 items being made license free and another 414 items to be imported against special import license. Duty exemption scheme was made more feasible as annual advance license system was introduced to take care of the entire import needs of the exporters. Besides, free trade zones were to replace export processing zones and were to be treated as outside the country's customs territory.[14]

Payments and Exchange Agreements

The Indian rupee has a unified exchange rate structure with its value being determined in the inter bank market. The Reserve Bank of India undertakes occasional market intervention in order to moderate excessive volatility in exchange rate and maintain orderly foreign exchange market conditions. For prescription of currency purposes, countries are divided into two groups—

(1) ACU member countries (except Nepal) where all eligible current transactions are to be settled *via* the ACU system. Export Import transactions financed out of loans from international financial institutions are settled outside the ACU mechanism. On July 6,1997 authorised dealers and commercial banks in ACU countries were allowed to transfer ACU dollars among themselves instead of routing the transaction through their respective central banks.

(2) The external group containing all other countries. The payments to these countries may be made in Indian rupees to the account of a resident of any of these countries or in any permitted currency, and receipt may be obtained in Indian rupees from accounts of a bank situated in any of these countries or in any permitted currency. [15]

Trade with ACU Countries

In the early eighties, India's exports to the ACU were relatively stagnant. Imports on the other hand increased nearly four-fold from 1975 to 1985 (Table 4.13). Bangladesh, Iran, Myanmar and Sri Lanka were the major trading partners during this period. India registered a steady growth in its trade with the ACU. countries in the 1990s. Its exports to the ACU increased from 744 mn US dollar in 1991 and 1605 and mn US dollar in 1997, nearly doubling. Similarly imports increased from 731 mn US dollar and 1023 mn US dollar for the same period.

Table 4.13: India's Trade with ACU Countries 1975-1997

(Millions of US Dollars)

Year		Bangladesh	Iran	Nepal	Myanmar	Pakistan	Sri Lanka	Total	Asia	World
1975	Exports	71.2	350.8	10.8	59.6	10.5	28.8	531.7	392.4	4364.1
	Imports	5.1	506.8	3.1	28.5	21.6	0.4	565.5	137.6	6254.1
1980	Exports	106.0	135	95	5.0	2.0	101	338.0	971.0	8441.0
	Imports	12.0	1350	21.0	-	76.0	32	1459.	1325	14822
1985	Exports	66.0	190.0	3.0	78.0	14.0	88.0	439.0	980.0	9214.0
	Imports	15.0	2012	6.0	6.0	43.0	102.0	559.0	2154.0	17813
1990	Exports	297.0	76.0	1.0	40.0	43.0	102.0	559.0	2154.0	17813.0
	Imports	15.0	482.0	90.0	15.0	45.0	22.0	669.0	2676.0	23990.0
1991	Exports	325.0	123.0	77.0	4.0	40.0	175.0	744.0	2761.00	17873.0
	Imports	6.0	585.0	19.0	51.0	58.0	12.0	731.0	1789.0	19509.0
1992	Exports	353.0	130.0	73.0	4.0	52.0	231.0	843.0	3177.0	185000.
	Imports	13.0	330.0	19.0	117.0	47.0	17.0	543.0	2201.0	21225.
1993	Exports	430.0	150.0	75.0	14.0	58.0	247.0	974.0	4308.0	20259.0
	Imports	13.0	330.0	19.0	117.0	47.0	543.0	2201.0	21225	
1994	Exports	521.0	142.0	85.0	24.0	59.0	334.0	1165.0	4926.0	24196
	Imports	34.0	476.0	14.0	120.0	47.0	17.0	543.0	2201.0	21225
1995	Exports	960.0	160.0	107.0	21.0	70.0	383.0	1701	6689	30537
	Imports	79.0	574.0	27.0	160.0	37.0	39.0	916.0	4788.0	34484.0
1996	Exports	832.0	196.0	158.0	46.0	141.0	458.0	1831.0	7562.0	32325.0
	Imports	58.0	810.0	49.0	148.0	39.0	35.0	1139.0	5267	36055.0
1997	Exports	649	169.0	145.0	45.0	129.0	468.0	1605.0	7688.0	33289.0
	Imports	***	704.0	71.0	184.0	22.0	42.0	1023.0	6211.0	38911.0

Source: IMF Directions of Trade Statistics Yearbook (various issues).

The trend was fairly well dispersed among the individual member countries with there being a uniform growth in India's exports and imports to most of these countries. Iran was a slight exception as both export and import growth was not as pronounced as in other countries. The overall trends were in tune with India's global trade which also nearly doubled during this period. However, India's trade with Asia far outpaced the growth in its global trade. While its exports to Asia increased nearly three times from 2761 mn US dollar to 7688 mn US dollar, the imports registered a nearly five fold growth from 1789 mn US dollar to around 6200 mn US dollar for the same period. More significantly India's trade with ACU as a proportion of its trade with Asia declined during 1975-97 (exports from 71 per cent to 20 per cent and imports from 87 per cent to 17 per cent). It clearly shows that the nineties have clearly witnessed a shift in India's trade away from the ACU countries in relation to the rest of Asia. Similarly there was a decline in India's ACU exports as a proportion of its global exports and for ACU imports as a proportion of global imports (Table 4.14).

Table 4.14: India's Trade with ACU Countries as a Proportion of its Trade with Asian Countries and Total World (1975-97)

Year	*Exports to ACU: Exports to Asia*	*Imports to ACU: Imports to Asia*	*Exports to ACU: Total Global Exports*	*Imports to ACU: Total Global Imports*
1975	71.54	87.76	12.18	9.04
1980	30.56	54.54	4.00	9.84
1985	37.52	54.25	4.76	13.57
1990	25.07	21.18	3.14	2.79
1991	25.80	30.79	4.16	3.75
1992	25.49	25.44	4.56	3.53
1993	21.85	21.45	4.81	2.56
1994	22.99	17.68	4.81	2.84
1995	24.84	17.08	5.57	2.66
1996	23.60	18.74	5.66	3.16
1997	20.43	14.79	4.82	2.63

Source: Iran IMF Directions of Trade Statistics Yearbook (various issues).

Iran

General Economic Outlook

Iranian economy during the 1970s was significantly affected by the oil prices hike. The period immediately after the hike led to substantial increase in oil revenues leading to increase in investment and accelerated economic expansion. However, the absorptive capacity for growth was limited by infrastructural bottlenecks. In the later 1970, efforts were made to facilitate expansion of imports to reduce pressure on domestic supplies.[16]

The reform process in Iran[17] in the 1990s coincided with an increasing trend in inflationary expectations due to the expansionary fiscal operations of the government in 1994-95 and intensified adverse external environment.

The GDP in the fiscal year 1998 was estimated to decline by 0.3 per cent compared with a positive 2.6 per cent growth recorded in the previous year. Despite the fact that the agricultural sector showed a much improved performance, GDP contracted because of sizable fall in the value added in industrial sector. The deceleration in the overall industrial sector was due to an estimated 14.9 per cent contraction in GDP from oil sector as a result of a fall in international price of oil. The merchandise trade surplus in Iran was at a peak level of $7.4 billion in fiscal year 1996. Oil and gas exports, comprising about 80 per cent of the total exports over the 1990-96 period however fluctuated in the range of $14.6 billion and 19.3 billion owing to the fluctuation in international price in 1997. The imports in the fiscal year amounted to $14.9 billion and showed virtually no improvement over that of 1996.[18]

Trade Policy

There is a drastic need in Iran to reduce heavy dependence on oil exports as the international environment in this sector has not been too conducive. Emphasis has to be given to production and export of industrial goods. This would require an increased level of competitiveness of industrial products in the international market. With regard to imports, the government has adopted a policy of limiting the imports of products which had domestic substitutes and favoured import of raw materials and intermediate goods.

Payments and Exchange Rate Policy

One of the major reform measures in the Iranian economy has been the unification of official and market exchange rate. Due to the wide divergence between the official and floating exchange rate during the war, the need for a unified exchange rate was felt all the more.[19] To achieve unification, government initially introduced 3-tier exchange rate system which was later converted to a dual rate. At present, exchange rate system consists of two rates. (i) The official rate, which is fixed at Iranian Rials 1750 per $1 applying mainly to the imports of essential goods, and (ii) the export rate which is fixed at Iranian Rials 3000 per $1 and applies to all other transactions. The exchange rates are managed floating and set by Bank Markazi. Iran has terminated all bilateral payments arrangements. The advance payment requirements range from 15 per cent to 100 per cent depending on the creditworthiness of the customer and the type of goods. The exporters of non-oil goods are required to repatriate to the banking systems 100 per cent of their foreign exchange earnings upon settlement effective January 28, 1998, 100 per cent of such earnings may be allocated to exporters for their imports.[20]

Trade with ACU Countries

Iran registered a steady increase in its exports to ACU in tune with its exports to Asia for 1975-1985 (Table 4.15). Its imports from ACU however declined during this period. The period also saw a number of trade and economic cooperation agreements between the two countries.[21]

Iran's trade with ACU has grown over the period 1991-1997. While exports have increased from 793 million US dollar to 935 million US dollar (after witnessing initial decline). Imports have actually declined from 341 mn US dollar to 296 mn US dollar for the same period. As far as individual countries are concerned, there was a net gain in exports and imports (except for Pakistan where imports declined and Sri Lanka where both exports and imports declined for the period 1991-1997). Iran's global exports increased whereas its global imports declined. Iran's trade with Asia grew steadily during this period.

Table 4.15: Iran's Trade with ACU Countries 1975-1997

(Millions of US Dollars)

Year		Bang-ladesh	Iran	Nepal	Myan-mar	Pakis-tan	Sri Lanka	Total	Asia	World
1975	Exports	12	461	1	—	33	28	535	980	18249
	Imports	12	322	—	1	30	15	380	612	10346
1980	Exports	36	1227	—	—	2	102	1367	1929	14018
	Imports	53	148	—	—	2	102	1367	1929	14018
1985	Exports	—	965	—	—	108	151	1224	2345	13952
	Imports	86	110	4	2	63	18	283	938	11145
1990	Exports	—	475	—	—	183	133	791	1979	19305
	Imports	34	84	2	—	34	73	227	1012	15903
1991	Exports	—	532	—	—	135	126	793	2349	18661
	Imports	—	92	—	—	182	67	341	1920	29678
1992	Exports	—	375	—	—	158	95	628	2270	19868
	Imports	—	242	—	—	101	87	430	2295	29870
1993	Exports	—	364	—	—	142	102	608	2736	18080
	Imports	42	224	—	—	40	41	347	2052	20037
1994	Exports	1	493	—	—	171	75	740	3070	19434
	Imports	38	214	6	—	53	19	330	1079	11795
1995	Exports	8	555	—	—	155	116	834	3134	18360
	Imports	22	722	10	—	33	1	771	3971	22391
1996	Exports	5	722	10	—	33	1	771	3971	22391
	Imports	66	231	—	—	54	28	379	1974	15117
1997	Exports	5	640	11	—	189	90	935	4789	25001
	Imports	64	186	—	—	21	25	296	2362	14624

Source: IMF Directions of Trade Statistics Yearbook (various issues).

Iran's exports to ACU as percentage of its exports to Asia have declined drastically from 1975 to 1997 from 54.59 per cent to 19.52 per cent (Table 4.16). Similar has been the case for its imports from ACU in relation to its imports from Asia. Iran's exports to ACU in relation to its global exports however increased from 2.93 per cent to 3.74 per cent while imports declined from 3.67 per cent to 2.62 per cent for the same period.

Table 4.16: Iran's Trade with ACU Countries as a Proportion of its Trade with Asian Countries and World (1975-1997)

Year	*Exports to ACU Exports to Asia*	*Imports to ACU: Imports to Asia*	*Exports to ACU: Total Global Exports*	*Imports to ACU: Total Global Imports*
1975	54.59	62.09	2.93	3.67
1980	70.87	41.75	9.75	3.57
1985	52.20	30.17	8.77	2.54
1990	39.97	22.43	4.10	1.43
1991	33.76	17.76	4.25	1.15
1992	27.67	18.74	3.16	1.44
1993	22.22	16.91	3.36	1.73
1994	24.10	30.58	3.81	2.80
1995	26.61	27.00	4.54	3.64
1996	19.42	19.20	3.44	2.51
1997	19.52	12.53	3.74	2.02

Source: IMF Directions of Trade Statistics Yearbook (various issues).

Nepal

General Economic Outlook

There has been a decline in growth rate in the recent times. The overall economic performance deteriorated in 1998, registering a 1.9 per cent increase, the lowest growth rate in more than a decade. The Eighth plan target of 4.3 per cent growth was revised and the new set cut down the average growth rate of the plan to 3.6 per cent.[22] There was stagnation in industrial production in 1998 largely because of continued decline in the growth of manufacturing sector and contraction in the construction and utilities sector. Besides, Nepal's dependence on foreign aid has increased in the recent years as share of foreign assistance in total development expenditure was expected to increase to 65 per cent in 1999. While exports recovered in 1998, increasing by 11.7 per cent, there was a decline in imports leading to better balance of trade.

Trade Policy

In Nepal, a liberal trade policy regime has been followed in the recent years. The import of luxury goods into Nepal has generally been discouraged with emphasis being given on imports of items of mass consumption, raw materials and capital goods. There are four tariff rates (5%, 10%, 30% and the 80% special rate for vehicles) with most goods subject to either the 20 per cent or the 40 per cent rate. The exports of certain items in Nepal is banned[23] most others coming under the free export product category, not being subject to any quantitative restrictions. Exporters are allowed to retain the export earnings on their foreign currency account with local banks. Commercial banks may grant export credit of up to 70 per cent of the F.O.B. value of the products specified by the government to all individuals and institutions holding irrevocable Letter of Credits opened or endorsed by foreign banks and acceptable to the Nepalese Banks.

Payments and Exchange Arrangement

Nepal follows a unitary exchange rate structure. The Nepalese Rupee is pegged to a currency composite. The reference rate of the dollar quoted by the Nepal Rastra Bank (NRB) is based on the average of the quoted rate of commercial banks. Exchange rates of other major currencies are quoted on the basis of overseas markets. Buying and selling rates are quoted daily for certain other currencies, with quotations based on the buying and selling rates for the dollar in the markets abroad.

Convertibility between the Indian rupee and the Nepalese rupee is unrestricted in Nepal. All current transactions with member countries of the ACU other than Indian must be effected through the ACU. Payments for selected imports from India may be settled in dollars. Other imports and import proceeds from exports to India must be settled in Indian rupees. Proceeds from exports to other countries must be received in convertible currencies.[24]

Trade with ACU Countries

Right from the 1970s, ACU has been a significant export market for Nepal. It registered a steady growth in exports to ACU for the period 1975-1985, India being the leading export destination. Similar was the case with imports (Table 4.17).

Table 4.17: Nepal's Trade with ACU Countries 1975-1997

Year		*Bangladesh*	*India*	*Iran*	*Myanmar*	*Pakistan*	*Sri Lanka*	*Total*	*Asia*	*World*
1975	Exports	1.0	25.6	0.8	—	—	—	27.4	31.1	39.0
	Imports	—	65.6	—	—	—	—	65.6	70.3	108.9
1980	Exports	0.9	19.0	—	—	3.6	3.1	26.6	28.4	80.4
	Imports	0.5	104.0	—	—	0.4	6.2	111.1	131.1	342.3
1985	Exports	—	39.3	—	—	1.8	4.0	45.1	49.4	135.8
	Imports	5.6	86.3	—	—	0.1	—	92.0	157.3	285.8
1990	Exports	1.0	14.0	—	—	—	—	15.0	27.0	216.0
	Imports	8.0	43.0	—	—	1.0	—	52.0	234.0	452.0
1991	Exports	—	17.0	—	—	4.0	—	21.0	30.0	257.0
	Imports	13.0	85.0	—	—	1.0	—	99.0	265.0	500.0
1992	Exports	—	21.0	—	—	3.0	22.0	46.0	51.0	352.0
	Imports	—	80.0	—	—	1.0	—	18.0	23.0	367.0
1993	Exports	—	17.0	—	—	1.0	—	18.0	23.0	367.0
	Imports	8.0	83.0	—	—	—	—	91.0	312.0	528.0
1994	Exports	—	13.0	—	—	—	1.0	14.0	19.0	351.0
	Imports	16.0	93.0	—	—	4.0	—	113	410.0	615.0
1995	Exports	4.0	25.0	—	—	—	1.0	30.0	33.0	324
	Imports	11.0	118.0	—	—	3.0	—	132.0	526.0	753
1996	Exports	5.0	45.0	—	—	—	—	50.0	56.0	358.0
	Imports	1.0	173.0	—	—	6.0	—	180.0	410.0	634.0
1997	Exports	10.0	65.0	—	—	1.0	5.0	81.0	93.0	394.0
	Imports	1.0	159.0	—	—	5.0	—	165.0	399.0	624.0

Source: IMF Directions of Trade Statistics Yearbook (various issues).

Nepal's trade with ACU has grown over the 1990s. While its exports to the ACU have increased from 21 mn US dollar to 81 mn US dollar between 1991–1997, imports have increased from 99 mn US dollar to 165 mn US dollar for the same period. One can clearly see that India constitutes for bulk of Nepal's trade with ACU.[25] There has been nearly a four fold increase in Nepal's exports to India during the given period, there being periods of relative decline in the mid-nineties. The imports too, have shown a gradual increase over this period, but it has not been as pronounced as exports. For other countries such as Pakistan, Sri Lanka and Bangladesh, not much significant trends are seen as they did not contribute substantially to Nepal's ACU trade.

As Table 4.18 shows, while Nepal's exports to ACU as a proportion of its exports to Asia has remained high since the 1970s at more than 80 per cent, the proportion of imports has drastically come down from 93.31 per cent in 1975 to 41.35 per cent in 1997. There has been a continuous decline in both its ACU exports and imports in relation to its global exports and imports.

Table 4.18: Nepal's Trade with ACU Countries as a Proportion of its Trade with Asian Countries and World (1975-97)

Year	*Exports to ACU: Exports to Asia*	*Imports to ACU: Imports to Asia*	*Exports to ACU: Total Global Exports*	*Imports to ACU: Total Global Imports*
1975	85.89	93.31	70.26	60.24
1980	93.66	84.74	33.08	32.46
1985	91.30	58.49	33.21	32.19
1990	55.56	22.22	6.94	11.50
1991	70.00	37.36	8.17	19.80
1992	90.20	30.94	13.07	17.19
1993	78.26	29.17	4.90	17.23
1994	73.68	27.56	3.99	18.37
1995	90.91	25.10	9.26	17.53
1996	89.29	43.90	13.97	28.39
1997	87.10	41.35	20.56	26.44

Source: IMF Directions of Trade Statisties Yearbook (various issues).

Myanmar

General Economic Outlook

The GDP growth in Myanmar slowed in fiscal year 1997 to 4.6 per cent from 6.1 per cent in 1996 and was estimated to decline to 1.1 per cent in 1998. The year 1998-99, the third year of the five-year short-term plan however achieved a growth rate of 5 per cent. Inflation was one of the major concerns as it increased from 33.54 per cent in 1997-98 to 51-56 per cent at the end of January 1999. Due to weak regional demand and low world price for commodities. Myanmar's exports of goods and services were expected to rise only by 2 per cent. However its total exports were expected to increase significantly in the coming years as a result of foreign investment in oil and gas sectors. Imports of goods and services were expected to fall as a result of import restrictions and acute shortage of foreign exchange.[26]

Trade Policy

Myanmar has sought to pursue a liberal trade regime over the years however several restrictions still operate. For instance in March 1998, export controls were imposed to limit trade in rubber, sugar, groundnut oil, sesame seeds and sesame oil and pulses to government agencies. Foreign exchange restrictions have been relaxed allowing traders to retain foreign exchange and open foreign exchange accounts.[27] The import tariffs range from zero to 40 per cent. Agricultural implements raw materials and other essential imports are taxed at low rates, while the highest rates are applied to imports of luxury goods. There exists an imports first system which links exports and imports together[28] with a few exceptions, private sector imports require import licenses for each transaction and are largely financed form the importer's foreign currency account.

Payments and Exchange Rate Policy

Myanmar has a dual exchange rate structure. In addition to the official exchange rate, foreign exchange certificates (FECS) are issued by the Central Bank of Myanmar in denominations of 1, 5, 10 and 20 units and exchangeable in the six hard currencies or with acceptable traveller's cheques. The FECS widely used by visitors and investors are available for Kyats at the market determined exchange rates. The Kyat is officially pegged to the SDR at K 8.50847 per SDRI. Myanmar applies margins of 2 per cent to spot exchange transactions based in the fixed Kyat-SDR rate.[29] The policy of maintaining a dual exchange rate however has been severely criticized. It has been pointed out that maintenance of a foreign exchange regime with a highly unrealistic official exchange rate at times overvalues the Kyat more than 20 times the free/black market rate.[30] The basic objective of such policy could be to gain greater foreign exchange from service firms. However, the main brunt of these policies has often been borne by native exporters in the phenomenal translation loss of their export proceeds in foreign exchange.

Trade with ACU Countries

Myanmar registered a declining trade in the ACU in the period 1980-85, with both exports and imports showing declining trends. However its trade with ACU has increased between the period 1991-97 (Table 4.19). While exports have registered more than three fold growth (from 52 million US dollar to 188 million US dollar). Imports have registered more than ten fold growth (from 6 mn US dollars to 72 mn US dollar). India has been the largest trading partner within the ACU with whom both exports and imports have shown a significant increase. Pakistan is the other significant partner, but its share in both exports and imports have fluctuated over the years.

Table 4.19: Myanmar's Trade with ACU Countries 1991-1997

Year		*Bangladesh*	*India*	*Iran*	*Nepal*	*Pakistan*	*Sri Lanka*	*Total*	*Asia*	*World*
1980	Exports	12.18	5.71	—	—	1.89	28.03	—	201.01	415.04
	Imports	9.35	4.76	.83	—	—	—		123.49	785.45
1985	Exports	9.24	10.03	3.73	—	3.18	4.14	—	230.20	501.04
	Imports	6.64	3.86	.09	—	2.26	0.01	—	166.21	646.46
1991	Exports	—	47	—	—	5	—	52	306	527
	Imports	—	4	—	—	2	—	6	762	1068
1992	Exports	2	95	—	—	29	3	128	447	684
	Imports	3	5	—	—	2	—	10	750	1046
1993	Exports	6	106	—	—	24	6	142	540	851
	Imports	14	16	—	—	3	—	33	964	1233
1994	Exports	7	109	5	—	11	1	133	533	916
	Imports	8	26	—	—	5	—	39	1226	1475
1995	Exports	4	146	—	—	28	1	179	756	1180
	Imports	1	50	11	—	2	1	65	1894	2515
1996	Exports	3	135	—	—	15	11	164	676	1189
	Imports	1	50	11	—	2	1	65	1894	2515
1997	Exports	2	168	—	—	13	5	188	602	1178
	Imports	1	50	12	—	9	—	72	2145	2675

Source: IMF Directions of Trade Statistics Yearbook (various issues).

Table 4.20: Myanmar's Trade with ACU Countries as a Proportion of its Trade with Asian Countries and World (1975-97)

Year	*Exports to ACU: Exports to Asia*	*Imports to ACU: Imports to Asia*	*Exports to ACU: Total Global Exports*	*Imports to ACU: Total Global Imports*
1980	23.78	12.02	11.52	1.90
1985	12.96	7.73	6.05	1.99
1990	25.07	21.18	3.14	2.79
1991	16.99	0.79	9.87	0.56
1992	28.64	1.33	18.71	0.96
1993	26.30	3.42	16.69	2.68
1994	24.72	3.18	14.52	2.64
1995	23.68	1.54	15.17	1.25
1996	24.26	3.41	13.79	2.58
1997	31.23	3.34	15.96	2.69

Source: IMF Directions of Trade Statistics Yearbook (various issues).

Myanmar's growth in trade with ACU has been in tune with that of Asia and the World. Its exports to ACU as a proportion of exports to Asia have increased from 23.78 per cent in 1980 to around 31 per cent in 1997. Its imports to ACU as a proportion to Asian imports however have been insignificant and have remained stagnant. Myanmar ACU exports in relation to its global exports have increased from 11.52 per cent in 1980 to around 16 per cent in 1997. Imports on the other hand have increased marginally (Table 4.20).

Pakistan

General Economic Outlook

Pakistan's economy went through a deceleration in economic activity in the mid-nineties, the year 1996-97 being regarded as one of the worst as far as economic situation was concerned.[31] The real GDP growth slowed down to 1.3 per cent as agriculture and large-scale manufacturing were stagnant. Subsequently the declining trend was reversed as the govt. undertook both supply side and demand management policies to attain macro stability and growth.

The real GDP was estimated to grow by 5.4 per cent in 1997-98 as both fixed investment and savings increased. The macro-economic targets were not changed despite the adverse fallout of the nuclear test. The exports and imports were projected to grow by 15.6 per cent and 4 per cent respectively.[32]

Trade Policy

Pakistan's trade policy in the 1970s was marked by several significant steps to reduce anti-export bias which includes devaluation, export bonus scheme and restrictive licensing. However the bias against imports remained. In the 1980s, other steps such as reduction of Non-Tariff Barriers, removal of quota on non-capital imports etc. were taken. Most significantly, a shift from fixed to flexible exchange rate system was adopted.[33]

The trade policy in the recent times has been aimed at economic revival through export led growth and reduction of trade imbalance in the merchandise trade. The policy sought to improve competitive edge of exports and expand the export base by promoting non-traditional items along with value added products. The trade policy in 1997-98 sought to liberalize import of raw materials and components for manufacturing engineering goods. Import of machines, tools and equipments required by gems and jewellery industry was allowed free of duty. No export duties are levied except for a nominal fee of 0.5 per cent chargeable on all exports. In 1998, the reduction in the margin deposit (for opening letters of credit) on imports from 30 per cent to existing ratio requirement -50 per cent at official rate and 50 per cent at floating interbank rate for exporters and importers buying and selling their currencies.[34]

Payments and Exchange Arrangement

Pakistan has a unitary exchange rate structure, which is managed floating. The State Bank of Pakistan sets the exchange rate of the Pakistani rupee. In 1998, commercial banks were allowed to quote their own exchange rates for the dollar within the SBP buying/selling band. At the same time, the spread between SBP buying and selling rates was increased to 1 per cent from 0.5 per cent. The managed rate system that has been followed since 1982 has been attributed to have helped Pakistan to avoid the severe external crisis often associated with fixed nominal pegs.[35]

Trade with ACU Countries

Pakistan's exports to the ACU increased in the late 1970s while imports registered a decline. Bangladesh, Iran and Sri Lanka were the leading trade partners in the 1980s. Pakistan has had a mixed record with regard to trade with ACU countries in the 1990s. There has been a net decline in its exports to ACU from 389 mn US dollar to 254 mn. US dollar for the same period (Table 4.21). The measures to reduce anti-export bias in Pakistan since the early 1990s appear to have diverted exports to other lucrative markets.

Bangladesh has been the largest source of exports for Pakistan which increased in the mid-nineties before declining in the later years. Iran has been the largest source of imports, which have shown a rather consistent increase in the late nineties. Its trade with India has been very erratic, not showing any consistent path. Although, there has been a gradual increase in its exports to Asia, the proportion of ACU exports have declined from 35 per cent to 14 per cent between 1975-97. Its share of ACU imports to Asian imports remained stagnant from 15 to 17 per cent. There has been a drastic decline in Pakistan's ACU exports as a proportion of its global exports from 8.82 per cent to 3 per cent for the same period, the proportionate decline for imports being from 13.50 per cent to 3.79 per cent (Table 4.22).

Table 4.21: Pakistan's Trade with ACU Countries 1975-1997

(Millions of US Dollars)

Year		*Bangladesh*	*India*	*Iran*	*Myanmar*	*Pakistan*	*Sri Lanka*	*Total*	*Asia*	*World*
1975	Exports	27.0	15.1	19.4	1.3	0.1	29.8	92.7	242.5	1051.1
	Imports	210.1	0.1	11.0	10.7	2.9	52.6	287.4	210.1	2129.0
1980	Exports	54.7	70.7	199.1	0.8	0.4	38.8	364.5	662.5	2617.9
	Imports	75.9	3.9	2.0	7.6	4.0	40.0	133.4	754.3	5349.5
1985	Exports	64.6	37.5	57.2	2.1	0.1	42.3	203.8	506.1	2738.4
	Imports	45.5	15.5	118.8	3.5	2.0	30.5	215.8	853.2	5858.5
1990	Exports	103.0	49.0	11.0	2.0	1.0	69.0	235.0	1166.0	5587
	Imports	38.0	46.0	20.0	2.0	-	37.0	143.0	1422.0	7383.0
1991	Exports	101.0	47.0	171.0	2.0	-	68.0	389.0	1474.0	6494.0
	Imports	5.0	44.0	144.0	6.0	4.0	34.0	237.0	1580.0	8431.0
1992	Exports	136.0	136.0	90.0	2.0	1.0	85.0	450.0	1819.0	7269.0
	Imports	7.0	52.0	185.0	32.0	4.0	33.0	313.0	1855.0	9375.0
1993	Exports	105.0	53.0	18.0	3.0	-	57.0	236.0	1323.0	6701.0
	Imports	10.0	67.0	149.0	26.0	1.0	41.0	294.0	2056.0	9492.0
1994	Exports	119.0	46.0	26.0	5.0	3.0	70.0	269.0	1547.0	7332.0
	Imports	11.0	72.0	129.0	12.0	-	42.0	266.0	2025.0	8884.0
1995	Exports	153.0	39.0	123.0	3.0	3.0	55.0	376.0	1849.0	7991.0
	Imports	15.0	81.0	188.0	31.0	1.0	50.0	366.0	2693.0	11460
1996	Exports	109.0	41.0	69.0	2.0	6.0	80.0	307.0	2175.0	9299.0
	Imports	28.0	212.0	267.0	16.0	-	45.0	568.0	2532.0	12150
1997	Exports	92.0	36.0	19.0	8.0	4.0	95.0	254.0	1752.0	8632.0
	Imports	33.0	142.0	208.0	15.0	1.0	40.0	439.0	2529.0	11595

Source: IMF Directions of Trade Statistics Yearbook (various issues).

Table 4.22: Pakistan's Trade with ACU Countries as a Proportion of Trade with Asian Countries and World (1975-97)

Year	*Exports to ACU Exports to Asia*	*Imports to ACU: Imports to Asia*	*Exports to ACU: Total Global Exports*	*Imports to ACU: Total Global Imports*
1975	35.40	129.99	8.82	13.50
1980	42.32	17.64	13.92	2.49
1985	36.18	22.20	7.44	3.66
1990	19.97	9.92	4.21	1.94
1991	23.65	13.75	5.99	2.81
1992	23.57	15.34	6.19	3.34
1993	17.60	13.33	3.52	3.10
1994	17.10	12.35	3.67	2.99
1995	19.07	12.70	4.71	3.19
1996	13.68	20.29	3.30	4.67
1997	14.34	16.04	2.94	3.79

Source: IMF Directions of Trade Statistics Yearbook.

Sri Lanka

General Economic Outlook

The Sri Lankan economy experienced a slowdown in economic growth in 1998 in the midst of a volatile external economic environment. It achieved a moderate 4.7 per cent economic growth in 1998 which was spread out across all economic sectors.[36] The inflation rate continued to decline in 1998 due to improved supply conditions, slowing down in growth of money supply and decline in prices of imported goods. The overall budget deficit however increased to 9.2 per cent of GDP in 1998 from 7.9 per cent in 1997. The export growth rate dropped from 13 per cent in 1997 to a mere 2 per cent in 1998 as products like rubber, coconut products, processed diamonds, gems and jewellery were also affected adversely by increased competition and demand contraction triggered by the East Asian Crisis.[37] One significant development on the external front has been Sri Lanka's success in achieving a significant shift from traditional exports to non-traditional exports in the post-1977 period with the latter increasing from 23.5 per cent of total exports to 76.5 per cent in 1996. However a significant industrial diversification was still required.[38]

Trade Policy

Sri Lanka's external trade and tariff policy in the recent times has focussed on rationalizing the trade and tariff system through lowering and simplifying the tariff structure while progressively reducing quantitative restrictions. The licensing requirements on exports and imports have been limited to a well defined narrow list considered necessary mainly for reasons of national security, public health, environmental protection and domestic producer protection. In November 1998 on the recommendation of the Presidential Trade and Tariff Commission, the earlier three band tariff system with 10, 20 and 35 per cent rates for imports was replaced with a system of 5, 10 and 30 per cent. All industrial raw material and machinery not manufactured in Sri Lanka are classified under the 5 per cent band. Further consolidation of the tariff structure to a two band system was expected to commence in the year 2000.[39]

Payments and Exchange Rate Arrangement

Sri Lanka has a unitary exchange rate structure. The Sri Lankan rupee operates under a managed float system with the Central Bank of Sri Lanka announcing the daily spot buying and selling rates of the dollar against the rupee for transactions with commercial banks within margins of 2 per cent and buys and sells the dollar on a spot basis at those rates. Payments to and receipts from the member countries of the ACU with respect to the current transactions and settlements are effected in dollars. For settlement with all other countries, payments for imports may be made in any foreign currency or in Sri Lankan rupees provided that the supplier maintains a non-resident rupee account in Sri Lanka. Other payments may be made either in the currency of the country to which payment is due or by crediting Sri Lankan rupees to a non-resident rupee account with the prior approval of the Central Bank proceeds from exports must be received either in designated foreign currencies, in Sri Lankan rupees from a non-resident account that a foreign bank maintains with an authorised dealer, or in any other non-resident account that a person-maintains with an authorised dealer as approved by the Central Bank.[40]

Trade with ACU Countries

The period 1975-85 did not see any drastic increase in Sri Lanka's exports to ACU. The policies of export pessimism of the early 1970s did not lead to a major export diversification. The imports however grew nearly three-fold during this period. Pakistan, India and Iran were the leading trade partners (Table 4.23). Its trade with ACU has not shown any significant improvement over the period 1991-97. While its exports to ACU have shown a tendency to decline (from 128 million US dollar to 126 million US dollar), the imports have shown a better trend (increasing from 443 million US dollar to 710 million US dollar). India is Sri Lanka's largest trading partner within ACU and there was a consistent increase in both exports and imports to the former. Iran, which is the nest significant partner, registered a decline in both the exports to and imports from Sri Lanka. Its exports to Pakistan increased, but the imports decreased, the situation with regard to Bangladesh being just the opposite. Sri Lanka's trade pattern with ACU has clearly not been in tune with that of Asia and rest of the world. While its exports to ACU have declined, the exports to Asia on the other hand have increased from 214 million US dollar to 389 million US dollar for the period 1991-97. Moreover its ACU exports as a proportion of Asian exports have been more consistent with the exports to Asia, although as a proportion have declined from 30 per cent to 25 per cent for the period 1975-1997. Its exports to ACU as a proportion of global exports has drastically declined from 12.13 per cent to 2.71 per cent for the same period, while the proportion of ACU imports to global imports has remained stable (Table 4.24).

Table 4.23: Sri Lanka's Trade with ACU Countries 1975-1997

(Millions of US dollars)

Year		Bangladesh	India	Iran	Myanmar	Nepal	Pakistan	Total	Asia	World
1975	Exports	1.7	0.4	16.5	—	—	48.9	67.5	67.8	556.5
	Imports	0.2	21.3	30.9	17.1	—	31.2	100.6	142.3	744.9
1980	Exports	4.0	34.3	33.0	—	—	34.2	105.5	141.9	1039.1
	Imports	3.0	96.7	112.0	—	0.4	29.9	242.0	430.2	2028.7
1985	Exports	14.5	6.2	16.1	—	0.1	27.3	64.2	142.6	1264.9
	Imports	2.0	74.7	166.1	4.6	4.4	33.8	285.6	431.3	1831.8
1990	Exports	10.0	20.0	67.0	—	—	32.0	129.0	183.0	1895.0
	Imports	113.0	118.0	222.0	6.0	—	32.0	129.0	183.0	1895.0
1991	Exports	5.0	13.0	78.0	—	—	32.0	128.0	214.0	1987.0
	Imports	4.0	220.0	145.0	—	—	74.0	443.0	1467.0	3061.0
1992	Exports	7.0	12.0	49.0	—	1.0	29.0	98.0	182.0	2488.0
	Imports	15.0	307.0	119.0	3.0	24.0	67.0	535.0	1798.0	3473.0
1993	Exports	7.0	20.0	20.	—	—	35.0	82.0	224.0	2859.0
	Imports	7.0	343.0	96.0	7.0	—	35.0	82.0	224.0	2859.0
1994	Exports	9.0	24.0	17.0	—	—	43.0	93.0	303.0	3210.0
	Imports	8.0	404.0	91.0	1.0	1.0	61.0	566.0	2171.0	4482.0
1995	Exports	12.0	32.0	25.0	—	—	43.0	112.0	352.0	3810.0
	Imports	6.0	469.0	86.0	1.0	1.0	61.0	566.0	2171.0	4482.0
1996	Exports	12.0	43.0	36.0	1.0	1.0	37.0	130.0	352.0	4097.0
	Imports	2.0	462.0	152.0	12.0	—	69.0	697.0	2502.0	5028.0
1997	Exports	11.0	44.0	31.0	—	2.0	38.0	126.0	389.0	4652.0
	Imports	2.0	560	99.0	6.0	5.0	38.0	710.0	2785.0	5654.0

Source: IMF, Directions of Trade Statistics Yearbook (various issues).

Table 4.24: Sri Lanka's Trade with ACU Countries as a Proportion of its Trade with Asian Countries and World (1975-97)

Year	*Exports to ACU: Exports to Asia*	*Imports to ACU: Imports to Asia*	*Exports to ACU: Total Global Exports*	*Imports to ACU: Total Global Imports*
1975	80.07	58.08	12.13	13.51
1980	60.32	44.63	10.15	11.93
1985	40.45	47.81	5.08	15.59
1990	51.60	39.60	6.81	19.35
1991	43.84	27.48	6.44	14.47
1992	42.42	27.91	3.94	15.40
1993	33.61	24.78	2.87	12.68
1994	29.06	25.02	2.90	12.63
1995	29.71	24.93	2.94	12.90
1996	33.51	26.26	3.17	13.86
1997	30.00	24.62	2.71	12.56

Source: IMF Directions of Trade Statistics Yearbook (various issues).

An analysis of the individual ACU countries' trade pattern with other members in relation to their trade with Asia and the world, thus, shows similar patterns. During the initial years of ACU's formation it was a major destination for both exports and imports of the member countries *vis-a-vis* the rest of Asia. However in the 1990s the relative significance of ACU declined as the member countries established greater trade linkages with the rest of the Asian countries. In fact only Nepal and Myanmar appeared to have maintained a stable proportion in their exports to ACU *vis-a-vis* the rest of Asia. All the other countries registered a steep decline. Similar was the case with ACU countries intra-trade *vis-a-vis* their global trade. All the member countries predictably had a very low share of ACU trade in the global trade in the 1970s. But that proportion has come down even further in the 1990s.

Annexure to Chapter 4

ACU Trends and Performance: Recent Figures

The present section updates and analyses the figures relating to performance of the ACU countries interms of their macro-economic aggregates and ACU transactions.

Table 4.1a: ACU Countries Total Exports 1999-2003

(Figures in parenthesis show per cent change from previous year)

(Millions of US $)

Countries	1999	2000	2001	2002	2003
Bangladesh	3.92	4.78	4.82	4.56	5.26
	(2.34)	(2.1)	(.8)	(.5)	(15)
India	35.92	42.64	45.14	50.57	60.94
	(9)	(18)	(5)	(12)	
Iran	21.03	28.46	23.90	28.18	—
	(-)	(35)	(-19)	(17)	
Nepal	.60	.80	.73	.56	.66
	(27)	(33)	(-9)	(-23)	(+.17)
Myanmar	1.13	1.64	2.38	3.04	2.48
	(5)	(45)	(45)	(36)	(-18)
Pakistan	8.4	9.02	9.23	9.91	11.9
	(-1)	(6)	(2)	(7)	(20)
Sri Lanka	4.59	5.43	4.81	4.69	5.12
	(-2)	(18)	(-11)	(-2)	(9)

Source: International Monetary Fund Directions of Trade Statistics, 2004.

As per Table 4.1a, figures for Total Exports during 1999-2003 by and larger show an increasing trend for most of the ACU member countries, with some of the most notable annual growth rates been seen in the case of Bangladesh, (2.34 to 15 %), India (9 to 19 %), Pakistan (-1 to 20%) and Sri Lanka (-2 to 9%) during the above period. India retained its position as the leading exporter in the ACU region followed by Iran and Pakistan.

Table 4.2a: ACU Countries Total Imports 1999-2003
(Figures in parenthesis show per cent change from previous year)
(Millions of US $)

Countries	*1999*	*2000*	*2001*	*2002*	*2003*
Bangladesh	7.69	8.35	8.34	7.91	9.51
	(9)	(8)	(.9)	(-5)	(20)
India	46.97	51.52	50.39	56.51	71.23
	(11)	(30)	(-.2)	(12)	(20)
Iran	12.68	14.34	17.62	21.18	—
Nepal	1.42	1.57	1.47	1.41	1.75
	(14)	(10)	(-6)	(-4)	(24)
Myanmar	2.32	2.40	2.87	2.34	2.09
	(13)	(3)	(20)	(-18)	(10)
Pakistan	10.20	10.86	10.19	11.23	13.03
	(.09)	(6)	(-6)	(10)	(16)
Sri Lanka	5.87	6.28	5.96	6.10	6.67
	(-.8)	(6)	(-.05)	(2)	(9)

Source: International Monetary Fund Directions of Trade Statistics, 2004.

With regard to Total Imports of ACU countries for 1999-2003 as per Table 4.2 a more or less a similar pattern was retained. All countries except Myanmar experienced a surge in their total imports, some of most notable being Bangladesh (9 to 20%), Pakistan (.09 to 16%), Sri Lanka (-.8 to 9%) and Nepal (14 to 24%). India continued to be the leading importer followed by Pakistan, Bangladesh and Sri Lanka.

Table 4.3a: ACU Countries Exports of Goods and Services as per cent GDP 1999-2003

Countries	*1999*	*2000*	*2001*	*2002*	*2003*
Bangladesh	13.9	15.9	15.0	14.7	15.6
India	11.4	12.9	12.9	13.9	14.0
Iran	8.9	.9.0	—	—	—
Nepal	25.3	24.0	20.7	17.3	17.8
Myanmar	0.5	0.5	0.5	0.3	0.2
Pakistan	15.2	14.3	15.8	16.6	17.8
Sri Lanka	35.5	39.1	39.2	36.1	35.8

Source: International Financial Statistics 2005.

As per Table 4.3 a, there was a moderate increase in the export to GDP ratio of the ACU countries for the period 1999-2003. While it witnessed an increase in case of Bangladesh (13.9 to 15.6%), India (11.4 to 14%), Pakistan (15.2 to 17.8%) and Sri Lanka (35.5 to 35.8%), for Myanmar (.5 to .2%) and Nepal (25.3 to 17.8%) it registered a decline.

Table 4.4a: ACU Countries Imports of Goods and Services as per cent GDP 1999-2003

Countries	*1999*	*2000*	*2001*	*2002*	*2003*
Bangladesh	.20	21.3	21.3	19.5	21.7
India	14	15.7	14.8	14.9	15.9
Iran	6.4	5.3	—	—	—
Nepal	34	33.5	31.0	30.7	32.6
Myanmar	.7	.6	.5	.3	.2
Pakistan	19.7	17.2	18.0	17.2	18.3
Sri Lanka	43.3	49.6	45.3	42.8	42.3

Source: International Financial Statistics 2005.

The import to GDP ratio between 1999-2003 as per Table 4.4a however showed a slightly different trend as it witnessed a decline in case of most of the ACU countries including Myanmar (.7 to .2%), Nepal (34 to 32.6%), Pakistan (19.7 to 18.3%) and Sri Lanka (43.3 to 42.3%). India (14 to 15.7%) and Bangladesh (.20 to 21.7) per cent registered a positive increase.

Table 4.5a: ACU Countries Trade Balance 1999-2003

(Millions of US $)

Countries	*1999*	*2000*	*2001*	*2002*	*2003*
Bangladesh	-2077	-1654	-2049	-1678	-2442
India	-8679	-10640	-6418	-3559	-8870
Iran	7597	13138	—	—	—
Nepal	-882	-814	-765	-793	-998
Myanmar	-887	-504	56	382	578
Pakistan	-1847	-1157	-610	-596	-109
Sri Lanka	-769	-1044	-560	-796	-872

Source: International Financial Statistics 2005.

As per Table 4.5a, the trade balance of nearly all the countries except Iran remained negative and registered an increase in that direction. This implies that though both exports and imports of ACU member countries surged during 1999-2003, the latter grew at a faster rate than the former, which by and large followed the trend of early decades.

Table 4.6a: ACU Countries Total Reserves 1999-2003

(Millions of US $)

Countries	*1999*	*2000*	*2001*	*2002*	*2003*
Bangladesh	1172	1144	1018	1242	1739
India	24203	29493	36902	50174	66984
Iran	—	—	—	—	—
Myanmar	202	179	327	354	378
Nepal	621	731	831	754	828
Pakistan	1174	1235	2970	6015	7436
Sri Lanka	1194	809	1033	1207	1530

Source: International Financial Statistics 2005.

The ACU countries' total reserves as percentage of the GDP for the year 1999-2003 as per Table 4.6a showed a positive trend with their being an increase in most of the countries. India accounted for the highest total reserves followed by Pakistan and Bangladesh. The figures for Iran are not available.

Table 4.7a: ACU Transactions Credited and Debited to Participant Central Banks (2000-2003)

(In Million US Dollars)

		Bangla-desh	*Bhut-an*	*India*	*Iran*	*Myan-mar*	*Nepal*	*Pakis-tan*	*Sri Lanka*	*Total*
2000	CR*	81.01	.07	1599.3	1412.2	2.3	4.8	197.2	86.3	3383.53
	DB**	1003.3	.11	1046.9	217.1	1.0	7.4	321.09	786.4	3383.53
2001	CR	76.4	1.5	1807.7	1426.3	1.7	4.4	176.08	59.21	3553.6
	DB	1189.7	.60	1105.6	219.2	7.2	15.2	347.14	668.7	3553.66
2002	CR	96.59	3.2	1900.1	1265.2	1.9	6.5	124.9	49.6	3448.4
	DB	1198.4	.28	952.3	214.9	1.0	7.7	317.94	755.6	3448.42
2003	CR	99.45	4.19	2487.6	1745.8	2.3	7.26	144.54	54.98	4546.3
	DB	1521.2	.50	1292.2	277.3	2.6	7.4	453.87	991.9	4546.3
2004	CR	104.3	7.6	3328.07	2929.1	2.05	5.4	215.9	87.19	6679.7
	DB	1773.04	.20	2415.1	335.1	.15	11.09	649.73	1495.5	6679.7

Source: Asian Clearing Union Annual Report, 2004.

* CR = Credited

**DB= Debited

Note: Some figures have been approximated to the second decimal.

Almost all the countries experienced growth in the transactions credited during 2000-2004 as per Table 4.7a. The transactions debited however showed fluctuations within countries as Myanmar and Nepal experienced a net decline during the period. Expectedly, India and Iran accounted for the largest share of the transactions credited and debited.

Table 4.8a: Transactions Credited and Exports 2000-2003

(*In Million US Dollars*)

		Bangladesh	*Bhutan*	*India*	*Iran*	*Myanmar*	*Nepal**	*Pakistan*	*Sri Lanka*	*Total*
2000	CR-a	81.01	.07	1599.37	1412.22	2.34	4.85	197.2	86.36	3383.53
	EX-b	125.5	—	2027	927	202.42	222.92	290	132.59	3927.43
	a as % of b	64.5		78	152.3	.01	.02	67	65	86.15
2001	CR-a	76.44	1.5	1807.74	1426.33	1.76	4.94	176.08	59.21	3553.66
	EX-b	127.89		2491	881	214.77	243.80	288	137.31	4383.26
	a as % of b	59.8	—	72	161	00	.02	61	43	81
2002	CR-a	96.59	3.2	1900.11	1265.23	1.98	6.56	124.97	49.67	3448.42
	EX-b	112.54		2640	854	231.59	265.74	267	245.79	4616.66
	a as % of b	85.7	—	71.9	146.4	00	.02	46.4	20	74.6
2003	CR-a	99.45	4.19	2487.66	1745.82	2.36	7.26	144.54	54.98	4546.30
	EX-b	145.81		3327	1090	288.33	335.18	348	330.13	5864.45
	a as % of b	68.2	—	74.7	160	00	.02	41.3	16.6	77.5

Source: Asian Clearing Union Annual Report (various issues) IMF Directions of Trade Statistics Yearbook (various issues).

The percentage of transactions credited to total exports remained significantly high during 2000-2003 as per Table 4.8a, ranging from 86.15 per cent to 77.5 per cent during the period. While the percentage was fairly high in case of Bangladesh, India, Iran, it was miniscule in case of Nepal and Myanmar, implying that non-ACU credited exports are much higher in case of the latter countries.

Table 4.9a: Transactions Debited and Imports 2000-2003

(In Million US Dollars)

		Bangladesh	*Bhutan*	*India*	*Iran*	*Myanmar*	*Nepal**	*Pakistan*	*Sri Lanka*	*Total*
2000	DB-a	1003.33	.11	1046.91	217.13	1.00	7.49	321.09	786.44	3383.53
	IM-b	1092.79		1078	2462	58.23	168.07	272	880.42	6011.71
	a as % of b	91.6	—	97.0	.08	.01	.04	118.04	89	56.2
2001	DB-a	1189.79	.60	1105.66	219.27	7.24	15.22	347.14	668.70	3553.66
	IM-b	1323.13		1186	3219	63.12	178.53	315	910.81	7689.08
	a as % of b	89.8	—	93.1	6	11.4	8	110	73.4	46.2
2002	DB-a	1198.49	.50	952.35	214.91	1.04	7.74	317.94	755.63	3448.42
	IM-b	1251.4		1325	3740	73.08	196.07	242	855.62	7683.17
	a as % of b	95.7		71.8	5.7	1.4	3.9	130	88.3	44.8
2003	DB-a	1521.29	.20	1292.24	277.37	2.60	7.47	453.67	991.92	4546.30
	IM-b	1656.95		1668	7096	85.41	238.05	323	1166.02	12233.43
	a as % of b	91.8	—	77.4	3	3	3	140	84.9	37.16

Source: Asian Clearing Union Annual Report (various issues).
IMF Directions of Trade Statistics Yearbook (various issues).

While the transactions debited as a percentage of exports during 2000-2003 showed a declining trend overall, from 56.2 per cent to 37.6 per cent for the period, there were variations in between. While India, Bangladesh, Pakistan and Sri Lanka accrued a high percentage, that of Iran, Myanmar and Nepal was miniscule, showing that bulk of their imports take the non-ACU route.

Table 4.10a: Cleared Trade as a Proportion of Total Trade

(*Million of US Dollars*)

Year	*Cleared Trade*	*Intra-ACU Exports*	*Global Trade*	*I as% of II*	*I as % III*	*II as% of III*
	I	*II*	*III*	*IV*	*V*	*VI*
2000	1634.36	3927.43	90260.4	41.6	1.8	4.3
2001	1643.56	4383.26	91207.2	37.4	1.8	4.8
2002	1446.40	4616.66	95216.9	31.3	1.5	4.8
2003	1877.95	5864.45	108661.8	32	1.7	5.3
2004	3163.25	—	—	—		—

Source: I. ACU Annual Report, (various issues) II and III. IMF, Directions of Trade Statistics Yearbook (various issues).

Finally, the transactions cleared as a percentage of intra-ACU and global trade presents an interesting picture. While the cleared trade as a percentage of intra-ACU exports has declined significantly, the ratio of cleared trade as a per cent global trade and that of intra-ACU exports to global trade has by and large stable (Table 4.10a).

Table 4.11a: Bangladesh's Trade with ACU Countries 1988-2003

(Millions of US Dollars)

Year		*India*	*Iran*	*Myanmar*	*Nepal*	*Pakistan*	*Sri Lanka*	*Total*	*Asia*	*World*
1998	Exports	55.02	43.14	.38	17.85	28.76	1.07	146.22	283.4	3821.0
	Imports	1178.83	7.59	12.19	14.27	73.37	6.28	1292.53	3861.7	77569
1999	Exports	49.51	32.91	1.25	5.24	24.87	6.53	120.31	230.1	4520.0
	Imports	1023.77	28.31	13.78	8.94	85.38	7.15	1167.33	3843.6	8352.4
2000	Exports	50.13	36.37	.70	1.32	34.51	2.47	125.5	29.49	5589.6
	Imports	954.45	19.90	22.03	3.98	93.16	8.27	1092.79	4272.1	9000.0
2001	Exports	60.80	36.84	.68	1.95	25.60	2.02	127.89	309.5	5735.6
	Imports	1195.49	10.27	19.72	4.15	85.63	7.87	1323.13	4669.3	9010.6
2002	Exports	39.33	38.24	.97	3.91	27.18	1.94	112.542	270.1	5443.3
	Imports	1145.83	9.99	23.77	5.38	59.78	6.79	1251.4	4324	7847.8
2003	Exports	55.34	36.55	2.44	2.98	42.70	5.80	145.81	325.4	6229.4
	Imports	1494.22	19.91	33.23	4.86	95.49	9.24	1656.95	5551.5	9672.3

Source: IMF Directions of Trade Statistics Yearbook 2004.

As per Table 4.11a showing Bangladesh's trading partners in ACU for 1998-2003, India ranked the highest, followed by Pakistan and Iran. Its total exports to ACU for the period declined marginally from 146.22 million US dollars to 145.81 million US dollars. Whereas imports from ACU surged from 1292.53 to 1656.95 million US dollars.

Table 4.12a: Bangladesh's Trade with ACU Countries as a Percentage of its Trade with Asian Countries and World (1998-2003)

(Millions of US Dollars)

Year	*Exports to ACU: Exports to Asia*	*Imports to ACU: Imports to Asia*	*Exports to ACU: Total Global Exports*	*Imports to ACU: Total Global Imports*
1998	51.5	33.4	3.8	17.5
1999	52.2	30.3	2.6	13.9
2000	42.5	25.5	2.2	12.1
2001	41.3	28.3	2.2	14.6
2002	41.6	28.9	2.0	15.9
2003	44.8	29.8	2.3	17.1

Source: IMF Directions of Trade Statistics Yearbook 2004.

As per Table 4.12a, Bangladesh's Trade with the ACU countries both as proportion of its Asian Trade and Global Trade registered a decline, showing it has not been able to enhance its trade with ACU *vis-a-vis* Asia and the world.

Table 4.13a: India's Trade with ACU Countries 1998-2003

(Millions of US Dollars)

Year		*Bangladesh*	*Iran*	*Nepal*	*Myanmar*	*Pakistan*	*Sri Lanka*	*Total*	*Asia*	*World*
1998	Exports	943	162	134	35	115	450	1839	6608	33663
	Imports	60	514	132	186	172	36	1100	7789	42162
1999	Exports	726	154	144	33	96	484	1637	7218	35920
	Imports	74	1057	178	172	105	43	1629	9020	47900
2000	Exports	860	208	143	48	163	605	2027	8797	42624
	Imports	80	471	238	179	65	45	1078	8657	50336
2001	Exports	1087	427	158	53	219	547	2491	10445	45144
	Imports	67	508	262	197	73	79	1186	12998	59364
2002	Exports	1042	464	172	58	148	756	2640	11879	50577
	Imports	43	541	285	214	54	188	1325	14545	67210
2003	Exports	1358	516	217	73	206	957	3327	15384	60641
	Imports	61	684	345	259	92	227	1668	19864	85294

Source: IMF Directions of Trade Statistics Yearbook 2004.

India's trade with ACU countries between 1998-2003 as per Table 4.13a shows an increase in both its exports (1839 to 3327 million US dollars) and imports (1100 to 1668 milion US dollars) with Bangladesh, Iran and Sri Lanka as the largest trading partners.

Table 4.14a: India's Trade with ACU Countries as a Percentage of its Trade with Asian Countries and World (1998-2003)

(Millions of US Dollars)

Year	*Exports to ACU: Exports to Asia*	*Imports to ACU: Imports to Asia*	*Exports to ACU: Total Global Exports*	*Imports to ACU: Total Global Imports*
1998	27	14.1	5	2
1999	22	18	4	3
2000	23	12.4	4.7	2.1
2001	23.8	9.1	5.5	1.9
2002	22.8	9.1	5.2	1.9
2003	21.6	8.3	5.4	1.9

Source: IMF Directions of Trade Statistics Yearbook 2004.

As per Table 4.14a, India's trade with ACU countries as a percentage of its Asian and Global trade registered a decline with the exception of its exports to ACU as a percentage of its global exports which showed an increasing trend. It indicates India has not been able to enhance its trade significantly with ACU in relation to its Asian and global trade.

Table 4.15a: Iran's Trade with ACU Countries 1998-2003

(Millions of US Dollars)

Year		*Bangladesh*	*India*	*Nepal*	*Myanmar*	*Pakistan*	*Sri Lanka*	*Total*	*Asia*	*World*
1998	Exports	—	365	—	—	66	92	523	2432	13118
	Imports	—	204	—	—	—	—	204	1943	14323
1999	Exports	—	718	—	—	112	128	958	4525	21030
	Imports	—	199	—	—	—	—	199	1945	12683
2000	Exports	18	428	—	—	296	185	927	7879	25064
	Imports	33	254	—	—	41	28	356	2462	14347
2001	Exports	9	462	—	—	198	212	881	7407	23151
	Imports	39	561	—	—		15	615	3219	17685
2002	Exports	9	492	—	—	186	167	854	6179	21438
	Imports	49	717	—	—	88	1	855	3740	22321
2003	Exports	18	596	—	—	274	202	1090	9120	31087
	Imports	40	797	—	—	90	1	928		

Source: IMF Directions of Trade Statistics Yearbook 2004.

Iran has registered an impressive increase it its trade, both exports and imports with the ACU countries for the period 1998-2003 as per Table 4.15a. Its most significant partners in ACU include India, Pakistan and Iran. In the recent years, it has had trade surplus with most of the countries except India.

Table 4.16a: Iran's Trade with ACU Countries as a Percentage of its Trade with Asian Countries and World (1998-2003)

(Millions of US Dollars)

Year	Exports to ACU: Exports to Asia	Imports to ACU: Imports to Asia	Exports to ACU: Total Global Exports	Imports to ACU: Total Global Imports
1998	21.5	10.4	3.9	1.4
1999	21.1	10.2	4.5	1.5
2000	11.7	14.4	3.6	2.4
2001	11.8	19.1	3.8	3.4
2002	13.8	22.8	3.9	3.8
2003	11.9	13.0	3.5	3.0

Source: IMF Directions of Trade Statistics Yearbook 2004.

As per Table 4.16a, while Iran's exports to ACU as a per cent of its Asian and Global exports have decreased for 1998-2003, its imports from ACU as per cent of Asian and global imports have increased.

Table 4.17a: Nepal's Trade with ACU Countries 1998-2003

(Millions of US Dollars)

Year		Bangla-desh	India	Iran	Myan-mar	Pakis-tan	Sri Lanka	Total	Asia	World
1998	Exports	9.60	145.50	—	—	.80	4.90	159.80	162.3	443.6
	Imports	5.90	439.70	1.50	—	6.20	2.20	455.50	995.2	1433.5
1999	Exports	8.12	161.52	—	—	.85	.08	170.57	182.6	575.6
	Imports	5.76	158.40	—	—	2.05	1.83	168.04	656.5	1199.6
2000	Exports	3.62	216.80	—	—	2.42	.08	22.92	244.9	676.4
	Imports	1.45	157.74	—	—	3.00	.88	168.07	679.6	1058.2
2001	Exports	3.77	239.34	—	—	.68	.01	243.80	261.3	613.7
	Imports	2.14	173.51	—	—	2.51	.37	178.53	552.7	907.7
2002	Exports	4.89	259.75	—	—	.93	.17	265.74	277.5	542.9
	Imports	4.31	188.31	—	—	2.48	.97	196.07	491.3	873.2
2003	Exports	4.42	328.76	—	—	1.78	.22	335.18	347.4	649.4
	Imports	3.28	228.29	—	—	5.30	1.18	238.05	551.9	996.6

Source: IMF Directions of Trade Statistics Yearbook 2004.

Table 4.17 a gives Nepal's Trade with ACU countries, Asia and the world. While its exports to ACU have increased for the period 1998-2003 from 159.87 to 335.18 million US dollar, its imports have declined from 455.50 to 238.05 million US dollars. India has been its largest trading partner followed by Bangladesh and Pakistan.

Table 4.18a: Nepal's Trade with ACU Countries as a Percentage of its Trade with Asian Countries and World Trade (1998-2003)

(Millions of US Dollars)

Year	Exports to ACU: Exports to Asia	Imports to ACU: Imports to Asia	Exports to ACU: Total Global Exports	Imports to ACU: Total Global Imports
1998	98.4	45.7	36.0	31.7
1999	93.4	25.5	29.6	14.0
2000	91.0	23.9	32.9	15.4
2001	93.3	32.3	39.7	19.6
2002	95.7	39.9	48.1	22.4
2003	96.4	43.1	51.6	23.8

Source: IMF Directions of Trade Statistics Yearbook 2004.

As per Table 4.18a, Nepal has one of the highest per cent of its ACU exports as a per cent of its Asian exports, which have however shown a declining trend from 98.4 to 96.4 per cent. Its exports to ACU as a per cent of its global exports however has shown an increasing trend from 36 to 51.1 per cent. This shows the Nepal's trade with rest of the Asia is witnessing an increase.

Table 4.19a: Myanmar's Trade with ACU Countries 1998-2003

(Millions of US Dollars)

Year		Bangladesh	India	Iran	Nepal	Pakistan	Sri Lanka	Total	Asia	World
1998	Exports	11.08	169.41	—	—	10.47	.91	191.87	504.2	1138.6
	Imports	.42	38.39	—	—	3.60	.59	43	1935.5	2358.5
1999	Exports	12.53	156.50	—	—	7.19	.76	176.98	613.1	1393.3
	Imports	1.38	36.41	—	—	2.20	.36	40.35	2125.2	2527.2

(Contd.)

(*Contd.*)

Year		Bangladesh	India	Iran	Nepal	Pakistan	Sri Lanka	Total	Asia	World
2000	Exports	20.03	162.89	—	—	18.41	1.09	202.42	817.9	1977.6
	Imports	.77	52.86	—	—	4.11	.49	58.23	2617.2	3039.1
2001	Exports	17.92	179.83	—	—	15.88	1.14	214.77	1369.9	2635.5
	Imports	.74	58.14	—	—	3.59	.65	63.12	2283.3	2661.2
2002	Exports	21.61	195.16	.02	—	13.73	1.07	231.59	1494.9	2652.8
	Imports	1.06	63.10	—	—	8.62	.30	73.08	2527.0	2952.1
2003	Exports	30.21	247.01	.03	—	8.36	1.36	288.33	1527.6	2641.7
	Imports	2.68	76.49	—	—	5.87	.37	85.41	2877.0	3204.9

Source: IMF Directions of Trade Statistics Yearbook 2004.

Table 4.19a shows Myanmar's trade with ACU countries for 1998-2003. It has consistently shown an increase in its overall exports as well as imports for the above period. India has been its largest trading partner followed by Bangladesh and Pakistan. It has enjoyed a fairly comfortable trade surplus with most of the ACU countries.

Table 4.20a: Myanmar's Trade with ACU Countries as a Percentage of its Trade with Asian Countries and World (1998-2003)

(*Millions of US Dollars*)

Year	Exports to ACU: Exports to Asia	Imports to ACU: Imports to Asia	Exports to ACU: Total Global Exports	Imports to ACU: Total Global Imports
1998	38.0	2.2	16.8	1.8
1999	28.8	1.8	12.7	1.5
2000	24.7	2.2	10.2	1.9
2001	15.6	2.7	8.1	2.3
2002	15.4	2.8	8.7	2.4
2003	18.8	2.9	10.91	2.6

Source: IMF Directions of Trade Statistics Yearbook 2004.

As per Table 4.20a, while Myanmar has registered a decline in its exports to ACU as a percentage to its Asian and global exports from the period 1998-2003, its ACU import percentages *vis-a-vis* Asia and the world have registered an increase. It is clear therefore that Myanmar is diversifying its export markets outside ACU.

Table 4.21a: Pakistan's Trade with ACU Countries (1998-2003)

(Millions of US Dollars)

Year		Bangla-desh	India	Iran	Myan-mar	Pakis-tan	Sri Lanka	Total	Asia	World
1998	Exports	107	203	13	3	8	95	429	1691	8433
	Imports	36	154	—	12	1	34	237	2690	9308
1999	Exports	106	87	6	2	2	105	308	1713	8439
	Imports	28	134	—	8	1	37	208	2476	10297
2000	Exports	139	58	5	4	3	81	290	1793	8870
	Imports	36	178	—	20	3	35	272	2427	10721
2001	Exports	119	66	23	3	2	75	288	1809	9205
	Imports	26	241	3	17	1	27	315	2520	10165
2002	Exports	104	49	33	8	2	71	267	1804	9883
	Imports	31	163	—	15	1	32	242	2904	11238
2003	Exports	166	84	4	5	5	84	348	2231	11929
	Imports	43	226	—	9	2	43	323	3684	13049

Source: IMF Directions of Trade Statistics Yearbook 2004.

Table 4.21a shows Pakistan's trade with ACU for 1998-2003. While its exports have declined from 429 million US dollars to 348 million US dollars, its ACU imports have shown an increasing trend from 237 to 323 million US dollars. India and Bangladesh are its leading trade partners within ACU.

Table 4.22a: Pakistan's Trade with ACU Countries as a Percentage of Trade with Asian Countries and World (1998-2003)

(Millions of US Dollars)

Year	Exports to ACU: Exports to Asia	Imports to ACU: Imports to Asia	Exports to ACU: Total Global Exports	Imports to ACU: Total Global Imports
1998	25.3	8.8	5.0	2.5
1999	17.9	8.4	3.6	2.0
2000	16.1	11.2	3.2	2.5
2001	15.9	12.5	3.1	3.0
2002	14.8	8.3	2.7	2.1
2003	15.5	8.7	2.9	2.4

Source: IMF Directions of Trade Statistics Yearbook 2004.

As per Table 4.22a , Pakistan has registered a decline in its ACU trade as a per cent of its Asian trade as well as its global trade (both exports and imports). It implies that Pakistan has not been able to raise its share of ACU trade *vis-a-vis* Asia and the world.

Table 4.23a: Sri Lanka's Trade with ACU Countries 1998-2003

(Millions of US dollars)

Year		Bangladesh	India	Iran	Myanmar	Nepal	Pakistan	Total	Asia	World
1998	Exports	10.44	37.69	18.33	.53	1.10	26.94	95.03	353.4	4819.9
	Imports	1.08	539.33	116.73	1.00	1.21	90.63	749.98	3350.7	62634
1999	Exports	11.65	48.62	25.07	.32	1.67	30.82	118.15	391.7	4621.8
	Imports	4.54	511.60	80.64	.83	.09	94.71	692.41	3275.5	6255.2
2000	Exports	10.22	58.03	33.40	.44	.80	29.70	132.59	500.2	5458.8
	Imports	3.56	600.14	203.26	1.20	.09	72.17	880.42	3723.7	6688.0
2001	Exports	10.08	71.99	29.45	.59	.33	24.87	137.31	389.5	4722.4
	Imports	2.05	600.48	233.2	1.25.	.01	73.82	910.81	3338.9	5730.8
2002	Exports	10.18	170.57	35.05	.27	.88	28.84	245.79	491.7	4679.9
	Imports	3.89	601.48	183.19	1.18	.19	65.69	855.62	3214.2	6022.8
2003	Exports	11.17	245.05	35.28	.24	1.66	36.73	330.13	602.0	5133.3
	Imports	5.64	832.07	249.51	2.29	—	70.98	1166.02	3741.8	6671.9

Source: IMF Directions of Trade Statistics Yearbook 2004.

Table 4.23a shows Sri Lanka's trade with ACU countries in relation to its Asian and global trade for 1998-2003. While it has shown an overall increase in its ACU exports (95.03 to 330.13 million US dollars) and its imports (749.98 to 1166.02 million US dollars), the latter have shown fluctuations in the intervening years. India, Iran and Pakistan have been its leading trading partners.

Table 4.24a: Sri Lanka's Trade with ACU Countries as a Percentage of its Trade with Asian Countries and World (1975-97)

Year	*Exports to ACU: Exports to Asia*	*Imports to ACU: Imports to Asia*	*Exports to ACU: Total Global Exports*	*Imports to ACU: Total Global Imports*
1998	26.8	22.3	1.9	11.9
1999	30.16	21.1	2.5	11.06
2000	26.5	23.6	2.4	13.1
2001	35.2	27.2	2.9	15.8
2002	49.9	26.6	5.2	14.2
2003	54.8	31.1	6.4	17.4

Source: IMF Directions of Trade Statistics Yearbook 2004.

As per Table 4.24a, there has been a steady increase in Sri Lanka's trade with ACU (both exports and imports) as percentage of its Asian and Global trade, with the latter growing at a faster rate. This implies that Sri Lanka has experienced a consistently higher growth in trade with ACU in relation to rest of Asia and world.

NOTES

1. The period covers the entire span of ACUs activities since its formation. The focus shall however be on the recent years which have coincided with reform measures in most of the countries.
2. Salim Jahan, Bangladesh: Macroeconomic Development during the Eighties in Rehman Sobhan (ed.), (The Decade of Stagnation: The State of the Bangladesh Economy in the 1980s) (Dhaka, 1991), p. 13.
3. *Asian Development Outlook* 1999, p. 125
4. Farishuddin Mahtab, State of Development Strategies and Resources Allocation in Rehman Shobhan, n.2, p. 111.

5. The reasons attributed mainly refer to non-convertibility of the capital account, lack of foreign institutional investment, low current account deficits and a moderate external debt burden that have largely insulated the economy from the instability of world capital markets.
6. See Joint Press Communique on Indo Bangladesh Protocol on the Balanced Trade and Payments Agreement, Dacca, 30 September 1974 in Satish Kumar (ed.), *Documents on India's Foreign Policy* (Delhi: Macmillan, 1974).
7. Article 1 of the Protocol on Credit Arrangements between India and Bangladesh, New Delhi, 16 May, 1974 in *ibid.*
8. Article 8 of the Protocol on Credit Arrangement between India and Bangladesh, New Delhi, 16 May, 1974 in *ibid.*
9. International Monetary Fund, Exchange Arrangements and Exchange Restrictions. *Annual Report* 1998 p. 67.
10. Asian Clearing Union, *Annual Report* 1997, pp. 15, 140.
11. CPD Occasional Paper Series No 20, Exchange Rate Policy of Bangladesh :Not Floating does not Mean Sinking, http://www.cpdbangladesh.org/publications/op/OP20.pdf
12. For an authoritative account of economic reforms and the subsequent impact on India's economic development, see Isher Judge Ahluwalia and I.M.D Little (eds.), (*India's Economic Reforms and Development. Essays in the Honour of Manmohan Singh*) (New Delhi, 1998). Also see Bimal Jalan, *India's Economic Policy: Preparing for the Twenty First Century* (New Delhi, 1996)
13. *Economic Survey* 1999, p. I.
14. *Ibid.* p. 97.
15. IMF n. 9. 418.
16. ESCAP, "The Iranian Economy: Oil and the Development in the First Half of the 1970s", *Economic Bulletin for Asia and the Pacific,* Vo1.29, No.2, December 1998, p.47 Also see Ehsan Yar Shater (ed.), *Iran Faces the 70s* (New York: Praeger, 1971).
17. See Muhammad Azhar, "Iranian Economy, Agenda for Reconstruction and Reform" in Girijesh Pant (ed.). *The Political Economy of West Asia. Demography, Democracy and Economic Reforms,* (Delhi, 1994). p. 157.
18. *Economic and Social Survey of Asia and the Pacific 1999-2000,* pp. 1, 149.
19. During the war while the official rate was 70 Iranian Rial = 1 US dollar, current floating rate was 15000 Rial = 1 US dollar.
20. IMF, n. 9., p. 68.

21. Iran and India discussed subjects relating to oil and other commodities, development of India's mineral resources for exports to Iran, extension of credit facilities to India etc. See the Joint Statement at the end of 4th Session of this Indo-Iran Joint Commission for Economic Trade and Technical Cooperation, New Delhi, 16 January 1974 in Satish Kumar, n.6.
22. See *Nepal Yearbook 1998*, p.33. There was however some contention regarding this rate of growth and was sent back for revision.
23. The banned export categories include articles of archaeological and religious importance, conserved wildlife and related articles, drugs, articles of industrial importance (explosives materials, material used in arms and ammunitions), Industrial raw material etc. For a detailed list see *Nepal & the World: A Statistical Profile 1998*, Federation of Nepalese Chamber of Commerce and Industry, Kathmandu, p.34.
24. IMF, n. 9, p. 641
25. In fact India is the largest trading partner of Nepal, a position it lost to USA and Germany in 1995-96 and 1996-97, but regained in fiscal year 1997-98. For further details see *Nepal Overseas Trade Statistics 1997-98.* Trade Promotion Centre, Kathmandu, p.159.
26. *Economic and Social Survey of Asia and Pacific 1999*, United Nations, p.36.
27. ESCAP Studies in Trade and Investment No.19, *Myanmar: Trade and Investment Potential in Asia, United Nations*, New York, 1996, p. 3.
28. See Mya Maung, *The Burma Road to Capitalism: Economic Growth,* versus *Democracy,* (Westport 1998), p. 69. Under this system, importer was issued a license on a consignment basis upon a condition, that within a specified period of time, usually 6 months, it must export domestic product to earn foreign exchange. In order to pay for the imports in foreign exchange, the importer must either establish a line of credit first with major foreign firm or pay for imports later after it earns foreign exchange from exports or purchase foreign exchange in the unofficial market to pay for the import.
29. IMF, n. 9, p. 627.
30. Maung, n. 27, p. 70.
31. *Economic Survey 1997-98.* Government of Pakistan, Finance Division, Islamabad, p.vii. 162.
32. State Bank of Pakistan *Annual Report* 1997-98, p. 10.
33. Ashfaq H. Khan, "The Experience of Trade Liberalisation in Pakistan", *Pakistan Development Review,* Vo1.37, Winter 1998, p. 675.

34. The Economist Intelligence Unit Country Report on Pakistan, First Quarter 1999, p. 30. Exporters were now allowed to sell 80 per cent at floating Interbank rate and remaining 20 per cent at official rate.
35. Nadeem U. Haq and Peter I. Montiel, Exchange Rate Policy in Pakistan: Recent Experience and Prospect, in Anjum Nasim (ed.), *Financing Pakistan's Development in the 1990s* (Karachi, 1996), p. 152.
36. Central Bank of Sri Lanka, *Annual Report* 1998, p. 2.
37. Sri Lanka, *State of the Economy*, October, 1998, p. 5.
38. Saman Kelegama, "Economic Development in Sri Lanka during the 50 Years of Independence: What went wrong?", *RIS Occasional Paper* No.53, p. 28.
39. Central Bank of Sri Lanka, n. 35, p. 151.
40. IMF, n. 9, p. 836.

Chapter 5

Asian Clearing Union: Critical Issues and Alternative Strategies

5.1 Introduction

At the time of its inception in 1975, the Asian Clearing Union was faced with a particular regional and global economic context. As elaborated earlier in chapter three most of the member countries were facing a deteriorating external economic environment with declining export growth, fluctuating terms of trade and declining capital flows. These regional developments coincided with a global economic climate characterized by a general economic slowdown and greater protectionism. At the same time, there were efforts underway within the ESCAP region to foster greater economic linkages among the developing member countries through intra-regional trade liberalisation along with monetary and financial cooperation. Formation of a clearing and payments arrangement among the member countries was seen as part of the steps aimed at overcoming the constraints posed by a deteriorating liquidity position among the member countries.[1]

As discussed earlier, one of the major objectives laid out at the time of ACU's formation related to promoting the use of participants' currencies in current transactions between their respective territories and thereby effect economies in the use of participants exchange reserves. In fact, the continued functioning of this mechanism till 1995 (with ACU switching over of dollar denominated transactions in 1996 due to emerging constraints[2] indicate that ACU was able to effectively function as a facility not only for settling intra-regional transactions, but also for conserving foreign exchange.

However, there were larger and broader issues envisaged as the ACU was set up. Apart from accomplishing the objectives stated above, it was also expected to promote monetary cooperation among the participants and closer banking relations among the banking systems in their territories, thereby contributing to the expansion of trade and economic activity among the countries of the ESCAP region.[3] Thus ACU was to act as one of the crucial links which was to give a further boost to the overarching process of regional economic cooperation in Asia and the Pacific. To what extent has the ACU really been able to address the broader agenda that was laid out? Have the periodic changes that have taken place in the ACUs functioning been able to address the fundamental problems that the facility has faced? Lastly, is there any role for ACU if at all it is to complement the larger efforts at regional integration that are underway in the South Asian region?

The present chapter is aimed at analysing these issues with regard to the present role and future directions of the ACU. It would examine the issues both at the macro and the micro level one by one before outlining a blueprint for its future. It shall analyse both the structural and the functional aspects of the mechanism to assess whether the system should continue in its present form or needs a major modification to justify its relevance. The chapter would derive extensively from the feedback from concerned institutions and individuals associated with the ACU mechanism apart from the conceptual analysis of the issues involved.

5.2 Structural Aspects

A critical analysis of the structural components of the ACU is in order as it enables us to understand better the institutional factors that guide its functioning. Besides it also gives us an insight into the internal dynamics of the organizations which pave the way for a deeper analysis. One would divide the structural aspects into two parts: (i) Administrative, and (ii) Procedural.

Administrative

The ACU has at its core the key decision making body—the Board of Directors (BOD, consisting, mainly of the Governors of the Central Banks of the members countries and a Chairman from among them) which meet at least once in a calendar year. All decisions of the BOD are to be taken by a majority of votes of all the directors unless a special majority is required by the Agreement.[4] When both a Director and his alternate are not present at a meeting of the Board, the Director in accordance with rules established by the board, may authorize another director to present his views and caste his vote. The Chairman does not have a vote except in the case of an equal divisions when he shall caste the deciding vote.

The executive function of the ACU is performed by the ACU Secretariat headed by the Secretary General who conducts the ordinary business of the ACU under the direction of the BOD. He is appointed by a two-third majority of the BOD for a period of three years. The Secretary General prepares and submits to the Board the documents necessary for its work, particularly the financial statements, the proposed annual budget and the draft annual report. Beside, he also acts as the representative of the Board of Directors within the limits prescribed by the Board.[5]

Given the broad administrative organisation of the ACU it appears that a clear-cut delineation of roles of its various components exists. The policy-making functions and the policy implementing functions are clearly demarcated between the Board and the Secretariat. However, it does appear that the decisions making process of the Board is often constrained by the limited agenda that is pursued. Apart from taking decisions on functional aspects of ACU when the need arises, the Board generally confines itself to a discussion of the monetary and financial developments among the member countries and is generally found lacking the outlining a pro-active agenda for the ACU. One of the possible reasons could be that in the recent times the meetings of the Board of Directors have rarely seen full representation by all the Central Bank Governors.[6] There are times when at the crucial annual board meetings, countries are represented by junior level officials who might or might not be associated with the ACU section of the Central Banks. Under such circumstances, there is the likelihood of a lack of proper exchange of ideas and the issues. The meetings, therefore, end up merely exchanging views on regional and global economic developments, rather than focussing on certain concrete issues. Although there have been certain exceptions such as the decision to assign a particular theme for each Board meeting, yet there is no indication that the discussions go beyond a mere exchange of views.[7] The decisions taken earlier had more to do with streamlining the functioning of the mechanism rather than having a broad-based agenda as such. These have, for instance, included decisions on extending of the settlement period from one month to two months in 1977, making the channelling of transactions compulsory in 1983, channelling of oil payments in 1985, commencement of dollar denominated transactions in 1995.

Thus there is a pertinent need for the Board of Directors to ensure participation at the highest level so that a greater focus and validity can be given to the decisions that are taken. Besides, the Board must also aim at redefining the scope of discussions undertaken, the broad elements of which shall be elaborated at a later stage in the chapter.

The other major component of the administrative machinery of the ACU is the Secretariat, which performs the executive role of the system. The Secretariat, headed by the Secretary General not merely undertakes the routine task of crediting and debiting the transactions of member countries, but also performs a much wider role pertaining to that of coordinating with other international and regional organizations and looking for prospective members. To that extent, the ACU Secretariat operating under heavy resource constraints,[8] very effectively performs the twin agenda assigned to it. Table 5.1 summarizes the meetings/initiatives by the ACU Secretariat towards enlarging the ACU in the late nineties. The only success achieved despite all efforts was the roping in of Bhutan as the ninth member in 2000.

Table 5.1: ACUs Representation Interaction with Other Bodies

Year	*Meeting*
1995	Sixth Meeting of Steering Group of Committee on Regional Economic Cooperation, Jakarta, 51st Annual Session of ESCAP.
1996	52nd Annual Session of ESCAP, Meeting with CIS countries such as Armenia, Turkemenistan and Kazakhstan.
1997	53rd Annual Session of ESCAP, Representation to Bhutan and Maldives, Invitation to State Bank of Vietnam, Orientation Course of the Turkish Mission at ACU.
1998	54th Annual Session of ESCAP, 27th Annual Board Meeting attended by, UNCTAD, Central Bank of Turkey and ECO.
1999	28th Annual Board Meeting, attended by China, Bhutan and the SAARC secretariat.

Source: ACU Annual Report (various issues).

As we can see, the Secretariat has tried to make use of the opportunities provided by multilateral and regional gatherings to highlight the role and significance of the ACU mechanism and made consistent efforts at attracting new members. For instance, at its regular presentations at the ESCAP annual meetings, the ACU has sought to explain the potential benefits of the mechanism and urged the other countries to become part of it. Besides it regularly interacts with individual countries which might be interested in knowing about the possible benefits of the ACU. However, its efforts in this regard have not been very successful given the limited mandate that it has. More recently, it has been making efforts to enable the members of the Economic Cooperation Organisation (ECO) to join the ACU as the former is in the process of forming a mutual payment arrangement among the member countries.[9] However, there have been times when its efforts to seek help and support from the members themselves have not met with immediate responses. For instance, the member countries have been often not too forthcoming in the Secretariat's repeated request for nominating members for the technical committees to study an enhanced role and functioning of the ACU. This not merely leads to a lack of proper communication within the Secretariat and its constituent members, but also prevents a constructive discussion among the members on the constraints and potential of the ACU mechanism. One possible way to overcome this limitation is by having a section within the secretariat which intensively deals with the policy issues relating to ACU and is able to give analytical support to the Secretary General. This would obviate the need for depending solely on the member countries for providing technical inputs when the need arises. Obviously this would require a further enhancement of the resources of the Secretariat.

Given the structural machinery of the ACU and the inherent limitations relating to the decision-making process, one feels that there is a drastic need for revision of the respective agendas and activities that both the Board of Director and the ACU Secretariat undertake. Such a revision has to be however linked to the broader role that the union sets for itself in the future. However, such a role has to be guided also by the procedural aspects of the ACU mechanism to which we shall now turn.

Procedural Issues

As we have seen from our discussion in the earlier chapters, ACU has functioned over the years primarily as a clearing facility for intra-regional current transactions among the member countries. Under the mechanism, the claims of the members were set off against each other and the net amount was paid in hard currencies *via* the ACU system. While initially, it was the Central Bank itself which facilitated payments for every transaction subsequently, due to growing number of transactions and added pressure, the commercial banks were directed to handle the transactions.[10] The central banks were now concerned primarily with the netting of payments and reporting them to ACU. Thus the three level coordination between the commercial banks, the central banks and the ACU formed the core of the clearing mechanism that operated.

The clearing facility as it operated over a period of time had manifold benefits. In an operating environment of inconvertible currencies and limited foreign exchange reserves among members countries, it provided the much needed breathing space to them to exercise some restraints over the foreign currency outflows albeit in a limited way. This apart from the other benefits such as saving on transaction costs and time as banking relationships within the region were made use of. Thus their appeared to be positive gains for the Central Banks, commercial banks and the traders as well. The Central Banks benefited out of economizing on the foreign exchange as the payments were restricted to only net amounts and also by the short-term credit facility to the members with deficit positions as settlement took-place in two months. Besides, the participating members were no longer dependent on international banks to service their trade with each other. The commercial banks benefited as the costs arising from service charges of international banks for handling export/import documents and on account of exchange conversion loss were considerably reduced. The importers on the other hand were no longer required to bear commission charges by foreign banks for executing the payments and had to pay only the commission charged by their domestic banks for issuing payment instructions.

For example, there were estimates that saving in cost of transaction payment was 0.25 per cent of the value of transactions. For the period 1981-89, total saving of cost on fee and commission on payment transactions worked out to US $11.98 million. Besides, the ACU mechanism also reduced the transit time which for bills drawn in rupees under ACU mechanism was about 4 to 8 days, while that for sterling bill took 15-35 days.[11] Besides, within the ACU area, the exchange rate margins were considerably reduced. This was mainly due to quotation by the concerned Central Banks of the very fine rates with a spread of only 0.20 per cent margin and partly to quotation by commercial banks of margins with a maximum spread of 0.15 per cent. Lastly, the political risk, if any, was stated to be indirectly borne by the Central Banks.[12]

While this arrangement continued effectively till almost two decades of ACUs functioning, the gradual transformation of the member economies and the consequent impact on foreign trade and payments started changing the environment in which ACU had hitherto been functioning smoothly. Most of the countries, as part of their respective reform programmes, moved towards gradual convertibility of their respective currencies, thereby opting for market based exchange rates. The ACU mechanism in its original form therefore appeared to be less favourable to the traders as well as bankers who saw the facility as depriving them in terms of both costs and time which initially were the exact reasons why ACU appeared more beneficial. The traders saw themselves at a disadvantage as they thought that invoicing in the ACU currencies, which dealt with rates three day old, made it unattractive to quote prices or draw documents of local currencies in view of the exchange risks involved. Similarly, they were not eligible for forward cover and pre-shipment and post shipment credit facilities denominated in foreign currencies as were enjoyed by exporters to freely convertible currency countries.[13]

In order to maintain its attractiveness to the traders, and ensure speedy settlement of payments the ACU switched over to dollar denominated transactions from January 1, 1996. The need for such change was recommended at the 12th Technical Committee for improving the ACU. Finally at the 24th Board of Directors Meeting at Colombo, the amendments to the ACU suggested by the consultant were approved. Accordingly preparatory arrangements were made by the ACU Secretariat to obtain the formal approval of member authorities. Subsequently ACU operational formats were put under the time table and almost all the formats were revised and sent to the member Central Banks for acceptance. This implies that all the transactions that are routed through the ACU mechanism are to be denominated in dollars and not in local currencies as it used to be.

The new arrangement therefore seeks to address the basic concerns of the traders as well as the bankers who felt more convenient in dealing with dollar as the medium of exchange. The system however, continues with the same institutional set up as was there under the old mechanism with minor modifications. While the unit of account has henceforth been changed to the US dollar and the banks are now expected to maintain. ACU dollar account with their correspondent banks, the entire process of clearing and netting of multilateral settlement remains the same. It is this particular feature that needs to be critically analysed in greater detail to make a correct assessment of the clearing role played by the ACU in the present context

The new dispensation was primarily aimed at overcoming one of the major grievance that the traders were having *vis-a-vis* the ACU, namely the inability to get repatriated earnings in dollars. While this limitation alongwith the associated shortcomings such as those relating to availing pre-shipment credit the time lag in announcement of exchange rates, inability to get forward cover etc., appear to have been overcome, there have been other sources of discontent in the recent times. The modified ACU mechanism now has to compete with an environment where currencies are freely traded in the foreign exchange market. At the same time, easing up of the foreign exchange position in major member countries has made access to foreign exchange resources much easier. Added to this is the introduction of latest techniques in payments settlement compared to the relatively slow mechanism through which the ACU operates, a point which will be elaborated a little later.

One of the most pressing problems faced under the ACU mechanism as of now is the delay that takes place even now in the final settlement of the exporters claim. For the transaction taking place outside the ACU mechanism, there is virtually no need for the involvement of the respective Central Banks.[14] This means that there is no need for the commercial banks to notify their respective Central Banks about remitting their export proceeds to their correspondent bank account in New York. On the other hand, under the ACU arrangement, the commercial banks have to notify their credit and debit position to their respective Central Banks, which in turn ask the ACU Secretariat to make surplus or the deficit accounting entry as the case may be. This entire process takes at least three days including the deal date. Whereas for the non ACU transactions, the settlement takes place on the same day itself. A delay of this magnitude for an exporter could mean a lot given the sharp fluctuations that exist in foreign currency markets. Besides, in certain cases (for instance in Sri Lanka), non-ACU exporters may retain their earnings abroad for a period of one year, whereas under the ACU mechanism, they have to get their export proceeds back (as the Central Bank has to report the transactions to the ACU).[15]

The commercial banks too, do not appear very enthusiastic about the present dispensation. The involvement at the level four banks (two commercial banks and two Central Banks) makes the process a lot more cumbersome. A commercial bank has to fund its nostro account in its correspondent bank in the other member country at the spot value. Since the transaction goes through various levels, it never reaches there at that date (takes three days). On the other hand, it allowed to purchase and sell foreign exchange in the free market, not only will the payment settlement system be fast, but also the rates would be the best possible available.

There have been times when commercial banks have advised their correspondent bank to fund the ACU dollar account of the exporter's bank, but funding of these accounts have got delayed—at times because of lack of availability of funds with corresponding bank as its Central Bank does not allow it to have overdraft facilities.[16] This often puts the credibility of the commercial bank at stake. Moreover, if the corresponding accounts are overdrawn, then one has to pay a lot more by way of interest charges.

At the Central Bank level however, there does not appear to be much difference as they continue with their earlier role of agent banks engaged with settling the net outstanding balances with other Central Banks through the ACU mechanism. Being at the core of ACUs functioning, the Central Banks through their representation on the ACU Board monitor the developments among the member countries. Besides, it is the Central Banks which effectively tend to make use of the only tangible benefit which the ACU mechanism seems to be offering, namely the interim credit facility of two months which may further be extended by two months as stipulated by the ACU SWAP mechanism. However, given the changing nature and status of Central Banks in the liberalising member countries, there is a need at the same time for an internal assessment as to whether the ACU mechanism in its present form does offer some concrete gains or not.

Thus one can clearly see that even in the present set up, the role of the ACU as a clearing mechanism has evidently been subject to certain limitations inherent in the Union. Despite modifications in tune with global/regional economic environment, persistence with the old institutional structure has left the mechanism more cumbersome and less user friendly. The problem is further compounded by the inadequate level of technological advancements among the member countries as far as payments systems are concerned. Some banks in the member countries are yet to be fully introduced to the modem methods such as SWIFT (Society for World-wide Interbank Financial Telecommunication) and RTGS (Real Time Gross Settlement) which can make up for the delays that take place in the payment systems.[17] It is precisely because of these limitations in the mechanism leading to undue delay in payments that there appears to be disenchantment among the traders and bankers who are operating through this facility. The need for an efficient payment system has been regarded as supporting changes in underlying trading and trade activities. Besides, with increasing economic global integration and operating linkages among national financial systems, payments systems are found to be interconnected.[18] It is not that the ACU meetings have not acknowledged this.[19] The 33rd Board Meeting held at Tehran identified some of the key aspects that needed to be remedied to make the facility more functional. This included among others : holding of sufficient ACU dollar accounts by member banks, faster settlement of Payments on the same day through SWIFT, to redress members complaints, similar benefits as extended to non-ACU traders. To ensure smooth flow of funds across various economies, payment mechanisms should not only have uniformity but must also save time.

Under such a scenario, there is a drastic need for the introduction of a more speedy and efficient payment system within the ACU if it is to continue its present role of clearing intra-regional trade transactions. Only then can one think of a greater role for the Union which we shall further discuss as we study the functional aspects of the ACU facility.

5.3 Functional Aspects

Having discussed the structural elements of the ACU mechanism which generally deal with the institutional set up within which the facility operates, we now come to the functional dimension of the mechanism, which has more to do with the way ACU has performed. The performance has to be seen in the light of some of the broad objectives that were laid out initially. We shall touch upon some of these issues while critically analysing each of them.

Economizing on Foreign Exchange—As stated earlier, saving on the hard currency while settling intra-regional transactions was among the major objectives of the ACU. Savings on foreign exchange by using ACU facility does not appear to carry much significance ever since it switched over to dollar denominated transactions. As a result, the savings of foreign exchange which could have amounted to a significant portion of the total trade no longer remain as the clearing trade too is to be denominated in dollars now. The only manifest advantage as far as foreign exchange savings is concerned is related to the benefit of deferred settlement for two months that is offered under the ACU system.

ACU as an Agent for Greater Monetary Interaction

As pointed out earlier, fostering greater monetary interaction among the member countries was among the major objectives that were laid out at the time of ACU's inception. It was expected to promote monetary cooperation among the participants and closer relations among the banking systems in their territories and thereby contribute to the expansion of trade and economic activity among the member countries.[20] Given the fact that ACU provided an appropriate forum for Central Bankers to meet every year and monitor and analyse the economic developments among the member countries, such expectations were, but natural.

However, a closer scrutiny of ACU's functioning over the years and the nature and level of Central Banker's interaction reveals that rather than as a forum for enlightened discussion on critical issues, these were more or less conducted like routine meetings where interaction remained mostly confined to discussing each other's economic performance. Not that the meetings did not discuss the important issues facing the member countries, but somehow the action never seemed to match the intent. For instance, most of the annual ACU meetings in the recent years have discussed growing instability in the global financial system and implications for the developing countries, yet they have hardly ever come out with a concrete action plan on how could the member countries take collective action to prevent such disturbances in their respective economies.[21] Probably the main problem has been the limited mandate that the meetings have had, which has prevented the board from going beyond the structured agenda that is to be followed.

While the Articles of agreement clearly state promotion of monetary cooperation among the participants as one of the key objectives, there has been no concrete progress on this front. In other words, ACU suffers severely from its limitations as a deliberative body as it is unable to take decisions beyond those which have a direct bearing on the mechanism as such. This has prevented ACU from taking major policy decisions on crucial issues such as exchange rate coordination, monetary management etc., which are generally taken as the basic elements of monetary cooperation in any regional arrangement. An agreement on these variables is key to the maintenance of balance in trade and capital flows in a region. To that extent, ACU has not emerged as an agency for enhanced monetary interaction among the member countries. While part of the problem arises due to the limited mandate that the ACU has on these issues, the other broad factor relates to the lack of coordination between the ACU and other regional integration initiatives which in any case are at a nascent stage. It is this particular theme that we now turn to.

ACU and Regional Integration Initiatives

The relative performance of a regional body is generally judged by the degree of regional integration that it seeks to achieve. To that extent, ACU, at the time of its inception was visualised as a body that would contribute to the expansion of trade and economic activity among the countries of the ESCAP region. Thus there was certainly an expectation that it would play a major role in supplementing regional cooperation initiatives although regional integration *per se* was seen as a rather distant objective at that time. Besides, it was considered that such a region-wise clearing facility could co-exist and function in cooperation with sub-regional or less than regional arrangements in Asia and the Pacific. The Board of Directors were also mandated to make arrangements to cooperate with other general, regional or sub-regional international organisations or other clearing arrangements among countries within or outside the ESCAP region.[22] The ACU therefore could not have merely interacted with other regional organizations, but also could have acted as a link between various regional groupings within Asia as its membership covered countries belonging to both West, South and South East Asia.

The ACU, however was not able to impart greater momentum to regional integration/cooperation efforts within the region. Neither could it really establish any formal linkage with such organisations outside. In fact the ACU has been the only clearing arrangement which has not been part of broader regional economic grouping. As Table 5.2 shows, all the other clearing arrangements have been part of a larger economic cooperation grouping.

Table 5.2: Clearing Arrangements under Regional Economic Groupings

Clearing Arrangement	*Regional Economic*
West African Clearing House	Economic Cooperation Organisation of West African States (ECOWAS).
Clearing House for the Eco nomic Community of Central African States (CHCAS)	Economic Community of Central African States (ECCAS)
Clearing House for Economic of Great Lakes.	Economic Community of Great Lakes (CEPGL).
Preferential Trade Area Clearing House (PTACH)	Preferential Trade Area for Eastern and Southern Africa.
Reciprocal Payments and Credit System (RPCS)	Latin American Integration Association (LAIA).
Central American Clearing House (CACH)	Central American Common Market (CACM)
Caribbean Multilateral Clearing Facility (CMCF)	Caribbean Community (CARICOM)

Source: Compiled from Handbook of Economic Integration and Cooperation Groupings of Developing Countries (Geneva: UNCTAD, 1995).

Unlike the other regional clearing arrangements where the efforts at broader regional integration were simultaneously pursued, the ACU functioned in relative isolation. As we shall elaborate a little later, this was both because of the inbuilt agenda that ACU pursued and lack of direct correspondence with any regional grouping. The regional cooperation efforts in this case often worked independently of the ACU process although occasional attempts were made to try to explore whether some linkages could be drawn between them.[23] It would be essential to explore the possible reasons for ACU not being able to complement the regional cooperation efforts in a major way.

First and the foremost, as stated earlier, the ACU itself sought to pursue a very limited agenda—namely that of acting as a clearing facility among the member countries. It never sought to expand its role beyond that of clearing. Its role as a possible credit/reserve fund facility was never really visualised in a serious manner despite several suggestions on the feasibility and desirability of such an arrangement.[24] As we know, credit arrangements and reserve funds are very essential components of regional cooperation efforts. Traditionally, they have been known to support the members facing short-term balance of payments problems. Such a facility has also been regarded as useful supplement to member countries who have exhausted their credit tranches from the IMF.[25] The role and relevance of such arrangements has attracted greater attention in the recent times especially in view of the East Asian economic crisis. The ACU on its part never really thought on lines of expanding its role as a payments union which would have been a step further from a mere clearing union. Such an arrangement could have given the requisite support to the member countries (especially smaller ones) in their liberalisation efforts in terms of enabling them to withstand occasional shocks. An expanded role of the ACU offering some kind of a short-term balance of payment support would certainly have been an attractive proposition for the regional integration efforts.

The other major reason appears to be the fact that ACU never really found itself directly overlapping with a particular regional cooperation initiative. The regional cooperation arrangements in Asia were by and large scattered, had different if not divergent agendas and were themselves at times constrained by their own long-term goals. For instance, the seven member countries of the ACU were at the same time members of three separate regional cooperation arrangements. Iran and Pakistan were the founding members of Economic Cooperation Organisation (ECO). Bangladesh, Nepal, India, Pakistan and Sri Lanka are members of the South Asian Association for Regional Cooperation (SAARC). Myanmar, not being member of any such arrangement for a long time, has recently been inducted into Association of South-East Asian Nations (ASEAN).

The ECO is at present giving a thought to form a mutual payments arrangement among the member countries, which would be on the lines of the erstwhile RCD Union for Multilateral Payments Arrangements. In fact, ACU even extended its invitation to the ECO member states to join the

ACU. The Central Bank of Iran was to host the first Expert Meeting on Mutual Payment Arrangement in February 1999.[26] The ASEAN had also a SWAP agreement with the purpose of providing immediate short-term SWAP facilities to ASEAN member countries with temporary international liquidity problems.[27] Paradoxically, of the three groupings, only SAARC appears to be significantly represented at the ACU. However, in absence of any formal linkage between the two, there has not been any kind of coordinated effort between them. Although SAARC has been represented at one of the ACU Board Meetings held at Kathmandu, yet there does not appear to be any formalisation of this institutional interaction at present.[28] The only visible development has been the meeting of SAARC FINANCE at the sidelines of the ACU Board Meetings.[29] Despite this, the fact remains that SAARC can very well make use of the ACU platform to complement its own regional integration efforts that are under way. This point needs to be elaborated a bit further.

SAARC has accorded high priority to achievement of a free trade area within the region. While one cannot go into the feasibility of this objective as it is beyond the scope of the present study, nonetheless, one can visualize a great need for monetary and financial coordination in the area once the intra-regional trade expansion gains further momentum. Not only would it call for a quicker payments and settlement system among the member countries but also a closer coordination among the Central Banks of the region so that a harmonious trade policy is effectively coordinated with a sound monetary and exchange rate policy. There has also been the view that ACU's role needs to be evaluated in the context of regional cooperation, strengthening the SAARC spirit and the role of proposed trade liberalization.[30] The ACU in its present form appears to be incapable of meeting these requirements. However, a bit of restructuring and fine-tuning of the present mechanism may provide just the right kind of institutional basis that is needed to forge greater integration within the region. There would be two major components of this restructuring. First of all, ACU must ensure that the delays in payment settlements are taken care of either by induction of new technology or by modifying the institutional mechanism. Secondly as pointed out earlier, it should seek an expanded role as a short-term credit facility that could take care of temporary balance of payment imbalances of the member countries arising out of intra-regional trade expansion.

There would be a critical area that would come in way of ACU complementing its efforts with SAARC. Bhutan and Maldives are the two SAARC countries which were not members of the ACU for a long time. While Bhutan has joined, there are no indications that Maldives might be considering joining the same.[31] Thus there is a need to continue efforts to include Maldives as a member so that SAARC finds full representation in the ACU. This way there would be no need for a separate clearing and payments arrangement for SAARC. The requirement of a regional monetary and payments mechanism in South Asia may thus be fulfilled by the remaining countries joining the ACU—a point which has been emphasised by several other studies.[32] This would also be consistent with the ACU charter which clearly allows for cooperation with other regional organisations.

5.4 The Issue of Enlarged Membership

A major area where ACU has not been able to achieve the desired objective has been its inability to attract new members despite its continuous efforts in that direction. Ever since its inception, ACU has been trying hard to rope in more countries as members, but somehow they have not been motivated enough to join the union. Part of the reason lies in the fact that other countries (especially from South East Asian region) have always considered the prevailing modes of international payments settlements as more beneficial in maintaining their linkages with rest of the world. For example, having correspondent banking relationships in financial centres such as New York and London enables them to integrate with the global financial system in a better way. The ACU mechanism was considered to be too archaic in times of convertible currencies and liberalising exchange rates.

This despite the fact that international monetary and financial developments in the recent times have created conditions whereby joining such a union could have been beneficial. At a time when volatile movements in exchange rates may have a debilitating impact on a country's balance of trade, a mechanism, that encourages use of bilateral currencies to settle mutual trade could provide a useful mode of conserving foreign exchange. For instance some of the post-Soviet Central Asian republics did express their keenness to join the union, yet they were constrained by the fact that they did not have a proper central banking and payment mechanism to enable them to become members.[33] Moreover, the South East Asian currency crisis in 1997, showed the hazards associated with unfettered currency movements. There were at one point of time discussions on some kind of a bilateral currency arrangement within the region to minimize the use of dollar—a kind of facility that ACU could have automatically offered. Yet there was no indication that the affected countries would go in for its membership.

Thus we see that by and large, ACU has been virtually left untouched by the global and regional economic developments in terms of its scope and feasibility. In fact, the responses of the ACU to the changing economic environment have been limited to the impact that they have had on the procedural mechanism rather than focussing on a transformed role for the Union *perse*. In other words, more specifically, neither has it been able to find a place in the broader under currents of regional economic integration process, nor has it been able to make use of the opportunity provided by the fluctuating regional financial environment to outline a new role for itself. It is exactly on this premise that there is a case for redefining the role of the ACU so that it is able to justify its relevance. This brings us finally to the broader elements of the strategy that ACU should follow to make it more relevant to the needs and requirements of the members nations.

5.5 Elements of the New Strategy

Our discussion in the previous section show that there is a two fold issue that the ACU faces today. The first has more to do with the internal dynamics of the facility in terms of its procedural functioning. The other is a more systemic one that tries to put the ACU in the scheme of broader regional economic environment. It is broadly on these two counts, the ACU should seek to redefine its role.

First and the foremost, there is an immediate need to address some of the basic concerns related to the present functioning of the mechanism itself. To be more precise, the ACU should look into the causes of the delays that still plague the payments settlement procedures. The delays arise on two counts. First due to the procedures adopted within the mechanism itself and second, due to the distinct payment procedures followed by the member countries which often leads to discrepancies in the settlement process. In this regard, the ACU could become an agency for smoother settlement. It provides an ideal platform to discuss the member's payments procedures and also redresses any grievance that members may have with regard to intra-regional payments settlement. As a step further, ACU could also enable the member countries to harmonise their respective procedures towards payments.

Secondly, the attempts towards enhancing the role of the ACU must focus on establishing facilities that favour regional integration efforts *per se*. In this regard, there is a strong case for strengthening the credit arrangement within the ACU, which at present is interim and is related merely to the clearing trade. An enhanced credit arrangement within the ACU that caters to intra-regional trade imbalances is very much required keeping in view the lopsided balance of trade that exists (esp. with regard to India and her neighbours). An enhanced credit facility would supplement the process of regional integration within South Asia, apart from allaying some fears of smaller countries with regard to the proposed free trade area.

Lastly, as envisaged as per the original objectives, ACU must become the coordinating agency for enhanced monetary interaction among the member countries. Given the greater vulnerability in the global and regional financial system, there is an urgent need for a coordinated approach on the issues of monetary and exchanges rate policies rather than the mere discussion and exchange that goes on at present. Besides, there is also a need for greater interaction among commercial banks in the region, better exchange of information on their respective procedures and a kind of mechanism which is able to settle any grievance of the traders with regard to settlement of their payments. ACU in its modified role would be the right kind of agency to perform this function. A positive development in this direction has been the decision at the last Board meeting held in Dhaka in May 2007 to form a technical committee, led by central bank of Sri Lanka, to examine a multi-currency settlement option in ACU transactions and possible ways to provide incentives to correspondent banks under ACU including interest in balances in ACU "nostro accounts."[34]

NOTES

1. See the extracts from the statement by U. Nyun, Executive Secretary of ECAFE, *Report of the meeting of Senior officials of the Government & Central Ranks for the establishment of An Asian Clearing Union,* TRADE/ACU/MOGCB/6, 12th March. 1973, p. 22
2. The primary constraints in the ACU mechanism related to non-availability of pre-shipment and post-shipment credit to ACU exporters, absence of any forward cover for the select currencies, time lag in the announcement of exchange rates etc.
3. Article I of the Agreement Establishing the Asian Clearing Union.
4. Article VIII Section 2 or the Agreement Establishing the ACU. The votes of all of the Directors means the votes of all the Directors and not merely of those present and voting
5. The Secretary General represents the Union at various regional and international for and acts as a critical link between the Union and potential members.
6. The last six meetings of the Board of Directors prior to 2000, have

rarely seen full representation by Central Bank Governors. At the 26th meeting of the BOD held at Teheran. Just two Central Bank Governors Represented their countries.

7. At the 26th Board meeting in Teheran in May 1997, it was decided that for each Annual Board Meeting, a topic which is of common interest and concern to the Central Banks for example monetary policy, balance of payments, exchange rate arrangements etc., may be selected for discussion and exchange of experiences of members countries. For the Annual meeting held in 1998, the subject of "Balance of Payments was selected. See the *ACU Annual Report 1997*, p. 96.
8. Interview with the ACU Secretary General. 7th April, 1999, Kathmandu.
9. Report of the Secretary General on item G Agenda Discussion on the enlargement of the ACU, p. 5, presented at the 28th *Annual Meeting of Board of Directors*. 5-6th April, 1999, Kathmandu.
10. The earlier provision of routing the transactions through respective Central Bank was done away with in 1980.
11. Based on the study on 'Payments Arrangements and Monetary Cooperation in South Asia' by B.K. Madan and Pritam Singh, cited in M.Y. Khan, "Asian Clearing Union: An Assessment", *RBI Bulletin*, February 1991.
12. Paper circulated to the Advisory Committee of Permanent Representatives and Other Representatives Designated by the Members of the Commission, 141st Session ESCAP OES/ACPR/ 69, 2 February 1990, p. 4.
13. R. Janakiraman, Critical Study of the Procedure Regarding the Operations of the ACU (Bombay, 1995), p. 4
14. Interview with official of thc Central Bank of Sri Lanka, 4th January 2000, Colombo.
15. *Ibid*.
16. Interview with Mr. D.B. Wijetunga, Head, Foreign Exchange Division, Commercial Bank, Colombo, 6th January 2000.
17. SWIFT is a cooperative organization created and owned by banks that operate a network that facilitates the exchange of payments and other financial messages between financial institutions (including broker dealers and securities companies) throughout the world. A SWIFT payment message is an instruction to transfer funds, the exchange of funds (settlement) subsequently takes place over a payment system or through correspondent banking relationships RTGS is a gross settlement system in which processing and settlement take place in real time (continuously).

18. Yawar Shah, "The changing payments landscape and its implications for Correspondent Banks", *International Correspondent Banking Review*, 1997-98. p. 4.
19. See ACU *Annual Report* 2004.
20. See Article II Section (c) of the Agreement Establishing the Asian Clearing Union.
21. The Address by Satyendra P. Shrestha, Governor Nepal Rastra Bank at the 28th ACU Board of Directors Meeting at Kathmandu, 5 April, 1999. The Governor called for a renewed and revamped role of the ACU in the light fluctuating international financial situation.
22. Article X of the Agreement Establishing the Asian Clearing Union.
23. For instance, the invitation to SAARC at the 28th Annual Board Meeting was implicitly aimed at exploring the possibility of linkage between the two.
24. Charan D. Wadhwa, Study on the Establishment of a Reserve Fund to Support the Activities of the Asian Clearing Union. UNIDO/UNDP — RAS/1/070-1101) 1987 as quoted by Ercan Uygur, 'The Asian Clearing Union: An Assessment and Prospects, RAS/81/070 May 1984, p. 23.
25. I.N. Mukherjee, "Towards Financial and Monetary Cooperation in South Asia". *South Asia Journal*, Vol. No.2, 1990, p. 145.
26. Report on Item 6 Agenda discussion on the enlargement of the ACU delivered by Mohammad Firouzdor, Secretary General, ACU at the 28th Board of Directors Meeting, Kathmandu, 5-6 April, 1999.
27. Article I of the ASEAN SWAP Arrangement in Michael T. Skully, *ASEAN Financial Cooperation Development in Banking, Finance and Insurance* (London, 1985).
28. Discussion with SAARC Secretary General, 8th May, 1999, Kathmandu
29. SAARC FINANCE, shall be explained further in the next chapter. It is the forum of Finance Secretaries and Central Bank Governors of member countries who discuss monetary issues in the region. The last such meeting was held in Dhaka in May 2007.
30. Synthesis Report of a Regional Workshop on Payments and Monetary Cooperation in the South Asian Region, 3-4th December 1994, Dhaka, p. 6.
31. The representative of The Royal Monetary Authority of Bhutan attended the 28th ACU Board Meeting at Kathmandu in April 1999. The earlier efforts of the ACU Secretariat to involve Maldives have evidently not borne fruit.

32. S.S. Colombage, *Monetary and Payments Cooperation* (Colombo, 1993), p. 91. Also see the Report of the Expert Group Meeting on South Asian Financial and Payments Cooperation, New Delhi 23 & 24 August, p. VII.
33. *ACU Annual Report* 1996, p. 4.
34. http://www.thebangladeshtoday.com/archive/May%2007/16-05-2007.htm.

Chapter 6

Post-Script: Political Economy of Monetary Cooperation in South Asia

There has been a renewed interest in the area of monetary and payment cooperation in South Asia in the recent times. This has been partly due to growing debates at the pan Asian level of deepening monetary and financial interaction as part of the larger Asian integration debate. The Asian financial crisis of the 1990s and the subsequent recovery necessitated a greater discussion on developing mechanisms and instruments that could preempt and counter similar crises having a contagion effect. The other reason has been the pace and nature of economic integration process underway within South Asia, where there has been a growing disenchantment with the inability of the SAARC process moving into certain core areas of economic cooperation. It is widely perceived that SAARC has not kept pace with the times and may lose out unless the spirit and practice of deeper economic cooperation is universally pursued. The area of monetary cooperation in South Asia therefore has to meet both the political and economic tests before it can become one of the key pillars of regional integration in the region.

6.1 Asian Monetary Cooperation: Recent Debates

As discussed in the initial chapters, monetary and financial cooperation has been one of the key themes in South-South Cooperation debates in general and the Asian cooperation efforts in particular. The contours of the debate however were shaped by the need and the desire for collective self-reliance in a world, which was still fragmented in terms of economic policy orientation and outlook. Most of the developing countries including those of Asia, undergoing post-colonial economic transformation saw regional cooperation as a safeguard for the respective national economic systems, which were often inward oriented. Being part of a regional initiative was in no way seen as compromising with national policy autonomy as the degree of intra-regional economic penetration was limited. Having a deeper monetary and exchange rate alignment in Asia was still seen as an alien concept which fitted more within the parameters of regional integration Europe was witnessing.

The later part of 1990s, coinciding with the culmination of the Asian Financial crisis and simultaneous opening of the hitherto closed economies of the region altered the context in which monetary cooperation issues were being discussed. The regional and sub-regional arrangements prior to the crisis mainly focused on research and training among central banks, clearing and settlement, reinsurance and small scale development financing and swap arrangements.[1] Subsequent to the crisis, greater interest emerged in exploring greater forms of monetary and financial cooperation particularly in the East Asian Region. The factors contributing to this were listed as[2] :

(a) *First* the unexpected and unprecedented contagion effect of crisis suggested that financial crisis in individual countries should not be a matter of indifference to other countries because such countries may have similar spillover effects;
(b) *Second,* since the crisis had its origin in weakness in financial and corporate sectors among several countries, cross country cooperation on financial sector reform issues is considered beneficial to all;
(c) *Third,* there is increasing awareness in the region that policy dialogue at the regional level can usefully complement national-level policy-making and global level policy dialogue.

Some of the initiatives that emerged in the region (particularly the East Asia-Pacific) included:

(1) *The Chiang Mai Initiative (CMI)* : The CMI, created in May 2000 established a system of SWAP arrangements within the ASEAN +3 countries.[3] These bilateral SWAP arrangements were intended to provide liquidity support for member countries that experienced short-term balance of payments deficits. The arrangement has worked relatively well over the recent years and the total bilateral SWAPS at the end of 2003 were estimated to be around $35 billion. The arrangement has enabled increasing availability of liquidity and encouraged greater informal mechanisms of policy dialogue and review among the ASEAN+3 countries.[4]

(2) *The Asian Bond Fund* : Developing of an Asian Bond Market was seen as an effective way to keep Asian savings in Asia rather than sending them to other countries and also to guard against future crises as they would be able to raise more funds in their own currencies. In this direction, an Asian Bond Fund (ABF) was launched in June 2003 by the Executive's Meeting of East Asia-Pacific Central Banks (EMEAP). The initial round of ABF was valued at around $1 billion and was earmarked for investment in a basket of dollar denominated bonds issued by Asian Sovereign and quasi sovereign issuer's in EMEAP.[5]

(3) *ASEAN Surveillance Process (ASP)* : The ASP was officially launched in October 1998 based on the principles of peer review for all member states and complimentarity with the global surveillance undertaken by the IMF. Under this mechanism, all ASEAN member states are to provide the ASEAN surveillance Process regular updates as is to be done for the IMF article six.[6]

Alongside these initiatives taken up to enhance monetary and financial cooperation in Asia, there has also been a fresh debate on whether Asia constitutes an optimum currency area, and therefore can the region have a common currency. Such discussions have generated keen interest among policy makers and academia following the launch of the Euro and comparative inferences have become inevitable. The analysis has focused on both the political and economic parameters that would determine the feasibility of the idea. As pointed out earlier, for a region to be an eligible candidate for a common currency and a monetary union, symmetric patterns of shocks, free mobility of labour and convergence of fiscal and monetary indicators are a prerequisite. The analysis has shown that the financial disturbance in Asian countries is the major source of asymmetric shocks and therefore provides the strongest argument against a common peg. It is pointed out that Asia's emerging economies need exchange rate flexibility and monetary independence to cope with financial disturbances.[7]

The other argument against a common currency borders more on the political logic. In Europe , the initial conditions for coordinated approach and eventual integration did exist. Despite frequent opposition to surrendering national policy autonomy and the desire to retain policy independence. Europe was able to work its way through to a minimum acceptable convergence in a phased manner as the integrationist tendencies got strengthened. In Asia on the other hand, neither the initial conditions, nor the events that took place thereafter provided the right basis for similar political and economic congruence.[8] As a result, the integrationist tendencies in Asia were premised more on loose networks of cooperation rather than strong supranational institutions and this was pretty much evident in the monetary domain. While Europe was able to create institutions such as the Committee of Central Bank Governors, the Monetary Committee, the European Commission, the European Monetary Institute and prospectively the European Central Bank, Asia has created SEANZA which conducts biennial central bank training courses, SEACEN, a ten member grouping holding annual meeting of governors and EMEAP, the eleven member grouping entrusted with sharing and collating information.[9]

Thus Asian countries thought it prudent to adopt a gradual approach towards monetary cooperation, focusing more on regular exchange of views on monetary matters, including reserve management, bank supervision, payments and settlement systems etc. While to a great extent such a gradual approach was necessitated by the internal preparedness (or lack of it), in certain instances it was the lack of support from outside which proved to be the deterring factor. A point in the case to substantiate the latter point was the issue of creating a reserve facility for Asian countries. While the issue of reserve management has always been high on the agenda of Asian monetary authorities, they have not always been clear on what would be the best way to manage the dollar assets running into billions of dollars prudently.[10] As mentioned earlier, the proposal for an Asian Monetary Fund (AMF) mooted by Japan after the Asian financial crisis to bring stability to Asian currency and financial markets was rejected by the IMF and the United States. The argument given was that it would create a moral hazard problem and could challenge the IMF leadership.[11]

Having discussed the developments in the field of monetary and payments cooperation in the larger Asia-Pacific Region I the recent times, it is interesting to note the debate and the policies within the sub-regional context of South Asia.

6.2 The South Asian Setting

South Asia has fared relatively better in terms of economic growth and financial stability in the 1990s, partly because the region was gradually opening up to economic reforms and liberalization and was therefore to a large extent immune to the financial crisis that engulfed the South East Asian Countries. The region experienced an average rate of growth of around 5.5 to 6 per cent in the 1990s and as per the latest available figures it ranked as the second highest growing region in the world during 2004-05, experiencing 8.7 per cent growth in GDP and 6.9 per cent growth per capita, next only to East Asia and the Pacific Region.[12] India , constituting more than three-fourth of the region's GDP, population and geography, led the charge with growth rate of 9.2 per cent and 7.7 per cent in GDP and per capita respectively.

Such impressive figures however mask two very important variables which will be key to South Asia's ability to sustain growth rates in future in a collective manner. First, the region still ranks fairly low in meeting certain basic human development parameters. As long as a majority of South Asians continues to face basic deprivation, a skewed pattern of growth will put a break on ability of the region to generate inclusive growth.[13] Secondly, despite nearly two decades of regionalism, South Asia is yet to experience deeper economic integration, which could again help in making grow together by sustaining the successes of the recent past. Shallow regionalism in South Asia therefore has prevented any meaningful and creative interpretation of regional cooperation which could have enabled the region to move to the next stage of its economic and political evolution. Cooperation in the field of monetary area therefore has to be judged against the backdrop of this paradox.

South Asia is often regarded as a region without regionalism, despite more than two decades of the formal institutional mechanism of SAARC. The grouping since its inception adopted a cautious approach to regional cooperation, particularly in those areas where two or more member nations could be anticipated as having differences. The association adopted a broad mandate of social and economic cooperation and decided to keep bilateral contentious issues out of the deliberations, outlining at the same time that all decisions were to be taken by consensus.[14] While this was ostensibly done to prevent differences between the two largest members —India and Pakistan from hampering regional deliberations, the actual functioning of SAARC over the years shows that political factors have indeed prevented cooperation in core economic matters in a major way. The creation of the South Asian Free Trade Area (SAFTA) which is perhaps the most significant and long awaited accomplishment of the grouping bears an ample testimony to that.[15] Deeper economic integration in South Asia therefore remained a non starter despite some of the very powerful arguments that have been given in favour of a economic union in SAARC. The SAARC Group of Eminent Persons, established in 1998 to advise on the new vision for SAARC proposed the ultimate goal of an Economic Union within SAARC by 2020 in a phased manner.[16] The actual developments at the ground level however left a lot to be desired.

Nevertheless there has been in the recent times a greater debate on the feasibility of greater monetary interaction within SAARC ranging from creating of regional institutions aimed at supplementing development finance to the feasibility of a full fledged monetary union and common currency within South Asia. A closer scrutiny of these development shows that while there might be a general consensus on creating regional mechanisms for development financing and consultation, time may not yet be ripe for envisaging a deeper monetary integration or a union within the region.

- *South Asian Development Fund* : One of the most concrete developments in South Asia on creating a regional fund has been in the form of the South Asian Development Fund (SADF) which was proposed at the sixth SAARC Summit at Male in 1991 to mobilize external funds for the development of South Asia. The basic objective of SADF is to provide finance for industrial development, poverty alleviation, protection of the environment, balance of payments support and promotion of economic projects in the SAARC region. SADF has three windows for (a) identification and development of projects, (b) institutional and human resource development projects, and (c) social and infrastructural projects. It has been proposed to establish a permanent Secretariat and create a substantially large core capital base for the consideration of its member states, besides the conversion of the same into a SAARC Development Fund.[17] There has however been a general disenchantment with the progress the Fund has made since nearly a decade and a half of its existence.[18] (See Annexure for detailed outline of SADF).
- *SAARC FINANCE:* The establishment of SAARC FINANCE has been the other major development

relating to monetary cooperation in South Asia. It is an organization of Governors of Central Banks and secretaries of SAARC member countries, with the broader objective of promoting cooperation among Central Banks and Finance Ministries. It envisages harmonizing banking legislations and practices, working towards a more efficient payments mechanism and higher monetary and exchange rate cooperation, forging closer cooperation on macro-economic policies, studying the impact of global financial developments in the region, monitoring international currency and capital flows and reforms in the system and undertaking research, training and network activities in the region.[19] (See Annexure for detailed mandate of SAARC FINANCE)

While creation of the first ever body on SAARC on monetary and financial issues is certainly a welcome development, its role has to go beyond the purely consultative mechanism that it provides rather than being a more policy oriented forum. One is yet to see how different and pragmatic such deliberations are than those already provided for by the Asian Clearing Union mechanism, with near overlapping membership, which has a similar mandate as far as the consultative process is concerned. Moreover, SAARC FINANCE deliberations at times have adopted an exclusivist position by being less inclined to involve official SAARC representatives and those of other regional bodies in its deliberations, a position that negates the very essence of deepening regional integration.[20] Nevertheless, SAARC FINANCE deliberations have indeed led to useful exchange of views on Exchange Rate Regimes, Balance of Payments Crisis, Reserve Management and Intervention Strategy and Monetary Policy and Exchange Rate Regimes.[21] It remains to be seen how India's recent chairmanship of SAARC FINANCE instills greater urgency in the mechanism.[22]

The above developments in the realm of institutionalized monetary cooperation in South Asia has been of late supplemented with a rudimentary yet thought provoking debate about the feasibility of monetary union and common currency in South Asia. Unlike the debates in the eighties and the early nineties, the recent works have had greater methodological and analytical rigour as is elaborated below.

6.3 Whither South Asian Monetary Union?

The issue of common currency and monetary union in South Asia acquired political significance (though short-lived) for the first time when the then Indian Prime Minister mooted the desirability of a common currency within SAARC in 2003.[23] Expectedly, there was a spurt of interest within the official and non-official circles on the idea as divergent opinions started flowing in. The immediate response by and large was guarded and it was pointed out that a lot more needed to be done of the exchange rate front before embarking on this exercise.[24] More detailed studies conducted much earlier more or less reached a similar conclusion.

In one of the pioneering works in the area, the criteria of symmetry or non-symmetry of different shocks affecting SAARC countries to determine economic feasibility of a common currency were used.[25] The assumption was if the member countries face symmetric shocks, then the policy response in form of a common monetary and exchange rate policy also could be similar, thereby making the region the right candidate for common currency, and *vice versa*. Thus symmetry or asymmetry of shocks would indicate the potential economic cost of a fixed exchange rate for SAARC member countries. The study concluded that the region is not yet a suitable candidate for a common currency as it does not face a symmetric pattern of shocks. Implementation of a single currency would result in significant economic costs, as the domestic countries would be forced to undergo a costly adjustment process to ring their respective balance of payments into equilibrium. It favoured a slow but sure path, which would allow at least as much time as it did in Europe for South Asia to reach similar convergence.[26] Building up on this work further, it was argued that the costs associated with monetary cooperation might decrease as the level of regional integration deepens in South Asia. Therefore, ultimate long-term goal of monetary union in the long run may still remain a desirable one.[27]

There were other studies that focused more deeply on the macro-economic convergence criteria that are seen as critical to the creation of an eventual monetary union. The assumption was that if the member countries could achieve low inflation, low interest rates, and fiscal discipline and control volatility of exchange rates, it would create the suitable premise for the formation of a monetary union.[28] It came out with the following conclusions :

- *Exchange Rates*: For the period 1997-2002, though there was a wide difference in the value of different national currencies, the movements are very smooth and are moving together.
- *Inflation Rates*: The inflation rates for 1997-2002 have been very low as compared to early nineties and the volatility has also reduced and are converging for most of the countries. This is a sign of convergence.
- *Fiscal Deficits*: Fiscal deficits in South Asian countries for the same period have generally stood at a high level but it has also shown a declining trend.

It was therefore concluded that harmonizing inflation and exchange rate may not be a difficult task, but controlling fiscal deficit may pose a major challenge.[29]

Analysis of certain supply shocks found that correlation coefficients of supply shock for South Asia ranged between — 0.46 and 0.42 which was much less compared to the other regions. From the positive correlations among different countries, it was found that the following groups may be suitable candidates for an OCA : Group 1. India, Pakistan and Sri Lanka; Group 2 : India, Nepal and Sri Lanka; Group 3: Bangladesh, Nepal and Sri Lanka, Group 4: India, Maldives and Pakistan.[30] Keeping in mind the speed of adjustments to the disturbance and also similar specialization in production of similar exports make South Asia a good candidate for common currency. Besides arguments have been given for common labour laws and expanded role of the ACU to make the idea of currency union in South Asia more relevant.[31]

The minor variations in the above studies regarding the feasibility and desirability of a common currency in South Asia, all the studies are unanimous in their view that any steps towards monetary integration in South Asia will have to be backed by an express political commitment and desire on part of the South Asian leadership to have deeper economic integration. Until or unless there is a larger political mandate for deepening regional economic integration in a meaningful way, any hopes of enhancing monetary interaction in South Asia, much less the ultimate goal of monetary integration in South Asia will remain a distant dream.[32] A functional mechanism such as ACU may at best be used as starting point, but will remain a mere procedural and discursive mechanism unless it instills a greater focus through SAARC and its affiliated agencies.

Annexure to Chapter 6

I. Terms of Reference of SAARC FINANCE

(Approved by Twenty-second Session of Council of Ministers, Kathmandu, 2-3 January 2002)

A. Structure

1. SAARCFINANCE will be a permanent body at the level of Governors of Central Banks and Secretaries of Finance of SAARC Member States.
2. SAARCFINANCE shall submit its report to the SAARC Council of Ministers through SAARC Finance Ministers.
3. Each Central Bank will establish a cell to coordinate the activities of SAARCFINANCE.
4. The SAARC Secretariat would assist and coordinate activities of SAARCFINANCE. The Cell in the Central Bank of the country holding the Chairpersonship of SAARC could function as the SAARCFINANCE Secretariat.
5. SAARCFINANCE meetings of Central Bank Governors and the Secretaries of Finance shall be held at least twice a year at the time of the spring and annual meetings of the IMF and the World Bank.
6. SAARC Secretary-General or his representative will attend the SAARCFINANCE Meetings of Central Bank Governors and Secretaries of Finance whenever they are held in the SAARC region.

B. Broad Objectives of SAARC FINANCE

1. To promote cooperation among Central Banks and

Finance Ministries in SAARC Member Countries by staff visits and regular exchange of information.

2. To consider and propose harmonization of banking legislations and practices within the region etc.
3. To work towards a more efficient payment mechanism within the SAARC Region and strive for higher monetary and exchange cooperation.
4. To forge closer cooperation on macro-economic policies of SAARC Member States and to share experiences and ideas.
5. To study global financial developments and their impact on the region including discussions relating to emerging issues in the financial architecture, IMF and World Bank and other international lending agencies.
6. To monitor reforms of the international financial and monetary system and to evolve a consensus among SAARC countries in respect of the reforms.
7. To monitor international currency and capital flows and to work towards a common SAARC position.
8. To evolve wherever feasible joint strategies, plan and common approaches in international fora for mutual benefit particularly in the context of liberalisation of financial services.
9. To undertake training of staff of the Ministries of Finance, Central Banks and other financial institutions of the SAARC member countries in subjects relating to economics and finance.
10. To explore networking of the training institutions within the SAARC Region specialising in various aspects of monetary policy, exchange rate reforms, bank supervision and capital market issues.
11. To promote research on economic and financial issues for the mutual benefit of SAARC member countries.
12. To consider any other matter on the direction/request of the SAARC Finance Ministers, Council of Ministers or other SAARC bodies.

Source: http://www.saarc-sec.org/main.php?id=63&t=2.1

II. The South Asian Development Fund (SADF)

The South Asian Development Fund (SADF) was created in 1996 with the merger of the SAARC Fund for Regional Projects (SFRP) and the SAARC Regional Fund, as recommended by the Twenty-first Session of the Standing Committee and endorsed by the Sixteenth Session of the Council of Ministers (New Delhi, 18-19 December 1995). The SADF objectives are to support industrial development, poverty alleviation, protection of environment, institutional/human resource development and promotion of social and infrastructure development projects in the SAARC region. The Fund is to be utilized for projects in one or more SAARC countries which are of significant economic interest of 2 or more countries.

SADF started with a resource base of US $5 million under SFRP contributed on prorata basis by the SAARC Member States. It has a fund of about $6.6 million. SADF has the following Windows:

First window	:	Identification and development of projects
Second window	:	Institutional and human resources development
Third Window	:	Social development and infrastructure development

The SADF Secretariat, which has been rotating among the Nodal Development Financing Institutions (DFIs), receives project proposals from Government/public/private sectors through Nodal DFIs/National Focal Points as well as from recognized SAARC Bodies. DFIs are to take necessary measures to identify sponsors for implementation of projects for which studies have been completed. SADF has so far financed about 16 project studies.

The SAARC Development Fund (SDF)

In the last few years, SAARC has been considering proposals

like Poverty Alleviation Fund, Infrastructure Fund, South Asian Development Bank, Media Development Fund, and Voluntary Fund for the Differently Able Persons, in addition to the SADF. In order to avoid proliferation of funds, the First Meeting of Financial Experts was convened in September 2005 to look at the entire gamut of issues relating to funding of SAARC projects and programmes.

The Meeting of Financial Experts, amongst others, agreed that proliferation of financing mechanisms would pose administrative, financial and operational difficulties, including the question of fund mobilization and management. It recommended that the SADF be reconstituted into the SAARC Development Fund (SDF), with a permanent Secretariat, with three Windows: Social, Economic, and Infrastructure.

The Thirteenth SAARC Summit (Dhaka, 12-13 November 2005) decided to reconstitute the SADF into SDF to serve as the umbrella financial institution for all SAARC projects and programmes. The Leaders directed the Finance Ministers to look into the operational modalities of the Fund.

The Second Meeting of the Financial Experts (Kathmandu, 23-24 February 2006) recommended an initial corpus of USD 300 million for the Social Window. It agreed on the broad principles and essential functional elements for the SDF. The Social Window would primarily focus poverty alleviation and social development projects. The Infrastructure Window would cover projects in the areas such as energy, power, transportation, telecommunications, environment, tourism and other infrastructure areas. The Economic Window would primarily be devoted to non-infrastructural funding.

The First Meeting of the SAARC Finance Ministers (Islamabad, 11 July 2006) considered the recommendations and approved the Framework for SDF. The Meeting agreed on a roadmap for the creation of the SDF. This was endorsed by the Twenty-seventh Session of the Council (Dhaka, 1-2 August 2006).

Subsequently, the SDF Board has been constituted. The First Meeting of the SDF Board was held at the Secretariat on 20-22 February 2007 to consider the inputs developed through the studies undertaken on legal architecture and mobilisation/ generation of funds and other essential operational issues. The Meeting deliberated on various aspects of creating the SDF as a legal entity.

As agreed, an Inter-governmental Meeting on the SDF was held at the Secretariat on 15-16 March 2007 to consider the recommendations of the SDF Board. It examined draft of an agreement establishing the SDF as a juridical entity. Another Inter-governmental Meeting is anticipated soon to finalise the text of an Agreement.

Source: http://www.saarc-sec.org/printable.php?id=183

NOTES

1. ESCAP *Meeting the Challenges in an era of Globalization by Strengthening Regional Development Cooperation*, United Nations, New York, 2004, p. 101.
2. Y. Iwasaki, 'Monetary and Financial Cooperation in East Asia: the Way Ahead' Presentation made at the Boao Forum for Asia Conference, Hainan, China, 2 November 2003, as cited in ESCAP n.1.
3. ASEAN +3 included the ASEAN member countries along with Japan, China and South Korea.
4. ESCAP n.1, p. 104.
5. Members of EMEAP include the Reserve Bank of Australia, People's Bank of China, Honk Kong Monetary Authority, Bank of Indonesia, Bank of Japan, Bank of Korea, Bank Negara Malaysia, Reserve Bank of New Zealand, Bangko Sentralng Philipinas, Monetary Authority of Singapore and Bank of Thailand.
6. Ramgopala Aggrawal, 'Towards Asian Economic Community: Monetary and Financial Cooperation, RIS Discussion Paper No.33/2002.
7. Barry Eichengreen and Tamin Bayoumi, Is Asia an Optimum Currency Area? Can it be one? Regional, global and historical perspectives on Asian monetary relations in Stefan Collongton, Jean Pisani-Ferry and Yung Chul Park, *Exchange Rate Policies in Emerging Asian Countries* (London,1999), p. 358.
8. *Ibid*. p. 361.

9. *Ibid.* p. 364. South East Asia New Zealand Australia (SEANZA) is the oldest Central Bank Group in Asia founded in 1957 by Central Banks of 5 countries formerly part of the British Empire: Australia, India, New Zealand, Pakistan and Sri Lanka. Later on it was expanded to thirteen other countries. South East Asia Central Banks (SEACEN) was created in 1966 with ten members: Indonesia, Korea, Malaysia, Nepal, Philipines, Singapore, Sri Lanka, Thailand, Myanmar and Thailand.
10. Masahiro Sugita 'Round table discussion: Prospects for regional monetary cooperation' in Barry Eichengreen and Tamin Bayoumi, n. 7, p. 371.
11. Ramgopal Agarwala, n. 6, p. 8.
12. World Bank, World Development Indicators, 2007, p. 16.
13. See Human Development in South Asia, 2005, p. 12.
14. See the SAARC Charter at www.saarc-sec.org
15. Trade liberalisation efforts in SAARC have often got protracted and stalled at times because of the pace and modalities of negotiations (preferential *versus* free trade approach, negative lists, non-tariff barriers) and at times because of purely political reasons such as Pakistan making grant of MFN and trade opening with India contingent upon resolution of Kashmir dispute.
16. Report of the SAARC Group of Eminent Persons, Shipra, New Delhi, 1998.
17. See SAARC: A Profile at http://www.saarc-sec.org
18. Views expressed at a Seminar on 'SAARC: 14th Summit and Beyond organized by Indian Council for World Affairs, 1-2 June 2007, New Delhi, during the session ' SAARC Development Fund: Projects under Social, Economic and Infrastructure Windows.
19. See SAARC FINANCE at http://www.saarc-sec.org
20. See Minutes of 14th SAARCFINANCE meeting held at Singapore on 20th September, 2006.
21. See the Report on the SAARCFINANCE Seminar on Issues in Exchange Rate Management, Kathmandu, 12-14 February 2001 in *South Asia Economic Journal,* Vol. 2, No.2, p. 346.
22. India's Central Bank Governor Takes Charge of SAARCFINANCE Chairman, http://www.allheadlinenews.com/articles/7007363265
23. PM for open borders, single currency in South Asia http://www.rediff.com//news/2003/dec/12sa.htm
24. Interview of Raghuram Rajan, Chief Economist IMF, *Economic Times,* December 23, 2003. Also see Kaushik Basu, India's Economy: Can the Boom Last? http://news.bbc.co.uk/2/hi/south_asia/3357957.stm

25. Nephil Matangi Maskay, South Asian Monetary Integration in Light of the Optimum Currency Area Criterion of Pattern of Shocks, *South Asia Economic Journal,* Vol. 2. No. 2, p. 205
26. *Ibid.* p. 217.
27. Sisira Jaysuriya *et al.* 'Monetary Cooperation in South Asia' South Asia Centre for Economic Policy Studies (SACEPS) *Draft Policy Paper,* July 2003 p. 14.
28. Sweta Chaman Saxena and Mirza Allim Beig, 'Monetary Cooperation in South Asia: Potential and Prospects' *RIS Discussion Papers* RIS—DP No.71/2004, p. 14.
29. *Ibid.* p. 16.
30. Cited in Sweta Chaman Saxena, No. 25, p. 10.
31 J. Ravikumar Stephen, Currency Union for South Asia: A SWOT Analysis, http://www.southasianmedia.net/Magazine/Journal/11_currency_ union.htm.
32. Rahul Tripathi, 'Political Economy of Monetary Cooperation in SAARC' in Nischal Pandey and Pushp Raj Dahal eds., *New Life with SAARC* (Kathmandu, 2005). Also See Rahul Tripathi, 'Towards a Common Currency in South Asia: A Rejoinder' *Economic and Political Weekly,* Vol. 40, No. 35

Conclusion

Monetary and Payments Cooperation has been a significant theme in South-South Cooperation, motivated by growing emphasis on collective self-reliance and socio-economic progress among the developing countries. The international economic system was often seen as inadequate in taking care of pressing concerns of developing countries such as declining share of trade, mounting debts and adverse terms of trade. Thus the importance of institutional arrangements within South that could not only assist in regional integration efforts, but also provide them with autonomous support mechanisms to meet specific financial requirements was realized. The present study has tried to examine in the context of monetary payments cooperation in South Asia, the role and prospects of the Asian Clearing Union.

Monetary and payments cooperation has been conceptualized in terms of both objectives and mechanisms underlying such arrangements in global as well as regional context. Such arrangements have been seen as not merely strengthening financial linkages, but as also providing adequate support mechanisms to existing institutional linkages in trade and investment.

Although monetary cooperation at the global level has been regarded as a difficult thing to sustain, yet Bretton-Woods international monetary system saw a certain stability being imparted by the dominant role of the dollar. In more recent times however, the idea of regionalisation of currencies in the form of currency blocs has gained wider recognition. Conceptualised under the theory of 'Optimum Currency Areas', to indicate regions having complete wage inflexibility and labour mobility, monetary unions having common currency are seen as eliminating transaction costs and exchange risks.

The theoretical premise of clearing and payments arrangements is seen in their impact on reducing restrictions on trade and on the use of foreign payment instruments in a situation of real overvaluation. Their role in promoting trade expansion is seen as complementary to that of more active instruments such as tariff reduction. These are seen as imparting certain benefits even without other forms of economic integration. They also create impulses for cooperation without compromising national policy autonomy.

The role and rationale of such clearing and payments arrangements, most of which were set up in the 1960s and 1970s had a specific context. Most of the developing countries, as part of their post-colonial economic development emphasized on building up of domestic resource base and expansion of trade as key to attain higher levels of growth. At the same time the need to conserve the foreign exchange reserves to meet the essential import requirements was felt all the more. Most of the clearing and payments arrangements that were established at that time therefore had the twin agenda of expansion of trade among the developing member countries and saving of the foreign currency by making use of the participants' own currencies in the settlement of these transactions. Besides, the clearing and payments arrangements were also sought to enhance greater monetary interaction among the member countries which could give a further boost to the regional integration initiatives in a major way.

While such arrangements continued to function effectively for a particular period of time, strains were evident gradually due to reasons which were both intrinsic and extrinsic. Within the arrangements due to the imbalances in intra-regional trade, the problem of arrears in payments usually crept in. This led to severe limitations on part of these payments arrangements to provide short term credit facility to the deficit members. Besides, they also got affected due to some of the economic reform measures undertaken by the member countries, particularly those relating to the exchange rate liberalisation and currency convertibility. Established at a time when currencies were inconvertible and foreign exchange availability was limited, the clearing and payments arrangements offered a suitable avenue to the developing countries to minimize the negative impact of overvalued currencies by making use of local currencies. However, with most of the countries going in for global convertibility, and foreign exchange being more readily available, the traditional role of the Clearing Arrangement was put to further test.

The case of the Asian Clearing Union has been no different. Ever since its inception in 1975, the organization has had to face the pulls and pressures generated by the ever changing global and regional economic environment. Yet, it was able to function effectively over the years by making specific changes and modifications in its functioning. Some of the major developments in the ACU may be summarized as follows.

The ACU entered into force on 9 December 1974 and commenced its operations on 1 November 1975. While Iran and Sri Lanka signed the agreement in 1973, India, Pakistan and Bangladesh became signatories in 1974. Burma was the last countries to join in 1977. While initially, the settlement period for transactions was kept at one month, it was subsequently, extended to two months in 1977. At the same time, the interim settlement period (accounting period) was extended from two weeks to one month). Till 1980, the mechanism operated through the respective Central Banks, but later due to growing burden, the transactions were allowed to be routed through commercial banks which kept ACU accounts with corresponding banks in other ACU countries. The Central Banks were now concerned only with funding or disposal of surplus balance in these accounts. While initially, the channeling of the transactions through the ACU was voluntary, in 1983 it was made compulsory to channel all eligible transactions (India making it compulsory in 1984). The exchange rates of Asian Monetary Units (AMUs) for the participants' currency were calculated initially on a fortnightly basis. However, due to rapidly changing exchange rate, they were subsequently calculated every ten days and finally everyday to ensure that exchange rates were in tune with the global alignments.

In one of the most significant development, channeling of oil payments was commenced in 1985 which led to a further boost in the transactions routed through the ACU. In another major development, the ACU switched over to dollar denominated transactions because of growing complaints by the ACU traders that they were not being treated at par with non-ACU traders in terms of the various facilities ordered.

The most creditable thing about the ACU during its entire span of functioning was that it did not register a single instance of default by members during its entire history of operations. However, what is the extent to which ACU has really been able to meet the original objectives as had been laid out? How effective have been ACU's responses to the ongoing changes that are witnessed in the regional economic environment? Besides, have there been any limitations within the organization that have prevented a major promotional role for the ACU. These are some of the issues that this study has attempted to explore.

First, the objectives. The original objectives as laid out during the time of ACU's formation were broadly, (a) to provide a facility for multilateral payments for current international transactions, (b) to promote the use of participants' currencies in mutual transactions, thereby help conserve foreign exchange, and (c) to promote monetary cooperation among participants, thereby contribute to the expansion of trade and economic activity. Given ACU's functioning over the past 25 years it is evident that it has been able to perform its role as a multilateral facility for payments settlements up to a satisfactory level. It has enabled multilateral settlement of member countries by aggregating their bilateral claims, allowing for payment of net amounts in foreign currency. To that extent the purpose of economizing on the use of foreign exchange was also satisfied. However, the role of the ACU has not really been able to go beyond that. It has not been able to play a major role in enhancing monetary cooperation among the member countries. Neither has it been able to play a major promotional role in enhancing intra-regional trade of the member countries. In fact, the intra-ACU trade as a percentage of its global trade has been quite low.

There are specific reasons which may be given for ACU not being able to expand its role beyond that of a mere clearing and payments facility. They stem from both structural and functional aspects of ACU's functioning. Firstly, the ACU found itself unable to pursue the given mandate as per the objectives that were laid out. Its major policy exercises were primarily focused on the basic role of the union as a clearing and settlement facility. Any discussions beyond that were purely deliberative in nature. That is why although the annual meetings of the Board of Governors did discuss the contemporary economic issues and the need for greater monetary financial interaction, yet no concrete action plans were ever spelt out. Secondly, ACU did not find itself directly overlapping with any major regional integration initiative unlike the other clearing and payments arrangements. As a result, the activities and programmes of the ACU often worked in absence of a broad based plan for regional integration which could have given signals for greater monetary interaction among the member countries.

Then there were reasons that stemmed from the functioning of the ACU mechanism *per se*. As originally set out, the ACU facility was to have facilitated the payment procedures through the correspondent banking accounts held with the member countries. This purpose was fulfilled effectively as long as the ACU involved the use of participants' own currencies in settlement of mutual trade. Since there was no market for regional currencies, the payments for intra-regional transactions had to be facilitated through the correspondent banking accounts whose requirements for regional currencies were met by the respective Central Banks. However, after switching over to dollar denominated transactions in 1996, the channeling of transactions through the ACU is being seen as more time consuming and there are indications of intermittent delays in the settlement of final payments. The prime reason behind this is attributed to the cumbersome process that is involved in payments settlement through ACU which still needs involvement at the level of two commercial banks and their respective Central Banks. This is in sharp contrast to the payments made outside the ACU mechanism where foreign exchange can be bought or sold freely in the market and payments be made directly to the commercial banks without any delay. The remedy therefore lies in ACU making use of the latest technological instruments to settle mutual payments which would minimize the delays that take place. Significantly, the ACU has initiated the process of studying the modifications that need to be done at the technological level to make the payments settlement more easy and fast.

Thus ACUs' present advantages can primarily be seen at the Central Bank level where the benefits of a two-monthly credit through deferred payments still exists. The deficit banks are therefore allowed to withhold payments for a period of two months. However, the scope of this facility needs to be enlarged if at all the ACU is to make any significant contribution to the intra-regional balance of payments deficits of the member countries. This would also enable the member countries to take further steps at meeting regional crisis situations.

One major limitation of the ACU has been its inability to attract new members in the last 25 years of its existence. This despite the fact that expansion of the membership has been one of the leading agendas of various ACU deliberations and its representations at various regional and global fora. This shows that ACU has not really been able to clearly highlight the benefits of joining the union to the potential members. One reason could be that with the greater trends towards foreign exchange and payments liberalisation, countries would find it much more attractive to make use of conventional channels for effecting their payments. A clearing facility like ACU might be considered archaic by some countries which would rather be part of a settlement system where payments are settled at the instant. However, this brings to the fore the need for ACU to outline a new agenda that bases its premises on providing a regional financial mechanism that extends its role to beyond that of clearing. The role of the ACU should be gradually transformed from being merely a deliberative body to more proactive body on regional monetary and financial issues.

The ACU in its modified role must have a broader mandate which would enable it to chalk out policy prescriptions for member countries within the wider regional context. This would enable it to address some of the very specific problems that the traders making use of the facility face on account of different procedural aspects. While such exercises do take place in the ACU, they operate only at an informal level. There is a need for a total formalisation of the mechanism which addresses to the concerns of the banks, traders etc., while making use of the facility. This would also promote closer relations among the banking community of the region as was originally laid out.

Lastly, but most importantly, ACU must try to seek in some way a harmonization of the monetary agenda with the trade agenda of the member nations. This would only be possible if it works in tandem with a broader regional integration initiatives as that would give a greater complementarily to the process. At present only SAARC appears to be capable of working in tandem with ACU on broader regional monetary and financial issues. This would however require overcoming considerable amount of procedural inertia that generally marks such initiatives. ACU needs to link up more pragmatically with institutions such as SAARCFINANCE to bolster the agenda of monetary and financial cooperation in South Asia as the ultimate goal of monetary union shall still need a lot of ground work before the ultimate goal of an Economic Union becomes a reality.

Appendix

Asian Clearing Union (ACU) Agreement Establishing the Asian Clearing Union

The central banks and monetary authorities of regional members and associate members of the UNITED NATIONS ECONOMIC AND SOCIAL COMMISSION FOR ASIA AND THE PACIFIC (ESCAP),

DESIRING to establish a facility to settle payments for current international transactions within the ESCAP region on a multilateral basis,

RECOGNIZING that such a facility would contribute to the expansion of trade and the promotion of monetary co-operation among their countries,

RECOGNIZING further that a facility designed to promote the use of the participants' currencies would reduce the use of extra-regional currencies to settle current international transactions within the region and thereby effect economies in the use of foreign exchange and reduce the cost of making payments for such current international transactions,

REALIZING that a region-wide clearing facility could co-exist and function in co-operation with sub-regional or less than regional arrangements in Asia and the Pacific,

CONVINCED that the regional clearing facility must be established and operated in a manner that will not prejudice the principles of multilateral trade and payments,

ON WHOSE BEHALF this AGREEMENT has been signed, HAVE AGREED as follows:

CHAPTER I
GENERAL PROVISIONS

Article I: Asian Clearing Union

The central banks and other monetary authorities on whose behalf the present Agreement is signed, hereinafter referred to as "participants", agree to establish a system for clearing payments among their respective countries on a multilateral basis, hereinafter referred to as the "Asian Clearing Union", which shall be governed by the provisions of this Agreement and by the rules, regulations and decisions agreed within its framework.

Article II: Purposes

The purposes of this Agreement are:

(a) to provide a facility to settle, on a multilateral basis, payments for current international transactions among the territories of participants;
(b) to promote the use of participants' currencies in current transactions between their respective territories and thereby effect economies in the use of the participants' exchange reserves;
(c) to promote monetary co-operation among the participants and closer relations among the banking systems in their territories and thereby contribute to the expansion of trade and economic activity among the countries of the ESCAP region; and
(d) to provide for currency swap arrangement among the participants so as to make Asian Monetary Units available to them temporarily.

Article III: Participation

Section 1. Eligibility to Participate

(a) Participation in the Asian Clearing Union shall be open

to the central bank or monetary authority of each regional member or associate member of ESCAP.

(b) Participation in another clearing group or arrangement is not precluded by participation in the Asian Clearing Union.

Section 2. Original Participants

Original participants shall be those central banks or monetary authorities that are eligible to participate in and which sign this Agreement not later than three months from the date this Agreement has been signed by the duly authorized representatives of five such central banks or authorities. Each shall become a participant on the date this Agreement enters into force.

Section 3. Other Participants

A central bank or monetary authority that is eligible to participate and is not an original participant may apply to the Board of Directors to become a participant and be admitted as a participant if the Board so decides by a two-thirds vote of all the Directors and upon such central bank or monetary authority signing this Agreement and accepting the rules, regulations and decisions of the Board of Directors. The Chairman of the Board shall determine the date on which the payments and transfers with respect to such a participant shall be included in the clearing facility.

CHAPTER II
OPERATIONS

Article IV: Unit of Account

(a) The accounts of the Asian Clearing Union shall be kept in a common unit of account hereby designated as the "Asian Monetary Unit", which may be referred to in the abbreviated form as "AMU".

(b) The value of one Asian Monetary Unit shall, with effect from 1.1.1996 , and until such time as it is changed by the Board of Directors in terms of sub-clause (c) of the Article, be equivalent in value to one US Dollar. The Asian Monetary Unit may also be denominated as 'ACU dollar'.

(c) The Board of Directors may change the value of the Asian Monetary Unit at any time by a unanimous vote of all the Directors.

(d) In the event of a change in the value of the Asian Monetary Unit by the Board of Directors, the outstanding net debtor and creditor positions as of the date of this change including accrued interest shall be settled on the basis of the value of the Asian Monetary Unit preceding such change.

Article V: Clearing of Individual Payments and Transfers

Section 1. Rules for Individual Payments and Transfers

(a) The Board of Directors, after consultation with participants, shall prescribe by appropriate rules consistent with this Agreement the procedures to effect the financial settlement of eligible payments and transfers through the clearing facility. In particular, these rules and regulations shall specify the procedures to be followed by persons, commercial banks, and central banks or monetary authorities. The Board shall prescribe the information to be supplied to the Secretary General for the operation of the clearing facility.

(b) Each participant, in so far as its monetary and exchange system permits, shall take all steps necessary to put into effect in its territories the procedures prescribed by the Board of Directors and to supply the information required by the Board for the operation of the clearing facility.

Section 2. Eligible Payments and Transfers

(a) The payments that are eligible to be made through the clearing facility are payments:

   (i) from a resident in the territory of one participant to a resident in the territory of another participant;
   (ii) for current international transactions as defined by the Articles of Agreement of the International Monetary Fund;
   (iii) permitted by the country in which the payer resides; and
   (iv) not declared ineligible under (b) or (c) below.

(b) The Board of Directors may declare specified payments to be ineligible to be channelled through the clearing facility and may terminate such ineligibility.

(c) A participant, at the time it signs this Agreement, may declare that payments for specified transactions are ineligible to be made by and to residents in its territories through the clearing facility. The participant shall consult with the Board of Directors with a view to the relaxation and eventual removal of this ineligibility as soon as circumstances permit.

Section 3. Duty to Complete Payment

Each participant undertakes that all eligible payments made through the clearing facility to residents in its territory will be accepted and completed.

Section 4. Use of the Clearing Facility

(a) A participant may require residents to make payments through the clearing facility, but such a requirement shall not be enforced in a manner that will restrict or delay the making of payments for current international transactions or create a discriminatory currency arrangement.

(b) Except to the extent that a participant requires its residents to make payments through the clearing facility in accordance with (a) above, the use of the clearing facility shall be optional.

(c) In order to promote the use of the clearing facility, participants may adopt measures designed to provide incentives to make payments for individual transactions through the clearing facility, provided such measures shall be consistent with the participant's undertakings under the Articles of Agreement of the International Monetary Fund. Thus, for this purpose, participants may allow the conversion of their currencies into Asian Monetary Units or into those of other participants in respect of payment receipts at rates which are more favourable than those for dealings outside the clearing facility.

Section 5. Instruments of Payment

The Board of Directors shall specify in its rules and regulations the types of instrument of payment that may be used and how each is to be used to make payment through the facility. Only instruments of payment denominated in Asian Monetary Units or the US dollar may be used to make payment through the clearing facility. A participant, after consultation with the Board may prohibit the use of particular instruments of payment by its residents for making payments through the clearing facility, but shall notify the Secretary General of such prohibition who shall notify all other participants.

Article VI: Settlement of Balances Among Participants

Section 1. Periodical Settlement

(a) Settlement shall be made of net positions and accrued interest at the end of each two monthly settlement period. Settlements shall be made in accordance with Section 3 of this Article.

(b) The Board of Directors may change the length of the settlement period by a decision taken by a unanimous vote of all of the Directors.

Section 2. Interest

(a) Interest shall be paid by net debtors and transferred to net creditors on daily balances outstanding between settlement dates. The accrued interest shall be included in the calculation of the net amounts to be paid and received at the end of each settlement period and shall be notified at the end of each settlement period along with the net position of each participant.
(b) The Board of Directors shall determine, from time-to-time, the rate of interest, which shall be the same for both net creditor and net debtor positions, on the basis of the return on balances held on similar availability in major financial centres.

Section 3. Notifications and Payments

(a) The Secretary General shall notify each participant of its net position, including accrued interest, and of the amounts it shall pay to, or receive from, other participants at the end of each settlement period.
(b) Each debtor participant, within four workingdays of the receipt from the Secretary General of the notice of the amounts to be paid, shall make the payments in international reserve assets specified by the Board of Directors for the purpose. Payments may also be made in the currency of the creditor subject to its specific consent.

Article VII: Maintenance of Value and Non-settlement of Balances

Section 1. Value of Payments and Transfers

The value of any instrument of payment or transfer of a currency for the purpose of the amount to be settled through the clearing facility shall be the amount in Asian Monetary Units or ACU dollars, as well as in the case of a transfer of currency, be equivalent in Asian Monetary Units or ACU dollars determined as of the date the transfer is considered to be made under the rules prescribed by the Board of Directors. The values of payments and transfers made and received with respect to participants and the resulting positions of participants shall be recorded by the Secretary General in Asian Monetary Units.

Section 2. Delayed Payments

If a participant fails to make any payment notified to it by the Secretary General under Article VI within the time required, interest shall be payable by the participant on the amount due at such rate as may be determined by the Board of Directors.

Section 3. Default

(a) In the event the payment referred to in Section 2 above remains unpaid after fifteen days from the date on which it was due in terms of Article VI Section 3(b), the participant shall be deemed to have defaulted and the Secretary General shall immediately notify the Directors and all participants. Thereafter no payments with respect to residents in the territory of the defaulting participant can be made through the clearing facility until the default has been fully discharged and the participant restored to full participation in accordance with (c) below.

(b) Unless the defaulting participant, within seven days of the date of default agrees with the participants to which it is obliged to make any payments due under Article VI on arrangements to make the payments, with interest, its participation in the Asian Clearing Union shall be suspended.

(c) After the default has been fully discharged, the Board of Directors may restore the defaulting participant to full participation in the Asian Clearing Union subject to any special terms and conditions that the Board may deem appropriate, or may require the defaulting participant to withdraw from participation. If the defaulting participant does not agree to continue participation on the terms and conditions specified by the Board within thirty days of the decision of the Board on this matter, it shall be deemed to have withdrawn. The special terms and conditions may be revoked at any time by the Board.

(d) In addition, the Board of Directors shall consider, in consultation with participants, other means by which the amount of the default may be recovered, and participants shall take such further measures as the Board deems appropriate in order to recover the amount of the default in the shortest possible time.

Article VIIA: Currency SWAP Arrangement

The Board of Directors may provide for a currency SWAP arrangement among the participants and specify in the rules the eligibility criteria, the terms including the rate of interest and the period for which the facility should be extended, the manner in which the participants should contribute and such other relevant conditions and procedures as are considered necessary.

CHAPTER III
ORGANIZATION AND ADMINISTRATION

Article VIII: Organization

Section 1. Joint Action

Representatives of the participants shall meet from time-to-time for the purpose of giving effect to those provisions of this Agreement which involve joint action and, generally, with a view to facilitating the operation and furthering the objectives of this Agreement. Whenever reference is made in this Agreement to the participants acting jointly, they are designated as the Board of Directors.

Section 2. The Board of Directors

(a) Each participant shall appoint one Director and one Alternate Director to represent it on the Board of Directors. Each Director and Alternate Director shall be appointed for a term of two years, may be reappointed, and may be replaced at any time during the term of his appointment. Each Director shall have one vote. An Alternate Director may attend the meetings but may vote only when his principal is not present or when his principal is acting as the Chairman. The Board shall elect a Chairman from among its members to serve for a period of one year, and a Vice-Chairman to serve in the absence or inability of the Chairman during the same period.

(b) The Board of Directors shall meet at least once in a calendar year. In addition, meetings of the Board shall be called by the Chairman when requested by two Directors or when the Chairman considers a meeting necessary.

(c) A quorum for any meeting of the Board of Directors shall be the Chairman or Vice-Chairman and two-thirds of the Directors.

(d) All decisions of the Board of Directors shall be taken by a majority of the votes of all of the Directors unless a special majority is required by this Agreement. The votes of "all of the Directors" means the votes of all the Directors and not merely of those present and voting. When both a Director and his Alternate are not present at a meeting of the Board, the Director, in accordance with rules established by the Board, may authorize another Director to present his views and to cast his vote. The Chairman shall have no vote, except in the case of an equal division when he shall cast the deciding vote.

(e) The Board of Directors may establish a procedure whereby the Chairman may obtain the votes of the Directors on a specific question without calling a meeting of the Board.

(f) The Board of Directors may adopt such rules and regulations as are necessary for the organization and operation of the Asian Clearing Union.

(g) The remuneration and expenses of a Director and Alternate Director shall be borne by the participant appointing them.

Section 3. Secretary General and Staff

(a) The Board of Directors, by a two-thirds majority of all of the Directors, shall select and appoint the Secretary General, who shall not be a Director, for a term of three years. The Board shall establish the remuneration and other terms of the contract of service of the Secretary General. The Secretary General may be reappointed and shall cease to hold office when the Board so decides by a two-thirds vote of all of the Directors.

(b) The Secretary General, under the direction of the Board of Directors shall conduct the ordinary business of the Asian Clearing Union. He shall be the head of the staff and, subject to the general rules of the Board, organize, appoint and dismiss members of the staff. He shall exercise such other powers as are assigned to him by the Board.

(c) The Secretary General shall prepare and submit to the Board the documents necessary for its work, particularly the financial statements, the proposed annual budget and the draft annual report.

(d) The Secretary General shall act as the representative of the Board of Directors within the limits prescribed by the Board.

(e) The Secretary General and the staff members, in the discharge of their official functions, shall owe their duty entirely to the Board of Directors and to no other authority. Each participant in the Asian Clearing Union shall respect the international charter of this duty and shall refrain from all attempts to influence any of the staff in the discharge of his functions.

Article IX: Agent

The Board of Directors may make arrangements with a central bank or monetary authority of a participant or with the Asian Reserve Bank when it is established to provide the necessary services and facilities for the operation of the clearing facility. The agreement establishing these arrangements with an Agent must be approved by a vote of two-thirds of all of the Directors.

Article X: Relations with Other Organizations and Clearing Arrangements

The Board of Directors may make arrangements to co-operate with other general, regional or sub-regional international organizations, or other clearing arrangements among countries within or outside the ESCAP region. Any such arrangement shall not apply to a participant which does not consent.

Article XI: Interpretation

(a) Any question of interpretation of this Agreement or of any rules, regulations or decisions of the Board of Directors arising between the Secretary General and a participant or between participants shall be decided by the Board whose decision shall be final.

(b) Should any disagreement arise between the Board of Directors and a participant which has withdrawn from the Asian Clearing Union or has been required to withdraw, and if efforts to settle the controversy by negotiation fail, such disagreement shall be submitted to arbitration by a tribunal of three arbitrators, the first appointed by the Board, the second by the participant and the third designated by the first two arbitrators. If they fail to reach agreement, the third arbitrator shall be appointed by the Executive Secretary of ESCAP. The third arbitrator shall be empowered to decide all matters of procedure whenever the other two arbitrators disagree with respect to such a question.

Article XII: Reports and Assessments

Section 1. Reports

The Board of Directors shall publish an annual report on its activities and the operations of the Asian Clearing Union. The report shall contain an audited statement of accounts and of the clearing operations. The Board may publish such other reports as it deems desirable.

Section 2. Operating Expenses

(a) The Board of Directors shall approve the annual budget and determine the formula under which expenses shall be apportioned among participants, on the basis of the actual use made of the Asian Clearing Union and of the services rendered to them.
(b) The Board shall specify the currencies or other means in which the assessments shall be paid by members as well as the schedule of payments for each fiscal year.
(c) The Board of Directors may request the Agent to make an advance to the Asian Clearing Union on behalf of the participants when such action becomes necessary to meet expenses, but the Board shall promptly make an assessment to meet the amount borrowed.
(d) All the decisions taken by the Board of Directors in accordance with this section shall require the affirmative vote of two-thirds of all of the Directors.

CHAPTER IV
MISCELLANEOUS PROVISIONS

Article XIII: Withdrawal from Participation

Section 1. Voluntary Withdrawal

Any participant may withdraw from this Agreement at any time by transmitting a notice in writing to the Secretary General. Withdrawal shall become effective three business days from the date such written notice is received by the Secretary General unless a later date is indicated by the participant in the notice. The Secretary General shall notify all other participants as promptly as possible.

Section 2. Compulsory Withdrawal

If a participant fails to fulfil any of its obligations under this Agreement, and if, after consultation between the Board of Directors and the participant concerned, the participant fails to correct the situation, the Board may require such participant to withdraw from participation. The participant shall be deemed to have withdrawn on the date of the decision of the Board or such later date as the Board may specify.

Section 3. Settlement of Accounts

(a) A participant shall remain liable for and shall meet all its obligations to other participants arising from its participation under the Agreement until the final settlement of accounts with it has taken place.

(b) Only instruments of payments for the settlement of transactions involving residents in the territory of the withdrawing participant issued on or before the date of its withdrawal shall be settled thereafter through the clearing facility. Settlements shall normally be made at the regular settlement dates until all outstanding instruments of payments have been cleared. The Board of Directors shall determine any further procedures needed to effect the final settlement of accounts with the withdrawing participant.

Article XIV: Amendment

(a) This Agreement may be amended by a decision of the Board of Directors taken by a vote of two-thirds of all the Directors.

(b) Notwithstanding the provisions of the preceding paragraph, the affirmative vote of each Director on the Board shall be required to approve an amendment to modify the provisions of :

(i) Article III on participation;
(ii) Article IV(c) on the modification of the parity of the Asian Monetary Unit;
(iii) Article V, Section 2(b) on specified ineligible payments;
(iv) Article VI, Section 1(b) on the change of the settlement period;
(v) Article VII, Section 1 on the value of payments and transfers;
(vi) Article XII, Section 2(a) on the formula under which expenses shall be apportioned among participants;
(vii) Article XIII, Section 1 on the right of a member to withdraw voluntarily from this Agreement at any time; and
(viii) Article XIV on the amendment of this agreement.

The absence or abstention of a Director shall be considered to be a negative vote.

(c) Any proposal to amend this Agreement shall be communicated to the Chairman of the Board of Directors who shall place the proposal before the Board for discussion. When an amendment has been adopted by the Board, the Chairman shall so certify in an official notice addressed to all participants and to the Executive

Secretary of ESCAP. Amendments shall enter into force one month after the date of dispatch of the official communication unless the Board specifies a different date.

Article XV: Suspension and Liquidation

(a) The Board of Directors may suspend operations by a decision of the Board taken by a vote of two-thirds of the Directors. All participants shall be notified immediately and no instrument of payment issued after the date of notice shall be settled through the clearing facility.

(b) After a decision under sub-section (a), if the Board of Directors does not decide to resume operations within six months, all operations and other activities shall be suspended, except those necessary for the orderly liquidation and the final settlement of accounts among participants as determined by the Board.

CHAPTER V
FINAL PROVISIONS

Article XVI. Signature and Custody

(a) The Executive Secretary of ESCAP shall be the depository of this Agreement and shall send certified copies of this Agreement and any amendments to it, to all regional members and associate members of ESCAP. Any amendments to this Agreement, as certified by the Chairman of the Board of Directors under the provisions of Article XIV(c), shall be appended to its text.

(b) This Agreement shall be open for acceptance by signature by duly authorized representatives of central banks or monetary authorities of regional members or associate members of ESCAP at the United Nations Economic and Social Commission for Asia and the Pacific. Each Central Bank or monetary authority on whose behalf this Agreement is signed shall deposit with the Executive Secretary, before signature, an instrument setting forth that it has full legal authority to accept this Agreement and to carry out all its obligations under it.

Article XVII. Entry into Force

This Agreement shall enter into force when it has been signed and the instruments provided in Article XVI(b) have been deposited by duly authorized representatives of at least five central banks or monetary authorities of regional members or associate members of ESCAP, but not before the date determined by Article III, Section 2.

Article XVIII. Commencement of Operations

(a) As soon as this Agreement enters into force, each participant shall appoint a Director and Alternate Director, and the Executive Secretary of ESCAP shall call the inaugural meeting of the Board of Directors.
(b) At its inaugural meeting, the Board shall:

 (i) elect the Chairman and Vice-Chairman; and
 (ii) make arrangements to proceed with the preparatory work necessary to commence operations of the clearing facility.

(c) The Chairman of the Board shall notify the participants of the date of the commencement of the operation of the clearing facility.

Article XIX. Notification

The Executive Secretary of ESCAP shall notify signatories and all regional members and associate members of ESCAP of :

(i) all signatures to this Agreement, and
(ii) the date on which this Agreement enters into force.

DONE in a single copy in the English language.

PROCEDURE RULES

ASIAN CLEARING UNION (PROCEDURE) RULES

1. These rules have been adopted by the Board of Directors of the Asian Clearing Union in terms of Article VIII Section 2(f) of the Agreement Establishing the Asian Clearing Union and shall be called the Asian Clearing Union (Procedure) Rules.
2. These rules shall come into force on such date as may be notified by the Board of Directors of the Asian Clearing Union.
3. *Definitions*: In these rules, unless there is anything repugnant in the subject or context:

   (a) "Agent" means the participant central bank or monetary authority with whom the Board has arranged to provide the necessary services and facilities for the operation of the clearing facility;
   (b) "Agreement" means the Agreement Establishing the Asian Clearing Union;
   (c) "Asian Monetary Unit" (AMU) means the common unit of account of the Clearing Union referred to in Article IV of the Agreement;
   (d) "Board" means the Board of Directors of the Asian Clearing Union referred to in Article VIII Section 1 of the Agreement;
   (e) "Clearing Union" means the Asian Clearing Union;
   (f) "Secretary General" includes the officer who is designated by the Agent to perform the functions of the Secretary General for the time being;
   (g) "Participant" means any central bank or monetary authority which is a signatory to the Agreement; and
   (h) "Currency Swap" arrangement means an arrangement among the participants under which a participant becomes eligible to draw Asian Monetary Units from other participants in specified proportion and in specified circumstances for settling imbalances in clearing.

4. *Ineligible Payments*: The following payments shall not be eligible to be made through the clearing facility:

   (i) Payments between Nepal and India;
   (ii) Payments which are not current international transactions as defined by the Articles of Agreement of the International Monetary Fund, except to the extent mutually agreed upon between two or more participants.

Participants have agreed that payments arising on account of import/export transactions on deferred payment terms will not be considered as ineligible payments.

5. *Eligible Instruments of Payment and the Currency in Which they are to be Denominated*: All instruments of payment denominated in AMUs or US dollars, may be used to effect payment through the clearing facility. Settlement of such instruments will be made by the commercial banks through operations of the accounts referred to in Rule 6.

6. *Clearing Operations*:

   (a) The participants will permit the banks in their respective countries to maintain ACU dollar accounts with their correspondent banks in the other participating countries. All payments other than ineligible payments will be settled by the banks concerned through these accounts. The operations on these accounts shall be governed by the prevailing Exchange Control Regulations and such other directions, rules, regulations or guidelines as the participants may issue or specify from time-to-time.
   (b) When a commercial bank desires to fund its ACU dollar account with its correspondent bank in another participating country, it may purchase the

required amount of ACU dollar either from a local commercial bank having a surplus in that participating country or from its central bank. In the latter case, it will surrender equivalent amount of US dollars or, at the option of the Central Bank, the equivalent in the local currency to its own Central Bank for remittance through the ACU mechanism. The participant receiving the amount will advise the participant in the country concerned to make available the amount in US dollars to the concerned bank in that country. After making the payment, the second participant will advise the Secretary General of the ACU to credit its account by debit to the first participant's account.

(c) When a commercial bank desires to repatriate funds from its ACU dollar account with its correspondent bank in another participating country, it may sell the desired amount of ACU dollar either to a local commercial bank which desires to fund its ACU dollar account in that participating country, or to its central bank. In the latter case, it will request that bank to effect the remittance through the ACU mechanism. The correspondent bank will surrender equivalent amount of US dollars to its own Central Bank for remittance. The participant receiving the amount will advise the participant in the country concerned to make available the equivalent amount to the concerned bank in that country. The Central Bank may , at its option, make the payment in US dollar or in local currency. After making the payment the second participant will advise the Secretary General of the ACU to credit its account by debit to the first participant's account.

(d) On receipt of the advices referred to in sub-rules (b) and (c) above, the Clearing Union shall effect the necessary transfers under advice to both the participants.

7. *Currency SWAP Arrangement*: A participant desirous of availing of the SWAP facility as defined in Rule 3 (h) should request the Secretary General in such format as he prescribes. The nature and scope of swap arrangement will be as described hereunder:

   (a) "Eligibility" Subject to sub-rule (d) of this rule any participant in deficit at the end of a settlement period shall be eligible to avail of the facility. Participants whose countries have special payment arrangements between themselves will not be eligible to avail of this facility from each other.

   (b) "Entitlement" Every eligible participant shall be entitled to the facility from every other participant upto 20 per cent of the average gross payments made by it through the ACU mechanism to other participants during the three previous calendar years. A participant shall not, however, draw more than its overall deficit at the end of a settlement period. The drawal by each participant from each other participant shall be in the same proportion as its overall deficit bears to its maximum entitlement.

   (c) "Rate of Interest" The rate of interest chargeable on each drawal would be equal to LIMEAN on US dollars for the period of 2 months. The reference LIMEAN will be of Barclay's Bank , London, at 11.00 a.m. applicable for the concerned value date. If the rate is not available from Barclay's Bank, the Secretary General shall ascertain it from any other London clearing bank at his discretion and if it is not available from any such bank, the rate of Barclay's Bank applicable for the immediately preceding value date will apply.

   (d) "Other Conditions" A participant may draw under the swap arrangement for a period of 2 months at a time. Such a participant shall not be entitled to draw under the arrangement at the time of the next following settlement.

8. *Accounts Kept by the Clearing Union*: The Clearing Union shall maintain an account in AMUs for each participant to which the payments advised by the participants will be debited or credited. Interest will be payable by the participants on the net debit balances and receivable on the net credit balances, calculated at the interest rate referred to in Rule 9 , on the daily balances outstanding.
9. *Interest*

   (a) Interest on the net debit and net credit balance will be calculated by the Clearing Union on the daily outstandings by the product method, taking a year as comprising 360 days and shall be debited or credited to the participants' accounts at the end of each settlement period. The rate of interest applicable for a settlement period will be the closing rate on the first working day of the last week of the previous calendar month offered by the Bank for International Settlements for one month Euro-dollar deposits. In the event that the Bank for International Settlements does not quote rates for such deposits, the last available rate will apply until such rates become available. However, the Board may decide upon a substitute rate if necessary.

   (b) In the case of delayed payments referred to in Article VII Section 2 of the Agreement and default referred to in Section 3 of the same Article, interest for the period of delay or default shall be calculated by the Clearing Union at:

      (1) One per cent per annum over the rate for the relevant settlement period or periods under sub-rule (a), or
      (2) One per cent per annum over the rate applicable on the day of default under sub-rule (a), whichever is higher.

10. *Notification of Net Position at the End of Settlement Period*: At the end of each settlement period, the Secretary

General shall notify each participant by telex or cable of its net position and accrued interest, and of the amounts it shall pay or receive from other participants.

11. *Settlement of Balances*: (a) Each debtor participant, within four working days of the resceipt from the Secretary General of the notice of the amounts to be paid, shall make the payment in US dollar or in any other mutually acceptable currency, under telex or cable intimation to the Secretary General.

    (b) If settlement is desired to be effected in a currency other than the US dollar, the participants shall, by mutual agreement, decide on the exchange rate to be made applicable for such settlement.

12. *Obligation to Accept Net Position Advised by the Secretary General*: The net position at the end of the settlement period, as notified by the Secretary General shall be accepted by every participant as correct and settlement shall be made accordingly. The participant shall, however, have the right to bring any discrepancy detected in such position to the notice of the Secretary General as soon as possible thereafter for eventual rectification and further settlement if necessary. Such rectification shall be made at the same rate of exchange at which the original settlement was made.

13. *Default*: In the event that a participant fails to make any payment notified to it by the Secretary General under Rule 10 within the time specified, the provisions of Article VII Section 3 of the Agreement shall apply.

14. *Amendment*: Unless otherwise provided in the Agreement, these rules may be amended by a decision of the Board taken by a majority of the votes of all of the Directors.

Bibliography

Primary Sources

Asian Clearing Union, Agreement Establishing the Asian Clearing Union and Procedure Rules as Amended by the Board of Directors during various Meetings up to May 1998 (Karachi: Asian Clearing Union Secretariat, May 1998).

Asian Clearing Union, *Annual Reports*, 1995-05 (Tehran).

Asian Development Bank, *Asian Development Outlook 1999* (Manila: Oxford, 1999).

Central Bank of Sri Lanka, *Annual Report 1998* (Colombo: Central Bank of Sri Lanka, 1998).

Central Bank of Sri Lanka, *Economic and Social Statistics of Sri Lanka 1998* (Colombo: Central Bank of Sri Lanka, 1998).

Federation of Nepalese Chamber of Commerce and Industry, *Nepal and the World: A Statistical Profile 1998* (Kathmandu: FNCCI, 1998).

Government of India, Ministry of Finance Economic Division, *Economic Surveys, 1997-98 to 1999-2000* (New Delhi).

International Monetary Fund, *Directions of Trade Statistics Year Book, 1991-1998* (Washington D.C.).

International Monetary Fund, *International Financial Statistical Yearbook, 1999* (New York: International Monetary Fund, 1999).

State Bank of Pakistan, *Annual Report 1997-98* (Islamabad: State Bank of Pakistan, 1998).

United Nations Conference on Trade and Development, A Review of the Main Features of Clearing Arrangements of Developing Countries, Document No. UNCTAD/ECDC/128, 22 November 1982.

United Nations Conference on Trade and Development, Clearing and Payments Arrangements among Developing

Countries: Recent Developments, Long-term Policy Considerations, Document No. UNCTAD/ECDC/238, 4 February 1994.

United Nations Conference on Trade and Development, Currency Convertibility and Monetary Cooperation within Integration Groupings of Developing Countries, Document No. UNCTAD/ECDC/250, 5 May 1995.

United Nations Conference on Trade and Development, *Handbook of Economic Integration and Cooperation Groupings of Developing Countries Vol. I: Regional and Subregional Economic Integration Groupings* (New York: United Nations, 1996).

United Nations Conference on Trade and Development, Payments, Clearing and Credit Arrangements among Developing Countries: Assessment and Policy Options, Report by the UNCTAD Secretariat, Document No. UNCTAD/ST/ECDC/40, 23 November 1998.

United Nations Conference on Trade and Development, Report of the Eighth Session of the Coordination Committee on Multilateral Payments Arrangements and Monetary Cooperation among Developing Countries, Document No. UNCTAD/ECDC/245, 24 August 1994.

United Nations Conference on Trade and Development, State of South-South Cooperation-Statistical Pocket Book and Index of Cooperation Organisations (New York: United Nations, 1995).

United Nations, *Economic and Social Survey of Asia and the Pacific* (1978).

United Nations, Regional Cooperation: Report of the Ministerial Conference on Asian Economic Cooperation held at Manila, Philippines, 3 to 6 December 1963 (New York: United Nations, 1964).

United Nations, Regional Economic Cooperation in Asia and the Far East: Report and Recommendations of the Seminar on Financial Aspects of Trade Expansion, Regional Economic Cooperation Series No. 6 (New York: United Nations, 1968).

United Nations, Regional Economic Cooperation in Asia and the Far East: Report of the Meeting of the Council of Ministers for Asian Economic Cooperation (Fourth Session), Regional Economic Cooperation Series No. 8 (New York: United Nations, 1971).

United Nations, Regional Economic Cooperation in Asia and the Far East: The Asian Development Bank and Trade Liberalisation, Regional Economic Cooperation Series No. 2 (New York: United Nations, 1965).

United Nations, Report of the Meeting of Government and Central Bank Officials on Trade and Monetary Cooperation: Consideration and Proposals for Trade and Monetary Cooperation in the ECAFE Region, Regional Economic Cooperation Series No. 7 (New York: United Nations, 1971).

Secondary Sources

Books

Amin, Samir, *Capitalism in the Age of Globalisatoin: The Management of Contemporary Society* (Delhi: Madhyam Books, 1997).

Amuzegar, Jahangir and M. Ali Fekrat, *Iran: Economic Conditions under Dualistic Conditions* (Chicago: Chicago University Press, 1971).

Anjaria, S.J., S. Eken and J.F. Laker, *Payments Arrangements and the Expansion of Trade in Eastern and Southern Africa, IMF Occasional Paper No. II* (Washington: IMF, 1982).

Athukorala, Premachandra and Sisir Jayasuriya, *Macro-economic Policies, Crisis and Growth in Sri Lanka 1969-90* (Washington D.C.: World Bank, 1994).

Auguste, Byron Gerald, *The Economics of International Payments Unions and Clearing Houses: Theory and Measurement* (London: Macmillan Press, 1997).

Balassa, Bela (ed.), *Changing Patterns in Foreign Trade and Payments* (New York: W.W. Norton & Company Inc., 1978).

Balassa, Bela, *The Theory of Economic Integration* (London: George Allen & Unwin Ltd., 1961).

Bhargava, K.K. (*et al.*), *South Asia: Towards Dynamism and Cooperation* (Bombay: Popular, 1994).

Bird, Graham, *The International Monetary System and Less Developed Countries* (London: Macmillan, 1978).

Blackman, C., *Managing Foreign Exchange Reserves in Small Developing Countries* (New York: Group of Thirty, 1982).

Bose, Sugata, *South Asia and World Capitalism* (Delhi: Oxford University Press, 1990).

Carlson, Jerker (ed.), *South-South Relations in a Changing World Order* (Uppsala: Scandinavian Institute of African Studies, 1982).

Centre for Policy Dialogue, Experiences with Economic Reforms: A Review of Bangladesh's Development 1995 (Dhaka: University Press, 1995).

Colas, Bernard (ed.), *Global Economic Cooperation: A Guide to Agreements and* (Tokyo: UNU Press, 1994).

Coleman, William D. and Goffrey R.D. *Underhill, Regionalism and Global Integration: Europe, Asia and the Americans* (London: Routledge, 1998).

Colombage, S.S., *Payments and Monetary Cooperation* (Colombo: FES, 1993).

Edwards Jr., Richards W., *International Monetary Collaboration* (New York: Transnational Publishers, 1985).

Eichengreen, Barry, *International Monetary Arrangements for the 21st Century* (Washington: Brookings, 1994).

El-Agraa, Al. M., *The Theory and Measurement of Economic Integration* (London: Macmillan, 1989).

Etinenne, Gilbert, *Bangladesh Development in Perspective* (Geneva: Graduate Institute of International Studies, 1977).

Feldstein, Martin, *International Economic Cooperation* (Chicago: University of Chicago Press, 1988).

Frieden, Jeffrey A. and David A. Lake, *International Political Economy: Perspectives on Global Power and Wealth* (London: Routledge, 1995).

Gamble, Andrew and Anthony Payne, *Regionalism and World Order* (London: Macmillan, 1996).

Ghatak, Subrata, *Monetary Economics in Developing Countries* (London: Macmillan, 1981).

Ghuman, Ranjit Singh, *Indo-Pakistan Trade Relations* (New Delhi: Deep & Deep, 1986).

Goacher, David J., *An Introduction to Monetary Economics* (London: Financial Training Publications, 1986).

Grauwe, Paul De, *The Economic Theory of Monetary Integration* (London: Oxford University Press, 1992).

Green, Christopher J. and David T. Llewellyn (eds.), *Surveys in Monetary Economics Vol. I: Monetary Theory and Policy* (Oxford: Basil Blackwell, 1991).

Guhan, S., The World Bank's Lending in South Asia, Brooking Occasional Papers (Washington D.C: The Brookings Institution, 1995).

Hamada, Koichi, *The Political Economy of International Monetary Interdependence* (Cambridge: MIT Press, 1987).

Haq, Khadija, *Crisis of the 1980s: World Monetary Financial and Human Resource Development Issues* (Islamabad: North South Roundtable, 1985).

Helleiner, Eric, *States and the Re-emergence of Global Finance: From Bretton Woods to the 1990s* (Ithaca and London: Cornell University Press, 1994).

Islam, Sarjul, *Bangaldesh, State and Economic Strategy* (Dhaka: Dhaka University Press, 1998).

Janakiraman, R., *Critical Study of the Procedure Regarding the Operations of the Asian Clearing Union* (Bombay, 1995).

Johnston, R. Barry, *Exchange Arrangements and Currency Convertibility: Developments and Issues* (Washington D.C.: IMF, 1999).

Jovanovic, Miroslav N., *International Economic Integration* (London: Routledge, 1992).

Kanesalingam, V. (ed.), *Privatisation: Trends and Experiences in South Asia* (Colombo: CSCD, 1991).

Kanesalingam, V., *Collective Self-reliance of South Asia* (Colombo: FES, 1993).

Kenen, Peter B., *Exchange Rates and Policy Coordination* (Manchester: Manchester University Press, 1989).

Kindleberger, C.P., *Foreign Trade and the National Economy* (New Haven: Yale University Press, 1989).

Lee, Jungsoo, *External Finance and the Role of Multilateral Financial Institutions in South Asia: Changing Patterns, Prospects and Challenges* (Manila: ADB, 1991).

Machlup, Fritz, *The Alignment of Foreign Exchange Rates: The First Horowitz Lectures* (New York: Praeger Publishers, 1972).

Madan, B.K., *The Asian Clearing Union: Towards Monetary Cooperation* (New Delhi: RIS, 1986).

Maung, Mya, *Burma and Pakistan: A Comparative Study of Development* (New York: Praeger, 1971).

Meller, P. (ed.), *The Latin American Development Debate* (Boulder: Westview Press, 1991).

Mukherjee, I.N., *Towards Economic Integration in Asia—An Evaluation of Trade Expansion Programmed of Developing Countries in Asia and Pacific* (New Delhi: Vidya Vahini, 1978).

Niehans, Jurg, *International Monetary Economy* (Baltimore: Phillip Allan, 1984).

O'Brien, Richard and Tapan Datta (eds.), *International Economics and Financial Markets* (New York: Oxford, 1989).

Orantes, Issac Cohen, *Regional Integration in Central America* (Massachusettes: Lexington Books, 1972).

Page, Sheila (ed.), *Monetary Policy in Developing Countries* (London: Routledge, 1993).

Panchmukhi, V.R., *et al.*, *Economic Cooperation in the SAARC Region: Potential, Constraints and Policies* (New Delhi: RIS, 1990).

Pavlic, Breda, *et al.*, *The Challenges of South-South Cooperation* (Boulder: Westview, 1983).

Poker, Nana and Lloyd Pettiford, *Redefining the Third World* (London: Macmillan, 1998).

Reejal, Pushkar R., *Monetary and Credit Policies of the Nepal Rashtra Bank & their Impact on the Nepalese Economy* (Kathmandu: Ratna Pustak, 1986).

Reis, Jaime, *International Monetary Systems in Historical Perspectives* (London: Macmillan, 1995).

Research and Information System for Non-aligned and Other Developing Countries (RIS), International Monetary Reforms-Issues Facing Developing Countries (New Delhi: RIS, 1987).

Robinson, E.A.G. and Michael Kidron, *Economic Development in South Asia* (London: Macmillan, 1970).

Serra, Jaime (*et al.*), *Reflections on Regionalism: Report of the Study Group on International Trade* (Washington: Carnegie Endwoment for International Peace, 1997).

Sheshadri, R.K., *From Crisis to Convertibility: The External Value of the Rupee* (Madras: Orient Longman, 1993).

Shrivastava, L.P.S., *Nepal at the Cross Roads* (New Delhi: Allied, 1996).

Silverstein, Joseph, *Burma: Military Rule and the Politics of Stagnation* (Ithaca: Cornell University Press, 1977).

Sindhwani, T.N., *Economic Feasibility of an Asian Common Market* (Delhi: Sterling, 1975).

Singh, L.P. *The Politics of Economic Cooperation in Asia* (Columbia: University of Missouri Press, 1966).

Skully, Michael T.S., *ASEAN Financial Cooperation: Developments in Banking Finance and Insurance* (London: Macmillan, 1985).

Sobhan, Rehman (ed.), *The Decade of Stagnation: The State of the Bangladesh Economy in the 1980s* (Dhaka; University Press, 1991).

Steinberg, David I. *Burma's Road Towards Development: Growth and Ideology under Military Rule* (Boulder: Westview, 1982).

Steinberg, David I., Burma: *A Socialist Nation of South East Asian* (Boulder: Westview, 1982).

Stewart, Francis, *North-South and South-South: Essays on International Economics* (London: Macmillan, 1992).

The Challenge to the South, The Report of the South Commission (New York: Oxford, 1990).

Thomas, Caroline and Peter Wilkin, *Globalisation and the South* (London: Macmillan, 1997).

Thorp, R. and L. Whitehead (eds.), *Latin American Debt and the Adjustment Crisis* (Basingstoke: Macmillan, 1987).

Tsoukalis, Loukas, *The Political Economy of International Money: In Search of a New Order* (New Delhi: Sage, 1985).

UNCTAD, *Financing of Trade Among Developing Countries: Report* (Geneva: UNCTAD, 1986).

UNCTAD, Preliminary Report on the Feasibility of Global Payments Arrangements Among Developing Countries by Jeorge Gonzalez del Valle (Geneva: UNCTAD, 1978).

Uygur, Ercan, *The Asian Clearing Union: An Assessment and Prospects*, Paper for the UNCTAD Secretariat, Project RAS/ 81/070, May 1994.

Wadhwa, Charan, *et al.*, *Regional Economic Cooperation in Bangladesh, India, Pakistan and Sri Lanka* (Ahmedabad: Allied, 1987).

Waqif, Arif, *South Asian Cooperation in Industry, Energy and Technology* (New Delhi: Sage, 1987).

Yar-Shater, Ehsan (ed.), Iran Faces the 1970s (New York: Praeger, 1971).

Articles

Agarwal, Manmohan, World Trading System and Developing Countries: Implications for the SAARC Region, *South Asia Journal*, Vol. 3, No. 4, April-June 1990, pp. 343-58.

Ahuja, Shobha and Rina Bhattacharya, "Trade Complementarities and Prospects for Regional Import Substitution Among SAARC ASEAN Countries", *Foreign Trade Review*, Vol. 23, No. 2, July-September 1998, pp. 186-99.

Akhlaqur, Rehman, M. Bhuyan, Auatur Rehman and Sadral Reza, "Trade Effects of a South Asian Customs Union: An Expository Study", *Pakistan Development Review*, Vol. 20, No., 1, 1981, pp. 61-80.

Balassa, B., "Trade Creation and Trade Diversion in the European Common Market", *Economic Journal*, Vol.77, No.2, pp. 1-21

Baldwin, Richard E., *"The Causes of Regionalism"*, The World Economy, Vol. 20, No. 7, November 1997, pp. 865-87.

Banerjee, Pranab K., "Crucial Aspects of North-South Relations", *Mainstream (Annual)*, 1990, pp. 107-8.

Batliwala, C.J., *"Financial Cooperation in South Asia"* in Asian Development Bank, Towards Regional Cooperation in South Asia (Manila: ADB, 1988).

Bergstren, C. Fred, "Globalizing Free Trade", *Foreign Affairs*, May/June 1996, pp. 105-20.

Bhagwati, Jagdish, "The Global Age: From a Sceptical South to a Fearful North", *The World Economy*, Vol.20, No.3, May 1997, pp. 259-83.

Bhuyan, A.R., "Regional Cooperation and Trade Expansion in South Asia" in Asian Development Bank, *Towards Regional Cooperation in South Asia* (Manila: ADB, 1988).

Bofinger, P. and D. Gross, "A Multilateral Payments Union for the CIS: Why and How?", *CEPR Discussion Paper*, No. 654, 1992.

Bofinger, P., "A Multilateral Payments Union for Eastern Europe", *CEPR Discussion Paper*, No. 458, 1990.

Bofinger, P., "Options for the Payments and Exchange Rate Systems for Eastern Europe", *CEPR Discussion Paper*, No.545, 1991.

Bokhari, Farhan, "The Will to Change", *Far Eastern Economic Review*, 25 September 1997, pp. 118-20.

Bressand, Albert, "Futures for Economic Integration Beyond Interdependence: 1992 as a Global Challenge", *International Affairs (London)*, Vo1.66, No.1, January 1990, pp. 47-66.

Chakravarty, Sukhmoy, "Vision of South Asian Region: A Medium Term Perspective", *South Asia Journal*, Vol. No.4, April-June 1990, pp. 325-42.

Chishti, Sumitra, "Crisis in International Economic Cooperation and Economic Development of the Third World Countries", *International Studies*, Vo1.26, No.2, April-June 1989, pp. 95-112.

Clark, P.B., "Optimal International Reserves and the Speed of Adjustment", *Journal of Political Economy*, Vo1.78, No.1, 1970, pp. 356-76.

Colambage, S.S, "Rationale of Regional Cooperation in Relation to External Debt Problems of South Asian Countries", *SAARC Perspectives*, Vol. No. 5, 1989, pp. 19-25.

Corden, W.M., "Economics of Scale and Customs Union Theory", *Journal of Political Economy*, Vol.80, No.2, 1972, pp. 465-75.

Dalal, Sucheta, "Winners and Losers", *Far Eastern Economic Review*, 25 September 1997, pp.114-16.

Debroy, Bibek, "Intra-regional Trade in the SAARC Region", *Foreign Trade Review*, Vol.23, No.4, January-March 1989, pp. 398-422.

Developing Countries and the International Economy: Issues in Trade Adjustment and Debt", *Journal of Development Studies*, Vol.27, No.3, April 1991, pp. 7-191 (Series of Articles).

Dodsworth, J.R. and J. Diamond, "Monetary Cooperation as a Source of Development Finance-ASEAN Case", *Journal of Development Economics*, September 1980.

Dornbusch, R, "Expectations and Exchange Rate Dynamics", *Journal of Political Economy*, Vol. 84, No. 4 , 1976, pp. 1161-76

Eichengreen, Barry and Douglas A. Irwin, "Trade Blocs, Currency Blocs and the Reorientation of World Trade in the 1930s", *Journal of International Economics*, Vol. 38, Nos.1-2, February 1995, pp. 1-24.

Fischer, Stanley, "The Asian Crisis and the Changing Role of IMF", *Finance and Development*, Vol. 35, No.2, June 1998.

Frieden, Jeffiy A, "Invested Interests: The Politics of National Economic Policies in a World of Global Finance", *International Organization*, Vol. 45, No.4, Autumn 1991, pp. 425-52.

Ghosh, Arun, "International Economic Disorder: An Action Programme for the South", *Economic and Political Weekly*, Vo1.26, Nos.1-2, 5-12 January 1991.

Gold, J., "The Multilateral System of Payments", IMF Occasional Paper No.6 (Washington: IMF, 1981).

Hilali, A Z., "Regionalism in South Asia: A Case Study of SAARC", *Asian Studies*, Vol.12, No.2, July-December 1994.

Kamaluddin, S., "Will-Power Needed", *Far Eastern Seminar Review*, Spring 25, 1997, pp. 122-24.

Kapstein, Ethan., "Global Rules for Global Finance", *Current History*, November 1998, pp. 355-59.

Kenen, P.B., "Transitional Arrangements for Trade and Payments among the CMEA Countries", *IMF Staff Papers*, Vol.38, No.2, 1991, pp. 235-67.

Keohane, Robert, "International Institutions: Can Interdependence Work?", *Foreign Policy*, Spring 1998, pp. 85-95.

Khan, M.Y., "The Asian Clearing Union—An Assessment", *RBI Bulletin*, February 1991, pp. 117-46.

Khan, Rashid Ahmed, "Indo-Pak Trade Prospects and Constraints", *Regional Studies*. Vol. 3, No.3, Winter 1994-95.

Khanal, Y.N., "Political Economy in South Asian Cooperation", *South Asia Journal*, Vo1.3, No.3, January-March 1990, pp. 273-78.

Krishna, Pravin, "Regionalism and Multilateralism: A Political Economic Approach", *The Quarterly Journal of Economics*, February 1998, pp. 227-50.

Krugman, Paul, "Latin Lessons for Asia", *Far Eastern Economic Review*, 25 September 1997, p. 34.

Lim, Linda Y.C., "Whose 'Model' Failed? Implications of the Asian Economic Crisis", *The Washington Quarterly, Summer 1998*, pp. 25-35.

Lorenez, Detlef, "Regionalisation *versus* Regionalism: Problems of Change in the World Economy", *Intereconomics*, Vol.26, No.1, January-February 1991.

Mishra, Pramod K., "South-South Cooperation and SAARC" , *Monthly Public Opinion Surveys*, Vol. 34, Nos. 10-11, July/ August 1989, pp. 9-15.

Mukherjee, I. N., "SAARC: Its Econòmic Achievements", *World Focus*, Vol. 14, Nos.11-12, November-December 1993, pp. 36-9.

Mukherjee, I.N., "Global Economic Environment: Implications for South Asia", *Mainstream*, Vol.31, No.31, 12 June 1993, pp. 9-13.

Muller, Henrik, "From Dollarisation and Euroisation: The Future of the Euro as an International Substitution Currency", *Intereconomics*, Vo1.34, November-December 1999, pp. 286-96.

Naqvi, Syed Nawab Haider, "Economic Integration: Meaning and Dimension", *South Asia Journal*, Vol.3, No.4, April-June 1990, pp. 307-24.

Panchmukhi, V.R., "Cooperation in Industrial Development in SAARC: Some Reflections", *South Asia Journal*, Vol. 4, No.1, July-September 1990, pp. 55-66.

Rao, V.L., "Clearing & Payments Arrangements and Other Forms of Financial Cooperation: Issues before SAARC" (unpublished paper).

Reforming the World's Monetary System", *Journal of Post-Keynesian Economics,* Vol. 15, No. 2, Winter 1992-93, pp. 151-260 (Series of Articles).

Reza, Sadrel, "Issues in Trade Cooperation in South Asia: A Bangladesh Perspective", *BIIS Journal,* Vol. 12, No. 1, March 1995, pp. 135-46.

Schokman, Yvonne, "Prospects for Investment Cooperation in South Asia", *South Asian Journal,* Vol. 3, No. 4, April-June 1990, pp. 411-30.

Shah, Yawar, "The Changing Payments Landscape and its Implications for Correspondent Banks", *International Correspondent Banking Review,* 1997-98, pp. 3-8.

Sobhan, Rehman, "Asymmetries in Adjusting to Global Change: Changing Perspectives in North South Economic Relations", *Journal of Social Studies,* January 1993, pp. 97-115.

Soros, George, "The Capitalist Threat", *The Atlantic Monthly,* February 1997, pp. 45-58.

Timberlake, R.H., "The Central Banking Role of Clearing House Association", *Journal of Money Credit and Banking,* Vol. 16, No. 1, 1984, pp. 1-15.

Wade, Robert, "The Asian Crisis and the Global Economy: Causes, Consequences & Cure", *Current History,* November 1998, pp. 361-71.

Wadhva, Charan D., "Regional Payments Arrangements: An Application to Asia and the Far East", *Yale Economic Essays,* Vol. 10, No. 1, Spring 1976, pp. 149-89.

Wadhva, Charan D., "Reserve Pooling in Asia and the Far East", *The Pakistan Development Review,* Vol. 9, No., 3, Autumn, 1969, pp. 309-29.

Young, Oran R., "International Regimes: Towards a New Theory of Institutions", *World Politics,* Vol. 39, No. 1, October 1986, pp. 105-11.

Index